Contents

Acknowledgements

There are many people whom I would like to thank and acknowledge for their support in the research and writing of this book.

I would like to begin by thanking certain former colleagues in the School of Dance and Theatre at Bretton Hall College, University of Leeds. My special thanks are extended principally to Linda Taylor, a close friend and provocateur who opened up certain post modernist discourses to me in a way that really stimulated my work on 'Queer as Folk' and 'Tales of the City'. I also want to thank Dougie Hankin, Maureen Barry and 'Mitch' Mitchell for their friendship and support. Furthermore, sincere thanks are extended to Tony Green and Paul Cowen, Wendy Johnstone and Arthur Pritchard for helping me to arrange my teaching commitments in such a way that facilitated the writing of this book to a very tight schedule.

I also wish to thank Dr Neil Sammells, Dean of Faculty and other new colleagues in the School of English and Creative Studies who have supported my transition into my new post at Bath Spa University College with such warm support and interest.

Other colleagues and friends whose help and interest is very warmly appreciated include Professor Beverley Skeggs and colleagues at the University of Manchester, Professor John Bull of the University of Reading, Dr Susan Painter of the Roehampton Institute and Bill McDonnell of the University of Sheffield.

Overseas colleagues and friends who have given warm support and help are Professor Percy Hintzen of the University of California and Carole Christensen (Copenhagen).

My deepest and sincere thanks must also go to Tony Garnett and Tony Marchant whose generosity of time and interest were essential for the successful researching and writing of the chapters on 'The Cops' and 'Holding On'. Thanks are also due to David Snodin and the BBC, World Productions, Red Productions, Channel 4, Productions de la Fete and Armistead Maupin for their interest, help and support of this project.

Finally, I must thank Sally Njampa Ashworth for overseeing the successful completion of this book for Intellect and Robin Beecroft for his faith in commissioning it from me.

This book is dedicated to Marilyn for her love and belief and to my wonderful family: Eve, Chris, Thomas, Sally, Leo, Ruth and William. Heartfelt thanks to you all for your love, patience and unending good will. May you all work towards building cities of love, justice, tolerance and equality.

Peter Billingham
Bath Spa University College
September 2000.

Sensing the City – Navigating a Journey
An Introduction

In this book, my central analysis concerns the relationship between contemporary ideological concerns relating to the experience of living within the city, and their construction and exploration in five case-studies from contemporary British and American television drama. From the vigorous examination of these television dramas, several issues have arisen which to varying degrees foreground the central discussion of this study. They are: sexual politics, gender, ethnicity, economics, urban alienation and – as a meta-frame – the global post-modern. In this introduction, I intend to define my core methodological and investigative approach. In so doing, I shall necessarily seek to identify and discuss the following key elements:

- My own *ideological viewing position.*
- The problematic constructs of the *viewer* or *audience.*
- The implications of the concept of the *geo-ideological.*
- The implications of the concepts of *dramatic value* and *dramatic realism.*

I would like to begin in a slightly more informal mode by outlining the early stages of this book's inception. 'Sensing the City' began its gestation as a concept that arose from research that I was conducting into Tony Marchant's 'Holding On,' an eight episode television drama commissioned by BBC2 in 1996/7. The series is set in contemporary London and explores the ways in which its diverse range of characters 'hold on' through the pressures and traumas of city existence. The territory of television drama was, at that time, relatively new to me, although I had both taught and published on the television dramas of Dennis Potter.[1] As I carried out multiple close readings of the performance texts of Marchant's powerful dramas, I became aware of the ways in which a multi-vocal narrative structure – foregrounded in some finely written central characters – seemed to expose and reveal a refracted, kaleidoscopic 'sense of the city.' Subsequently, a central component of my methodological and investigative approach has been the thesis that, though the deconstruction of character formation and the dialectical matrix of narratives, a 'sense of the city' is exposed in which the politics of location is inextricably interwoven with the politics of identity. It became clear to me, therefore, in an increasingly vivid and compelling sense, that this award-winning drama might be interpreted as exposing and examining certain crucial ideological anxieties about the city, and related issues of urban identity and the politics of place. Excited and challenged, I began to search for other examples of contemporary British and American television drama that might, in their own complementary ways, be also engaged in a similarly dynamic dialectic of investigation, exposure and revelation. Through the systematic excavation of these ideas, I then developed the concept of the *geo-ideological* as a means of defining the dialectic of literal notions of place and location, transposed with their ideological marking, signing and delineation. I shall discuss this concept and its implications for my analysis later in this chapter. Through my investigative research and the simultaneous questioning of my criteria and frame of reference, I began to question the means by which the process of this refracting of the city was motivated and mediated. This in itself stimulated me to interrogate and extend my own understanding of the critical model on which my analysis and viewing position was based. From this came the slightly disorientating sense of vertigo that accompanies the navigation of new territories. Extended discussions with my good friend and former colleague, Linda Taylor, at Bretton Hall College, provoked me into what proved to be the most creative encounter with the theories of Michel Foucault and Julia Kristeva. This in itself provided me with a kind of compass with which to delineate the territory of 'Queer as Folk' and 'Tales of the City,' as well as opening my broader gaze of vision in other creative and challenging ways.

Before writing this book my background was, and remains, Drama and Performance Studies. Therefore this study is focused upon the five cases studies as dramas and performance texts. In the early stages of my research and preparation, I recognised the requirement, challenge and value of engaging in certain crucial issues arising out of the eclectic disciplines of Cultural Studies. In this respect, I wish to extend my thanks to Professor Beverley Skeggs and colleagues at the University of Manchester for sharing ongoing discoveries with me arising out of their 'Dangerous Erotics' research project. Following helpful advice from my former colleague, Dr Kelvin Taylor at Bretton Hall College, I have been particularly enriched and helped by such excellent anthologies such as *Post-modern Cities and Spaces* (eds. Watson and Gibson, Blackwell) and *Place and the Politics of Identity* (eds. Keith and Pile, Routledge). Also immensely helpful in terms of my chapters on 'Queer as Folk' and 'Tales of the City' was *Lesbian and Gay Studies* (eds. Medhurst and Munt, Cassell).

Viewing positions and audiences

It is clearly necessary, before I begin to offer some brief introductory discussion of the five case-studies and the principal issues arising out of them, to try and identify my own ideological, interpretative viewing position. I should first of all state that I am a white man in my early middle age who grew up in a close knit, British east midlands working class family and environment. I am now, through education, profession and income, middle class. I am heterosexual. I subscribe to an ideological position that is broadly Marxist in a left pluralist context. I also acknowledge associated constructs and perspectives from liberation theology and Quaker value systems, essential elements in my ongoing struggle with the problematic metaphors of the subjective and transcendent.

In any study of television as a medium of mass communication, the question of the viewer or audience is central, problematic and the site of ongoing ideological debate. In terms of my developed understanding of the term viewer/viewing, I believe that the phenomenological act of viewing is inseparable from the ideological context and marking in which that viewing exists. In seeking to extend and clarify my understanding of this socio-cultural phenomenon, I have been stimulated and supported through Fiske and Hartley's discussion of audiences and the bardic function of television in *Reading Television* (Fiske and Hartley, Routledge, 1978, reprinted 1994). I discuss this concept further towards the end of this chapter

I believe that the ideological context and marking of viewing for the audience is inevitably subject to considerations of class, sub-class and the complex relationship of cultural/sub-cultural infrastructures of identification and expression. I do not wish to engage in a vulgar simplification of this inherently Marxist model. I am not proposing a crude stratification of autonomous, constitutive audience bases marked by either economic income or socio-geographic demography. Furthermore, I also recognise the constraints of space and opportunity for a wider debate within the confines and function of this introduction. Nevertheless, in terms of these efforts to navigate the metaphorical minefield of debate concerning audience, viewer and class, Fiske and Hartley (1994) make the following observation, which I find most concise and helpful:

> Class *in itself*, [Fiske and Hartley's italics] deriving from inequalities based on economic 'conditions of existence,' exists irrespective of how people themselves (whether they be victims or beneficiaries of inequality) see and respond to their class condition. But people's response to their objective class situation does give rise to the secondary notion of class *for itself*. This is the (sometimes only potential) awareness among people of a common identity springing from their common experience. It is important… to have made this distinction because we suggest that in the world of television, divisions between classes *in themselves* are rarely if ever presented as such. Television articulates the responses of people to their class condition, not the class condition itself. Hence it is primarily a medium for the expression of classes *for themselves*… This is television's starting point: its 'mass code' is merely a recognition of the basically similar 'social conditions of existence' that obtain among apparently widely disparate groups.'[2]

Given these ways in which television as a mass medium de-politicises notions of audience and viewer, it is clear, I believe, that the production, encoding and broadcasting of most television drama as a complex cultural product, is expressed in my concept of the *viewing public* as *a site of marketed homogeneity determined by dominant cultural-economic interests*. Within the economic (global multi-national) and cultural (post-modern) conditions of late capitalism, the construction of the allegedly *privileged consumer* is but one primary aspect of other similar myths such as the *public*. Not surprisingly, this construct of *the public* is inherently – even 'naturally' – a centre-right, home-owning bourgeoisie. In mainstream television production terms, this translates in British television into a preoccupation with the active leisure of home and garden improvement, the pleasurable contemplation of overseas holidays, and melodramas of hospital and police station locations. This form of programming, along with the ideological idealisation of urban and rural communities in soap operas such as 'Eastenders,' 'Coronation Street,' 'Brookside' and 'Emmerdale', acts as a reinforcing reflection of bourgeois positioning. Furthermore, in terms of the strategies of Thatcherism and their continued implementation by New Labour, this programming serves as 'evidence' of the 'absence' of class in providing 'consensual,' mediated images of social stability and the possibility for material – and socio-cultural – advancement. I would argue that these fictional or quasi-documentary television formulas serve to heighten and ameliorate the disruptive, 'external' traumas of unemployment, ill health or crime, and the threat that such intrusions pose to that homogenous haven. It is one of my central arguments in terms of both 'The Cops' and 'Homicide – Life on the Street,' that this compensatory function of the convention of 'cops and docs' drama is provocatively unsettled and challenged. In that key respect, the mythology of the moral and strategic efficacy of the police to enforce dominant agendas of law and order are simultaneously and seriously undermined.

I have chosen to use the term 'viewer' rather than 'audience' predominantly throughout this book. In doing so I am aware of the issues of *dominant* and *marginalised* viewing positions, which are themselves relative and fluid. Indeed, it is one of my principal contentions that, for example, in 'Queer as Folk,' the centrality and dominance of not only homophobic centre right, but liberal left perspectives of gay, queer and lesbian sexuality, are challenged and 'marginalised' by the ideological viewing frame of the scriptwriter and producers. It goes without saying that the totality of my evaluation of the dramas discussed in this book is an expression and consequence of my own viewing position. Therefore, in foregrounding this meta-perspective of choice of case-studies and their detailed analysis and discussion, I do not present this viewing position as inviolable or *privileged*. To the extent that I value and recognise the privilege as *opportunity* to write this book, I acknowledge the wider historical meta-perspective of my own class transition, effected as it has been by the increased educational opportunities afforded the working classes in the immediate post-war decades. In respect of the terms of 'audience' and 'viewer', my preference for the latter term lies in that it carries the possibility of individualised *reception* and *interpretation* of the cultural product, within and through the production and reception of cultural product as a site of struggle. This certainly reflects my own past, personal experience of the transforming impact inherent within television drama. As a working class teenager excited by literature, I can recall the visceral influence of Potter's 'Son of Man' and Jeremy Sandford's 'Cathy Come Home,' directed by Ken Loach and produced by Tony Garnett. As a 'viewer' in this sense therefore, I am inevitably and imperceptibly a constituent and characteristic of an 'audience' in what I believe is an *active, transitive* and *transformative* process. I acknowledge my debt of thanks to my family and their class in their support and belief, within the wider struggle for equality of opportunity, to be able to participate in this dialectic of struggle for growth and change.

The Geo-ideological

Perhaps one of the crucial discoveries that I have made during this study is my development of the term *geo-ideological* as a means by which to express my growing sense of the interface between the literal and metaphorical constructs of location. This concept is central to the theoretical and methodological strategies in this book. It delineates the fundamental sense in which our perception of the geographical-as-location inevitably carries within it a prevailing sense of the ideological signing of that location. Throughout the research and preparation process for this book, I came to believe increasingly that television, as a medium of mass communication, is inextricably both part of that mapping phenomena and also a *prime initiator*. There are issues attendant upon this concept concerned with the extent to which a constituent group or sub-group either actively define the limits and boundaries of that geo-ideological space/formation, or are willing or resistant participants within that process. There are clear connotations with Foucault's concept of the *heterotopia* and these connections are more fully explored in the chapters dealing with, respectively, the San Francisco of 'Tales of the City,' and the Manchester of 'Queer as Folk.'

Dramatic Value and Dramatic Realism

In terms of the post-Fukuyama debate concerning the closure of ideology and its meta-histories, with its advocated primacy of liberal democratic consumer capitalism, it is not surprising to see that much television broadcasting reinforces the constructs of bland bourgeois conformity and assimilation. It is my conviction that the five case-studies that I have chosen – 'The Cops' (BBC2/World Productions), 'Holding On' (BBC2), 'Tales/More Tales of the City' (Channel 4/ Working Title Productions/ Productions du Fete), 'Queer as Folk' (Channel 4/ Red Productions) and 'Homicide – Life on the Street' (Channel 4/NBC) – are all examples of television dramas that serve to disrupt conventional and dominant ideological perspectives, on issues ranging from law and order through to sexual, racial and ethnic identities. In so doing, they raise issues of the motivation of their commissioning, production and broadcasting. Consequently, they also return the reader once more to considerations of the potential/targeted 'audience(s)' and 'viewer(s)'. It is also important to recognise that, with the preponderance of lobotomising mediocrity masquerading as quiz programmes such as 'Who Wants to be a Millionaire,' these programmes might be seen as oases of aesthetic quality and oppositional probity. Before offering some brief, introductory discussion of the five dramas, and as an important part of that process, I want to try and further define the ideological underpinning informing my analysis. Within this, I want to address some of the problematic associations of dramatic value and dramatic realism.

Firstly, the following quotation from Terry Eagleton provides an excellent summary of my own critical framework within both this book and my wider research:

> Criticism, in other words, is now politics by other means, encompassing as it does questions of mass culture, literacy, popular education, power formulations and forms of subjectivity as well as more narrowly, the artistic text… if this third wave of Marxist criticism can best be described *ideological*, it is because its theoretical strengths lie above all in exploring what might be called the *ideology of form*… that it is possible to find the material history which produces a work of art somehow inscribed in its very texture and structure.[3]

In this book, I have sought to examine the *ideology of form* as exposed in the narrative strategies, thematic sites and fictive constructions of principal dramatic characters across the five programmes. It is my contention that, though a careful deconstruction of the dialectical interplay of these constituent elements, an analysis may be made of the wider meta-frame of contemporary social, cultural and political experience(s) of 'Sensing the City' through aspects of contemporary television drama. Furthermore, I would assert that, through this deconstructive analysis, it is possible to discern a material, ideological history inscribed within their texture and structure.

My second quotation returns once more to that seminal analysis of modern television drama, Fiske and Hartley's *Reading Television*. Whereas Eagleton serves to define the meta-perspective of my understanding and implementation of critical theory, the following quotation from Fiske and Hartley usefully highlights the inherent, structural contradiction between the seemingly socio-cultural experience of viewing television, with the inscribed ideological ordering structures of both the product and its reception:

> Television is taken to be wholly commercial, conventional and conservative. But that is only another way of saying that as a medium it is normative, a casual part of everyday experience. In fact, it is the very familiarity of television which enables it… to act as an agency for defamiliarisation…. The myths which operate as organising structures within this area of cultural intersubjectivity cannot themselves be discrete and unorganised, for that would negate their prime function; they are themselves organised into a coherence that we might call a mythology or an ideology.[4]

From this employment of 'myth'/'mythology' in Barthes' sense of the dominant ideological reading/construction of normative coherence, it is possible to see how television – and television drama – acts as a metaphorical re-enactment and displacement of myths of 'real' or 'normal' life and behaviour. There is, within this reading, a sense of dominant ideological displacement and verification. However, as signaled by their equal use of the Brechtian concept of 'defamiliarisation' or 'alienation,' Fiske and Hartley are also alerted to the means by which those myths of anaesthetising, coercive cultural discourse might be subject to subversive deconstruction. This surely links to Tony Garnett's admission, in an interview with me, that 'The Cops' functions as a form of what he called 'Trojan Horse drama.' I discuss this issue more fully in Chapter One, 'Policing the Imagination,' which examines the first two series of that controversial, award-winning police drama.

Throughout the writing of this book, my understanding of the potential role and function of contemporary television drama has been extended, with, perhaps, some former optimism as to its efficacy for social change tempered, whilst revitalising a belief in its potential for, and realisation of, high-quality *performative aesthetic*. This inevitably raises issues both of what might be meant by dramatic value and also the extent to which the five case-studies are examples of dramatic realism.

In quoting from Connor (1992:32) Nelson makes the following observation that:

The question of *value* [my italics] will always exert an imperative force which disturbs us from our safe inhabitation of ourselves, impelling us to question beliefs, certainties and values with a view not only to their potential betterment, but to the revaluation of the very notions of better or worse.[5]

When I first began to develop the original concept and proposal for this study, one of my central defining preoccupations was the question of the value of contemporary television drama. This was both in its aesthetic context and also, from my broadly Marxist viewpoint, its *social and ideological* value in the sense that Raymond Williams might have defined that concept. In his seminal analysis, *Television – Technology and Cultural Form* he observed:

> Though the surviving theatres still commanded and received cultural prestige, much of the best new work of the younger generation of dramatists was by the mid-sixties in Britain going straight into television. It was predominantly a radical dramatic movement, drawing on and developing two major kinds of possibility: the drama of internal dissolution and the drama of public action or public-and-private tension…. The existence of very large audiences for disturbing and controversial plays of this kind, was in many ways embarrassing to the broadcasting authorities and to orthodox public opinion.[6]

In the decade or so following on from Williams' analysis of the cultural and ideological value of television drama, significant changes occurred both within the culture of the BBC with more or less simultaneously, the election of Margaret Thatcher's right wing, monetarist Tory government in 1979. The implications for the commissioning and production of controversial, oppositional television drama were significant, both for the BBC and for Independent, commercial television. In the excellent collection of interviews celebrating and commemorating the late Alan Clarke – surely one of British television's most outstanding and unique directors – David Hare asserts that the circumstances surrounding the banning of Clarke's direction of Roy Minton's controversial borstal-drama 'Scum' (1977) were significant:

> I believe 'Scum' is – well, I would stand by what I said at Alan's memorial service. 'Along the fault line created by the banning of 'Scum' flowed all the lousy decisions and abject behaviour which left the BBC ten years later having to fight to justify its very existence to government.' Meaning that the decision about 'Scum' was particularly craven, it was a pure political decision dressed up as an artistic decision. And there wasn't any real justification for it, except sheer fear of government…. To not back your own creative people when they hadn't done anything wrong and everybody knew they hadn't done anything wrong was a very grim moment in the history of the BBC.[7]

There are clear and far-reaching implications in Hare's analysis for the conditions and circumstances in which the five dramas under discussion were made and these are discussed both within the individual chapters and also reviewed in my conclusion. Williams nevertheless identified the social value of the 'radical' television drama from the mid 1960s onwards, a value inseparable from its counter-cultural value and status. I of course recognise the problematic issues that post-structuralist and post-modernist discourses provoke in terms of notions of signifying 'value' to the term *value*. Certainly, from these critical viewpoints, the very notion of a fixed sense of aesthetic value is profoundly questionable, being so conditioned by matters such as class, gender, culture(s) and ethnicity. Nevertheless, as I seek to review the value and significance of the five dramas under discussion, I want to propose that their *value* might be defined as:

The extent to which, through the dynamic dialectic of the written text and performative aesthetic, the television drama critically self-reflects both dominant and counter-dominant ideological positions.

My definition thus implicitly informs the treatment and critical evaluation of all five case-studies and I shall revisit some of the implications of that approach in my concluding chapter. However, there is one final important consideration that I want to raise in this respect before continuing to a summative introduction of the dramas themselves. That is, the implications of the notion of dramatic realism in terms of assessing the value and impact of those dramas. One of the self-evident characteristics of most, if not all, popular television drama lies in its verisimilitude to normative, consensual notions of 'real life.' Thus, the lives of the middle and working-class characters in the ever popular 'Brookside' are assumed to accurately reflect both the specific north western English location of Liverpool, but also – by implication – the lives of similar individuals and families throughout the country. Its themes of, for example, marital breakdown, drug abuse and the anxieties and implications of unemployment are common across many other urban communities. It is significant, perhaps, that when the programme makers introduced more controversial issues such as a lesbian relationship and child abuse that the tabloid press moralists were provoked while simultaneously – and predictably(?) – audience figures soared for those episodes.

Fiske and Hartley established a key critical concept and vocabulary to discuss this crucial issue of how television's function as a mediated representation of constructs of socio-cultural homogeneity in their notion of *bardic* television. Whilst it is not possible in the context of this introduction to enter into a detailed discussion of the seven elements that they define with that generic term, I want to offer the following quote as a concise summary of that term's usage:

> Television performs a 'bardic function' for the culture at large and all the individually differentiated people who live in it. When we use the term *bard* it is to stress certain qualities common both to this multi-originated message and to more traditional bardic utterances.[8]

Fiske and Hartley proceed to define the seven different – but mutually inter-dependent – purposes that this homogenising and centralising process seeks to achieve. To the extent that they argue for television effecting a 'ritual condensation' of economic disparities and inequalities into a Barthian construct of validating mythologies, I would argue that each of the five case-studies in this study represent *differing* but *equivalent* attempts to disrupt and reveal that process. What remains of crucial interest within this model and the debate that it has generated, is the extent to which all forms of dramatic representation are iconic. Given that this is the case, it invites a discussion of how a drama such as 'The Cops' exploits its own genre of social realism in a self-reflective way, to both sustain a notion of 'documentary realism' while simultaneously exposing the ideological constructs *within* that generic representation of social reality. To return to Fiske and Hartley once more:

> The more closely the signifier reproduces our common experience… the more realistic it appear to be. The signified is determined by our culture, not by some external natural reality. Denotation is visual transfer while connotation is the result of human intervention in the process – camera distance/angle, focus, lighting effects etc.[9]

In this important respect therefore, my own definition and use of the *performative aesthetic*, whilst entailing the denotative visual transfer of the signification of themes and issues, is simultaneously connotative in the interpretative matrix of the drama's technical and performative aesthetic.

The Five Case-study Dramas

The first two series of 'The Cops' have been produced against a social and political backdrop of transition from eighteen years of far-right Thatcherite economic and social policies within Britain, to the supposed new dawn of Tony Blair's New Labour. The emphasis upon 'New' – redolent from the sound bites of the term's inception – has conveyed a worrying but wholly accurate sense of political debate as product signing. As Tony Marchant observed, in an interview with me, 'Everyone's marketing their finer feelings.' In terms of the neutralising and 'modernising' influence upon the British police force, the last decade of the twentieth century witnessed the serial revelations of corrupt police practices in, for example, the cases of the Birmingham Six and the Guildford Four. Furthermore, through the courage and tenacity of the parents, family and friends of Stephen Lawrence and Michael Menson, a growing revelation of the institutionalised racism inherent within the Metropolitan Police Force has, like Pandora's Box, once opened, defied closure. Significantly, having occupied and subsequently colonised the centre-right ground of Thatcherite 'Middle-England' in order to secure the devastating electoral victory of May 1997, New Labour's Home Secretary, Jack Straw, has sought to prioritise Law and Order issues. In so doing, he has sought to occupy territory that observers such as myself had imagined were the natural domain of extreme right-wing Conservative politicians such as Michael Howard and Anne Widdicombe. Thus, at the time of writing, (May, 2000), there are regular media pronouncements about cracking down on 'bogus' asylum seekers and curfews for young people on the run-down housing estates of Britain's depressed urban areas. Meanwhile, in a spirit of Dickens' 'Hard Times,' the Home Office attracts condemnation from a major support agency such as Oxfam for providing – from the government's mediated viewpoint – the presumably 'authentic' refugees from the war in Kosovo – with vouchers, rather than money, to support themselves. Not surprisingly, against this backdrop of increasingly centralised and reactionary policies on law and order, by the time that Tony Garnett and his team had started shooting on the second series, the support that they had received from the Greater Manchester and Lancashire Constabulary on the first series had disappeared. Nevertheless, as I discuss in some detail in Chapter One, Garnett is not seeking to engage in simplistic judgments or criticisms of the police. His production company, World Productions, carried out extensive research into the conditions and problems facing contemporary policing, with all cast and crew spending some time with the police force on day-to-day duty. In an interview, one of the directors of the series Alrick Riley spoke about this experience and its implications for him:

> We all went out and spent time with the police, you get things that you'd just never get
> from simply reading the script. I think that with Roy [Brammell], who's tremendously
> charismatic – even with all of his faults – the 'but' is, when he's bad, he's dealing with
> bad people – and that makes it all right? The danger is that, in the police force, when
> someone like that bends the rules, they have the power and, of course, they get it wrong.
> It can never be all right… It's been an incredibly liberating experience… and what I've
> learnt is that drama can have many, many layers and still remain powerful. In 'The Cops'
> the characters are viewed from an oblique angle, fragmented, and that helps to make the
> drama more interesting.
>
> (Alrick Riley, interviewed by the author, June 1999.)

Tony Garnett's reputation as a producer of ground-breaking film and television drama is well known and documented. Of particular interest is his long-standing professional relationship with the left-wing British film and television director, Ken Loach. The two met while working under the auspices of what, not only in retrospect, may be seen as a 'Golden Era' of liberal/radical programming opportunities under the benevolent, non-interfering guidance of Sidney Newman. Newman was a Canadian who had enjoyed considerable success in his home country of producing quality television drama. Initially brought to Britain to develop the Independent Television series 'Armchair Theatre' (which helped to launch and develop the careers of dramatists such as Harold Pinter and David Mercer), he was appointed Head of Drama by the BBC in 1964. Newman instigated the now legendary 'Wednesday Play' series on BBC 1 which provided a platform for young radical writers, directors and producers like Loach, Garnett and Alan Clarke. When the transmission day changed to Thursday in 1970, the series was re-named 'Play for Today,' with writers such as Jim Allen, John Hopkins and Dennis Potter all receiving important early commissions. As George Brandt observes:

> The producer most associated with the use of film (16mm associated with lightweight
> filming equipment) on the 'Wednesday Play,' Tony Garnett, worked with authors like

David Mercer, Charles Wood, Jim Allen and Jeremy Sandford. The play that epitomised this realistic trend was Sandford's 'Cathy Come Home.' Produced by Tony Garnett and directed by Ken Loach, when it was first transmitted on 16 November 1966 it entered into television mythology instantly.[10]

The use of 16mm film was significant in that, prior to Garnett and Loach, it had been used exclusively in outside broadcast news footage and documentary. The jump-shot, staccato editing and discontinuous camera work of early work such as 'Cathy Come Home' is revisited and explored to create a memorable, if challenging, ideological aesthetic in 'The Cops.' Garnett was, of course, also involved in the origins and development of the landmark 1960s television police drama, 'Z Cars,' with its monochrome grained social realism, and a sense of both police officers and criminals as human beings caught in a problematic post-war society. More recently, in the early 1990s, Garnett also produced 'Between the Lines,' a hard-hitting television drama centred upon the police force's attempts to monitor its own institutional corruption and malpractice. 'The Cops' is set in a fictional northern English town called Stanton and is actually filmed on location in the North West town of Bolton, some twenty minutes north west of Manchester by train. In this respect, the series is the only one of the five case-studies not to be city located. However, I very much wanted to include this powerful drama as a case-study, largely because of its idiosyncratic qualities in terms of contemporary British television drama dealing with issues of policing and law and order. Furthermore, I also wanted to use 'The Cops' as an example of the ways in which social and economic issues of drug abuse, long term unemployment and crime were not solely confined to metropolitan areas. This migration of what had formerly been considered as 'inner city issues' to larger satellite urban areas such as Bolton/Stanton is an important consideration within this study. Finally, the contrast between the questionably 'exotic' southern capital location of Marchant's 'Holding On' with a Northern urban conurbation not noted for its fashionable, cosmopolitan credentials, seemed important and effective by contrast. In this respect, the location of one of my American case-studies, 'Homicide – Life on the Street,' is also significant. Whilst Baltimore is one of America's oldest cities, its placement on the eastern sea board and chilling reputation as one of the major American homicide sites, denies it any kind of fashionable reputation. By contrast, San Francisco, location and backdrop for Armistead Maupin's 'Tales of the City' could not be more credit-rated for liberal and radical sensibilities. In the same sense that the decline of traditional manufacturing industries – especially the Cotton Mills – in North West England precipitated both rapid employment and subsequent urban degeneration, Baltimore was one of the first significant American cities to suffer serious economic decline in the second part of the twentieth century:

> By the late 1960s the inner city [of Baltimore] was as economically depressed as it had been in during the Great Depression. The downward swing hit bottom in 1968 when riots laid further waste to the city following the assassination of Martin Luther King, Jr.[11]

In a critical essay entitled 'You're Nicked!' which examines television police series and the fictional representation of law and order, Alan Clarke observed that:

> The flood of police movies which came out of America in the late 1960s and early 1970s constructed a view of policing in which violence was represented as a way of life for the police in modern cities. This more explicit portrayal of the violence could be seen as completely gratuitous unless it gained a symbolic value as the necessary background to the war against crime, which the police was fighting.[12]

This concept of the 'symbolic value' of violence as a seemingly inescapable and necessary element of policing cities and other urban sites is a significant construct. Whilst there are relatively few instances of explicit police-initiated violence in either 'The Cops' or 'Homicide – Life on the Street,' when they do occur, they are always presented as profoundly problematic and contingent upon other evidence of serious compromise and corruption. Thus, the strategies and motives surrounding such actions by PC Roy Brammell in 'The Cops' and Detective Paul Falsone in 'Homicide' are framed in such a way as to provoke potential moral unease and uncertainty in the viewer. Even where, in the case of Falsone, his victim is an arrogant and unrepentantly brutal rapist, the quasi-legitimacy of the detective's impetuous, even moral, anger is implicitly questioned. Nevertheless, in the series' unrelenting resistance to simplistic moral or ethical judgments, it is significant that his Commanding Officer, Giardello, is primarily concerned that the use of violence during interrogation will undermine any hope of a conviction against the criminal. Simultaneously, the viewer is presented with a location of moral indeterminacy, where personal agenda of justifiable violence are placed equidistantly with wider, liberal, public concerns of the impartial and just execution of the law.

A significant aesthetic commonality that 'Homicide' shares with 'The Cops' is that they are both filmed on 16mm film, using hand held cameras and eschewing the fixed stable gaze that the tripod ensures. 'Homicide' employs fast action double and triple take editing, used to grimly powerful effect in sequences such as the narrative and visual revisiting of the mass murder in the 'Saigon Rose' episode, discussed in Chapter Five. It is also significant that the camera in both series does not offer a fixed viewing frame for the speaking actor(s) but rather darts and loops to inter-cut fractured visual images, frequently with out of vision, or part-vision dialogue. Interestingly, in terms of audience feedback to both series, many viewers complained – at least initially – of the difficulty they faced in trying to stay with and 'read' this complex aesthetic flexi-narrative, to borrow Robin Nelson's term from his informative and stimulating 'TV Drama in Transition':

> Flexi-narratives do not seek to channel a singular ideology but are plural in their very structures in recognition that audiences comprise a range of people with differing perspectives. Whilst TV drama texts are by no means innocent in their discursive positions, flexi-narratives particularly evidence a model of negotiation of a range of meanings rather than an inoculation theory of ideology.[13]

Nelson's concept of the flexi-narrative clearly carries with it both an aesthetic and ideological value. In terms of any post-modern reading of contemporary British and American society and culture, the fractured, discontinuous discourse of location, image, text and identity is most telling tellingly communicated through the flexi-narratives of 'The Cops,' 'Homicide' and, adapted to a more modernist formalism, in Tony Marchant's 'Holding On.'

In the chapters dealing with 'The Cops' and 'Homicide' my principle concern is to explore the ways in which issues of law and order and crime are mediated, offering a refracted and oblique sense of the city and urban locations that serve as a site for their enactment. Furthermore, this sense of the city as foregrounded in the construction of both character and narrative presents the viewer with a series of ideological contradictions and anxieties. These relate to both the complex causes of crime, and the problematic question of what constitutes adequate and impartial policing of those city and urban sites. Furthermore, there is the issue as to whether crimes caused as a malign symptom of structural and historical inequalities *can* be viewed and policed 'impartially.'

In Chapter Three, in which I examine and discuss 'Holding On,' the issue-based focus becomes less centred. Issues in the series such as sexual harassment and the brutal murder of a young Afro-Caribbean man with its racist connotations, while providing a matrix of anxieties about life in contemporary London, serve more to locate the deeper concerns of characters struggling to navigate their survival and express their humanity.

The central character of Shaun, the crusading Inland Revenue investigator, acts as the central narrative and ideological spine of this eight-part drama. Marchant acknowledges his debt to some of Dickens' great London-based fictional landscapes such as in *Our Mutual Friend*. In 'Holding On,' I think we have a late twentieth century equivalent of searching moral analysis and impassioned concern, at the impact of late capitalist, post-modern political culture upon the inhabitants of that city awash with evocations of history and destiny.

Finally, in chapters Three and Four respectively, I analyse and discuss 'Tales of the City' and 'Queer as Folk.' Inevitably, one of my principal concerns is the way in which sexual identities and their expression, which have been systematically marginalised and even demonised by the dominant ideological system, are constructed and represented. In 'Tales of the City' there is an essentially radical liberal argument for tolerance and openness whilst simultaneously offering a satirical critique of a Californian high culture of excess and denial. The series, based upon Maupin's novels which themselves grew out of a newspaper serial, is located significantly pre-AIDS and evokes the latter days of the counter-culture decade of Haight-Ashbury and Woodstock. However, and more significantly in terms of this series, San Francisco had already earned a reputation as an organised site of resistance to homophobic discrimination and oppression. In the early and mid 1950s, the Mattachine Society, possibly the first properly organised homosexual rights movement in America, opened a chapter in San Francisco. During this period, the Daughters of Bilitis, America's first lesbian movement was founded in the city in 1955. Whilst the

Stonewall Riots in New York's Greenwich Village in 1969 are generally regarded as the defining *leitmotif* of the Gay Liberation movement, San Francisco's Gay community had by that time already secured a number of hard won battles against police harassment. Called the 'gay capital' of the United States in an article in 'Life' magazine in 1964, San Francisco provides the most appropriately eclectic setting for this series.

'Queer as Folk' became a controversial *cause célèbre* when it was first broadcast in Britain on Channel 4 in 1998. Situated in Manchester's Gay Village, centred around Canal Street, the opening episode of the first series managed to outrage the reactionary tabloid press and even served to unsettle some liberal media commentators, both gay and straight. The principal reason for this outcry was the explicit portrayal of gay sexual intercourse between Stuart, a man nearing thirty years of age and Nathan, a fifteen year old boy that he has picked up that evening. The outrage was such that Becks brewery, who had sponsored the series, withdrew their funding after the first episode, clearly making a calculated value judgment in more senses than one in terms of the fashion credos of gay and lesbian sexuality and the 'Pink Pound.' If there is a sub-textual undercurrent of tolerance and assimilation in 'Tales of the City,' then the diametrical opposite must surely be argued for 'Queer as Folk,' which has all of the outrageous, camp confrontation of a queen generously fueled by vodka and caffeine-energy mixers. As I explore and discuss in some detail in the chapter, there is an intriguing conflict between more conventionally liberal gay assimilationist strategies and, by contrast, queered politicised confrontational agendas within the series. Certainly, whatever other conclusions might be reached about the series and its two-episode sequel, it has undoubtedly set a marker for future explorations and representations of gay, queer and lesbian sexuality on British television.

In choosing my five case-studies, I have selected dramas that I believe to have a fundamental, if eclectic, sense of aesthetic, authorial and ideological integrity. They are dramas that, in their various ways, have sought to speak from an oppositional margin into an increasingly authoritarian, controlled, reactionary centre of public debate and consciousness. All of the three British case-studies were broadcast on either BBC2 ('Holding On' and 'The Cops') or Channel 4 ('Queer as Folk'). Both of these channels (the BBC publicly funded through the licence fee; Channel 4 relying upon advertising revenue but with a brief to offer alternative programming to the mainstream commercial channels) have established deserved reputations in Britain for the quality of much of their commissioned drama, film and documentary programming. It is also significant that Channel 4 broadcast both American case-studies on British television, albeit that 'Homicide' was scheduled either for insomniacs or those expert with video tape recorders. Similarly, it is important to recognise that 'Tales of the City' was broadcast on a national public channel, with 'Homicide' broadcast by NBC. However, even with the cachet of this major prestigious American broadcasting company, it is scheduled for the ten o'clock evening Friday slot, normally seen as something of a 'graveyard' for programmes. As Hoffman observes:

Even though 'Homicide' stands up reasonably well to its head-to-head competition… it can't compete in the overall ratings with shows presented at more coveted times. Ratings as of mid-April 1998 gave 'Homicide' 80th place out of 168 network programs. What has secured its survival is a consistent, loyal following within that important demographic [i.e. 'hip urbanites between the ages of twenty five and forty'].[14]

I have enjoyed immensely researching and writing this book. In an ongoing and fundamental sense, that process has entailed that many of my discoveries and judgments became vividly alive for me in terms of their emerging directly out of my encounter with five outstanding examples of contemporary British and American television drama. I owe many thanks to many people who have directly or indirectly supported, encouraged and challenged me over the fifteen months of this book's inception, research and writing. These thanks are expressed in the accompanying Acknowledgments, but I must take the opportunity here to thank Marilyn, for her ceaseless belief in the project and for Robin Beecroft at *Intellect* for exercising the faith in my proposal and commissioning this book.

Notes

1. Please see *The Angel in Us: Dennis Potter's* Blackeyes, published in Occasional Papers in the Arts and Education, National Arts Education Archive, Vol.5, (1996).
2. John Fiske and John Hartley (1978, reprinted 1994) *Reading Television*, Routledge, pp.102–3.
3. Terry Eagleton and Drew Milne (eds.) (1996) *Marxist Literary Theory*, Blackwell, pp.10–11.
4. Fiske and Hartley, p.19.
5. Robin Nelson (1997) *TV Drama in Transition*, Macmillan, p.228.
6. Raymond Williams (1975, reprinted 1990, edited by E. Williams) *Television – Technology and Cultural Form*, Routledge, p.58.
7. Richard Kelly (ed.) (1998) *Alan Clarke*, Faber and Faber, p.105.
8. Fiske and Hartley, p.85.
9. *Ibid*. pp.38–9.
10. George Brandt (1981) *British Television Drama*, Cambridge University Press, p.19.
11. Tod Hoffman (1998) *Homicide – Life on the Screen*, ECW Press, Toronto, p.34.
12. Alan Clarke (1992) 'You're Nicked! –Television police series and the fictional representation of law and order, from Strinati and Waggs', (eds) *Come on Down? – Popular Media Culture in Post-War Britain*, Routledge, pp.234–5.
13. Nelson, pp.41–2.
14. Hoffman, p.86.

1 Policing the Imagination
Tony Garnett's 'The Cops'

In this opening chapter I intend to analyse and discuss in some detail the two series of Tony Garnett's 'The Cops.' The first of these police dramas was broadcast over eight fifty-minute episodes from Monday 19 October 1998 on BBC2. The second series began broadcasting, again on BBC2, on Monday 11 October 1999 and consisted of ten fifty-minute episodes. Both series were produced by World Productions with Garnett as Executive Producer and Eric Coulter as Producer.

In June 1999, Tony Garnett invited me to Bolton both to interview him about the making of the first series and to spend a day on location viewing the second series in production. During that day, I was also able to interview other members of the production team. All references to Tony Garnett in interview in this chapter are from that meeting. In my interview with Garnett he explained that:

> We wanted to do a 'cop show' where the characters are not playing their uniforms – where we're dealing with human beings that are more than the uniform. Now of course, putting that uniform on effects who you are when you have the uniform on, and it even effects you after a while when you've taken it off. It also effects the way in which the world perceives you and then reflects back to you, because how we perceive others is partly made up of how we perceive the world perceiving us.

It is one of my principle contentions in relation to 'The Cops' that at the heart of this two series drama is a profound moral ambiguity concerning the issues of law and order and their enforcement. As I mentioned in my introduction, 'The Cops' is urban based, rather than city based. The programme, filmed on location in Bolton, Lancashire in the north of England, constructs a fictional town named Stanton. Much of the dramatic action is located on or around the fictional, run-down housing estate known as Skeetsmoor. As Garnett noted in relation to this question of location when I asked him about its significance:

> We wanted it to be urban but not metropolitan. What I particularly wanted was a fictional town that was large enough to throw up the kinds of problems we wanted to deal with, but small enough to allow regular and semi-regular characters to occur. I didn't want the anonymity of a metropolitan centre because that is a different kind of drama.

Within this fictional setting therefore, the dramatic action is defined in terms of a location that is beyond the city and yet exhibits problems and issues that one might relate to a metropolitan centre. Such issues are the use and abuse of illegal drugs, homelessness, petty crime, prostitution and a pervading sense of wider material deprivation. In an important sense, the intrusion or transplanting of these major social and economic issues within an urban setting highlights wider concerns within contemporary British society about the increase and spread of these problems beyond London and the major regional cities such as Birmingham, Manchester, Newcastle and Bristol. As Anne Power reported in an article for the *The Guardian* entitled 'Streets of Shame':

> In the inner areas of Manchester and Newcastle, almost half the population of working age is outside the labour market or education – double the national average. Nearly half of all households are poor, compared with a fifth nationally…. Although unemployment dropped in the 1990s, it dropped far more rapidly for women than for men. There is a surplus of men with a manual work background.[1]

Manchester is the named city in the series, the third largest city in England outside of London and Birmingham, and Stanton's proximity to it ensures a symbiotic relationship between the two. The migration of these major socio-economic problems from the city into the conurbation carries with it also endemic implications for issues of law and order and the surveillance and punishment of criminal behaviour. In this chapter, through a closely detailed examination of both series, I intend to discuss the extent to which 'The Cops' interrogates and exhibits some principal concerns relating to the urban location as a site of ideological struggle. I shall examine firstly the eight episodes constituting the first series, seeking to identify some key and defining characters, conflicts and narratives. A self-reflexive, critical interrogation operates throughout the series and signifies a complex interaction of subject – the Police Force – constructed as myth but simultaneously, through a dialectical tension between the camera point-of-view and editorial values, subverting and questioning the status and function of that myth. In that important respect, 'The Cops' shares similar territory to 'Homicide – Life on the Street,' which I discuss in Chapter Five. In terms of my concept of the geo-ideological, both series map a geographical terrain of urban degeneration. What is significant is that some of the kinds of issues of urban neglect and impoverishment located within the city setting of Baltimore ('Homicide'), are viewed within the regional urban setting of Bolton/Stanton in 'The Cops.' This confirms my assessment made slightly earlier in this chapter, that the demarcation of the geo-ideological terrain of the city, as opposed to the urban, is diminishing with a bewildering rapidity that has profound implications for social services and various schemes of both urban planning and inner city regeneration. So, in terms of the ideological marking of their terrain, both series implicitly address the wider meta-idelogical and socio-economic conditions in which crime and its palpable causes is enacted. In Barthes' use of myth as a theoretical construct, he was, to quote Masterman (1984) 'demonstrating the centrality of power relations – of patterns of dominance, oppression and subordination – to the process of signification.' In television drama, the proximity between the signifier and our sense of everyday experience becomes equivalent to our valuing of the drama's 'reality' or 'realism.' This process of the construction and reception of meaning is itself, of course, a function and outcome of our own culturally determined subjectivity. I shall argue that in terms of the performative aesthetic of both 'The Cops' and 'Homicide – Life on the Street,' both series seek to effect a deconstruction of those prevailing myths of the police and the concomitant constructs of law and order.

'The Cops' – Series One

In the opening sequence of Episode One, the visual narrative invites the viewer on a geographical journey from night-club to police station, which is correspondingly a journey for Mel Draper – the young WPC – from the anima of her private world into the persona of her formalised, public identity. Accordingly, the viewer is presented with a contradiction of expectations, powerfully communicating the tensions that Garnett identified in both the actual and ideological wearing of the police uniform. Therefore, within two minutes screening time of this opening episode, this sequence is signaling a world of ambiguity and disclosure. In so doing, it also exhibits complex, connotative layers of public duty and rhetoric with other, contradictory, subjective agendas. In 'Notes' that Garnett distributed to the production crew and actors he stated that "The moral ambiguity thus created is to be a defining attribute of the show and central to our relationship with the audience."[2]

I believe that the location and function of this 'moral ambiguity' reflects a political and cultural climate, in which the fixed positions of activists and practitioners on the left have been subject to substantial review and reformulation. This ideological re-configuration is a symptomatic response to the strategies of a dominant political culture, which seeks to deny ideology itself. Declaring that 'the class war is over,' the Blair 'project' accordingly seeks to define a debate in which no opposing view is articulated. It is important to recognise that it is within this context of the ascendancy of the centre right, with its accompanying penetration of the management and production of the political and popular mass media that Garnett observed:

> More and more in television you have to do 'Trojan Horse' drama if you want to be political. Thirty years ago I could produce films and television that were overtly political. You can't do that now, partly because the broadcasters won't allow it, and partly because the audience is difficult to get and to keep. If I'd gone to a broadcaster and said that I wanted to do a series that is largely set on a really tough, difficult housing estate somewhere in the north of England… they'd have said there's no audience for that. But if I say that I want to do a cop show, they say that's very interesting because 'cops and docs' are the mainstays of the schedule.

This function and strategy of 'The Cops' as 'Trojan Horse' drama is hugely significant exemplifying the potential and actual constraints of expressing an oppositional critique within those fields. This is not to present a simplistic model of direct censorship or interference. As worryingly, it is the exertion of indirect control and influence through the 'audience led' management of the means of cultural production, which prevails. Nevertheless, in terms of the demographic constituents and range of many television audiences, television drama, as a medium of popular mass communication, offers one of the most effective means of engaging in discourse about – and with – those urban communities that are, in Garnett's own words, "untouched by Blair's Paradise."

I am going to continue my immediate examination of these issues through a more detailed analysis of three characters in an inter-locking narrative from Episodes One and Two. These characters occupy significant positions within both the plot narrative and also the ideological discourse of these episodes. The characters are WPC Mel Draper, PC Roy Brammell and Nico a young, unemployed, working class man living on the Skeetsmoor estate. The fictive constructions of these characters and their dramatic interaction exemplify crucial ideological anxieties concerning the scale and extent of urban deprivation and crime and the rationale of its surveillance, policing and control.

The opening sequence of Episode One reveals that Mel's personal life is located in a popular sub-culture of recreational drugs and the club scene. The clash between that lifestyle and the demands of her role as a young policewoman are vividly expressed by the panic intensity of her journey between those meta-locations. The consequences of Mel's near-failure to self-reconstruct from the private into the public domain are traumatic not only for her, but also for the meridian expectations of the police and law enforcement. This dichotomy that is WPC Draper therefore constitutes an anxiety about both the efficacy of law enforcement in late capitalist urban society, and also about the increasingly indeterminate boundaries of the constructs of order and disorder. This dialectical tension, typified by Mel along with certain other characters, is a central narrative and ideological spine defining both series. Consequently, I shall be examining and discussing other examples of its presence and implications throughout this chapter.

It is significant that Draper is a newcomer in an established social order undergoing radical internal change. Her dominant motivational drives are an instinctive social concern expressed through humane values which, at crucial moments, collide with the pragmatic expediency of the old order, embodied most completely in the character of PC Roy Brammell. Brammell represents the type of policeman and policing which is perceived as dated and unacceptable by both the liberal left and the ascendant new management class within the police. Synonymous with the ideological strategies that led to both New Labour and the Birtist revolution within the BBC itself, these police inspectors are characterised through management-speak and a preoccupation with image. The character who embodies this generic class is Newland, whom I shall I discuss at greater length later in this section and chapter. Suffice to observe that Newland, in Episode Eight of the first series, against the background of a death in custody and insurrection upon Skeetsmoor, occupies himself with humiliating catering staff for the absence of exotic fruits at a police conference buffet. Placed almost subliminally in his office is a framed photograph of Tony Blair.

Roy Brammell acknowledges that both his own and the old order's existence are fundamentally threatened by this culture change within the police. Grieving for a former friend and senior colleague, Sergeant Poole, who has collapsed and died while pursuing a criminal, the series opens with Roy seeking to exact his own revenge for Poole's death. Believing – without any significant evidence – that the criminal being chased was a local house thief, Vince Graves, Brammell determines to fit Graves up for a criminal offence. A crucial stage in Roy's plan is to stop and search Nico, whom he knows to be acting as a small-time drug courier across the estate for the drug-dealing Caffrey brothers. In taking the drugs that Nico is carrying in order to plant them on Graves and secure a wholly dishonest conviction, Brammell's actions are seen to have serious and inevitable consequences for Nico, as the viewer sees in Episode Two. The predominant use of off-centre close ups, juxtaposed with the final cut to a mid-range framing of Nico's abject exposure and vulnerability, reinforces the aesthetic and ethical confusion endemic within the problematic objectivity that this sequence presents to the viewer. There are voyeuristic implications in the viewing of Brammell forcing Nico to undress in public, the police officer threatening an uncompromising rectal examination if his suspect doesn't co-operate. Equally, the sequence also provides another excellent example of the strategic tensions between camera-point-of-view that is that of the police, with the editorial viewing which translates into an ideological and ethical critique of the events witnessed. At the end of Episode One, Brammell drags a bloodied and evidently beaten-up Vince into the police station. Simultaneously, he slams onto the duty desk the plastic wrapped drugs that the viewer has previously witnessed him taking from Nico. There is a subtle layering process of possible meanings and resonance in this scenario. Self-evidently, the viewer is obliged to read into Brammell's actions a complex web of personal vendetta and covert police brutality with a public display of law enforcement. The unlawful and humiliating searching of Nico and his subsequent framing of Vince are unquestionably corrupt and serve only to fulfil Brammell's own, private need for his understanding of 'justice' to be executed and prevail. In Episode Two, Draper happens upon the badly beaten Nico in hospital and discovers that the Caffrey brothers have punished him for, as they construe, selling or using their drugs for his own purposes. Her righteous indignation and anger is, however, partially undermined by the viewer's privileged knowledge of her own use of illegal drugs with all of its implications. This compromised position has been reinforced when, also in Episode One, Draper allowed a female drug addict to have one final, illicit fix prior to Draper taking her into custody. In this crucial sense, the editorial commentary is deliberately ambiguous, rejecting simplistic binary positions of the ethics of law enforcement – including those of the *Guardian*-reading, liberal left. What does become increasingly and unmistakably clear throughout the series, is that personal agenda and private histories are continually in conflict with the demands of both dominant public expectations of the police, and the impact of the uniform upon those who wear it. As Garnett again stated in our interview:

> What I'm trying to do is to build up a tension – an ambivalence – between seeing from their [the police] point of view literally, but editorially not seeing it from their point of view and it's in that tension that we hope to find the show itself. It does not mean coming at this subject from the left that we are never tempted into pat, knee-jerk, left-liberal attitudes towards the police, or if we are tempted into those, the discipline of the show pulls us up short.

Returning to the character of Nico, it is perhaps an inevitable consequence of the framing device of the camera that the perception of the poor, disenfranchised, working class characters is as marginalised subjects. Nevertheless, the construction of Nico is given an additional dimension and resonance through the revealing of a pre-existing friendship between him and Mel. It transpires that they share a common background of class, schooling and friends. In the mutual surprise, bewilderment and – for Mel – discomfort that the characters express at meeting in the circumstances of the hospital ward, a shared and equalising correspondence of that former friendship militates against Roy's view of Nico. For Brammell and others like him, Nico is just another expendable 'scrote': the worthless, treacherous shirker of regular, Tory party conference rhetoric. More disturbingly, a similar form of reactionary rhetoric is, at the time of writing, being used by the New Labour Home Secretary, Jack Straw, in relation to asylum seekers.

Mel's attempts to bring news of Roy's corruption to light are irretrievably compromised and undermined when Roy makes it clear to her that he knows about her own illicit, recreational use of drugs. Furthermore, in later episodes, the viewer is offered other, more benign views of Brammell when, for example, he buys breakfast for a homeless young male prostitute, displaying an unexpected and practical concern for the boy's welfare. Whilst he rationalises his concern to colleagues by joking that his actions save him the drudgery of paperwork attendant upon an arrest, the incident highlights one of the strengths of the series. This is the extent to which these apparent contradictions and tensions resist the predictable polarities of given ideological positions. In the case of the thematic narrative involving Mel, Roy and Nico, the viewer is left to contemplate, with a sense of moral disquiet and impotence, the frustration, anger and discomfort of Mel's inner turmoil.

Another matter raised in Episode One deals with the concerns of the modernising Newland with the issue of the presence and representation of ethnic and racial groups within the police force. The character of PC Jaz Chundhara represents the only non-white officer at the Stanton station. Like Draper, he is relatively new to the force and is clearly both ambitious and frustrated with being consigned to a beat in Stanton's Asian community known as Wadsam. After trying to deal, unsuccessfully, with a case involving criminal damage to a Ford Escort owned by a young Muslim man, he goes to visit his father who owns a small car parts store and garage. The following short sequence of dialogue between father and son encapsulates the father's common-sense pragmatism with an oblique hint of his son's naive materialism and latent ambition:

Jaz: It's still fifteen thou a year, but it goes up when my probation ends...

Mr. Chundhara: It's a secure salary though. Put something away each week, you can leave at thirty, turn to business...

Jaz: I don't want a business Dad, I want to stay in, specialise, maybe CID, or diving...

Mr. Chundhara: It's okay for a young man, when you get older you may feel different...

The scene ends tellingly when a Muslim customer enters to buy an air filter for his *Orion* and disrupts their conversation. Seeing Jaz in his uniform, he jokingly enquires whether there has been a robbery at the store. When Mr Chundhara smiles proudly and says "My son", the customer replies:

(Incredulous) Your son! (Mutters in Urdu) What kind of a man puts his son in the police...

This short sequence raises, with an economy of dialogue and visual grammar, potential conflicts of expectation within both the family and also between differing ethnic groups within multi-racial communities. In a later scene in the same episode, some of the implications of these issues are further developed with a sharp, underlying irony. Jaz is continuing to talk with his father about his frustration at being used as a pawn in the liberal politicising of Newland and others:

Jaz: It's so everyone up here can see the police allow Pakis in...

Mr. Chundhara: (Injured) You're not a 'Paki' – you're a Gujarati...

Jaz: To them it's all the same. I'm just a walking recruitment poster...

Mr. Chundhara: You're the only Asian boy down there, aren't you?

Jaz: Yes.

Mr. Chundhara: They'd be embarrassed then if you resigned. They know what people would say.

The father advises his son to go and "play politics" with Chief Inspector Newland whom Jaz has described as "fast track, three years university and he's a Sergeant before his feet have touched the ground. Never even seen someone locked up." It is against this background that the scene is framed in which Jaz acts on his father's advice and arranges an appointment to see Newland. The following extract from this encounter demonstrates the superb sense of a satirical critique unknowingly engendered by Newland in his efforts to be a progressive, modernising manager:

Newland: Our community liaison initiative in Wadsam keeps reporting a lack of ethnically compatible officers as a major grievance.

Jaz : I'm not particularly interested in community relations sir.

(Newland arches his eyebrows at this heresy)

Jaz: Also, I'm not ethnically compatible. Most of the Wadsam community is Muslim, I'm Hindu.

Newland: Yes, but we hoped at least you'd be seen as more sympathetic to the problems of minorities.

Jaz: I'm not a minority, my father was born in India that's all, I'm English…

Newland: Nonetheless you're culturally from a minority group.

Jaz: I don't want to be treated that way… That's why you keep assigning me to Wadsam beat. As an advert!

Realising that he is making little or no progress with Newland, Jaz attempts to use his trump card: the threat of resignation from the force. Newland, slightly perturbed, offers at the conclusion of the interview to convey Jaz's 'misgivings' to Sergeant Giffen. These three sequences convey the complexities of seeking to redress historical and structural inequalities within recruitment to the police force. Newland is constructed in such a way that his concerns over these issues can only be expressed in the formal euphemisms of a Hendon training manual[3]. From Newland's ideological viewpoint, Jaz represents a schematic type of both a 'problem' – his ethnicity – and of that 'problem' as primarily an issue of presentation. It is as if Jaz can only be validated in those terms, denying him any other alternative, individual delineation. The programme successfully avoids replicating the glaringly patronising inconsistencies of Newland's construction of Jaz by presenting his character in a refreshingly open-ended manner. The character is not simply used as a formulaic cipher for either left-liberal or reactionary ideological positions. His passion for fast, attractive cars is presented simultaneously with his assertion that Hindu arranged marriages are acceptable because "You get to see them. It's just like picking a fridge… they all look a bit different but they all perform the same function." As with the construction of all the principal characters in 'The Cops,' the tensions present within Jaz's justifiable frustration at being the subject of liberal stereotyping, set against his own dismissive, reactionary attitude towards women, creates an interpretative space that is simultaneously unsettling and liberating.

I want to return to the character of WPC Mel Draper in terms of this discussion of Episode One and address a narrative line that I referred to earlier in this chapter. This concerns the young woman Theresa, a drug addict whose father has died and whom she has knowingly left to decompose in his council flat. Alerted by a neighbour living below the dead man's flat by both a terrible stench and discoloration of ceiling plaster, Draper is called to the scene on the very morning that she rushed to her morning shift, hung-over through lack of sleep and her use of drink and drugs. After some delay, with the irate neighbour breaking down the door, Draper is violently ill on finding the corpse. With Sergeant Giffen arriving and restoring a sense of order and focus to the situation, Draper discovers that the young woman, despite having endured sexual abuse by her father throughout her life, had maintained some nominal care of the old man. Nevertheless, on finding him recently dead some months previously, she has taken both his Giro cheques and his prescribed tamanzapan tablets for her own illicit use. The scene in which Draper confronts Theresa with her criminal actions presents a bleak and despairing insight into the seedy urban sub-culture of drug addiction. The camera focuses on Theresa, framing her gaunt, emotion-bleached features, presenting the viewer with a quietly insistent, dispassionate gaze that perfectly accompanies Mel's understated but necessary probing of the circumstances of the father's death. Just as Draper is about to take Theresa for further questioning and probable arrest at the station, Mel discovers her anxiously and hurriedly taking one last fix, which the young WPC should censure and prevent. Nevertheless from Draper's point of view, looking down upon the crouched figure of Theresa, the camera lingers uncomfortably to observe her desperate probing for a vein. This dark and appalling vignette conveys once again the tension implicit in the viewer as a complicit voyeur within a micro-narrative of confused empathy, pity and guilt. We are presented with a fictional world in which the strident judgments and prejudices of the tabloid press are challenged, whilst the assurances of a detached, affirming liberal tolerance are also questioned.

At the conclusion of Episode One we witness the barely constrained antagonism between Brammell and Giffen, the new sergeant who has been brought in by Newland to replace the recently deceased Poole. Giffen is clearly concerned about the circumstances surrounding the arrest of Graves and confronts Roy on the matter. Giffen is viewed by Newland as an efficient means of implementing the modernising process of the Stanton force. Nevertheless, there is a sense of Giffen's character functioning as more than just a management cipher. This conflict between Giffen's public role and private past is skilfully developed throughout the two series. Within that process, the relationship between Giffen and Brammell also undergoes a slow but significant, change as well. Nevertheless at this early stage in the series, Roy's views are cogently expressed in the following brief encounter between himself and Danny with whom Roy is on duty:

Danny: You don't rate him [Giffen] eh?

Roy: Nah, tosser.

Danny: That's an acute psychological insight Dr Brammell...

Roy: You know the score yourself. Newland's gone outside the Division to bring in his own man...

   (Danny shrugs, not disagreeing)

Roy: Be a 'modernising influence'... Y'know what that means?

   (Danny looks at him)

Roy: It's the end of the road for the real bobbies.... Anyone with balls is out....

The implications of this personal feud between Giffen and Brammell are made horribly and tragically clear in the opening of Episode Two when a young, suicidal man is seen to be standing precariously on the roof of a Stanton town centre building. As he urinates onto the passers by below, the police are dispatched to try and talk him down. Giffen and Brammell arrive on the rooftop and, whilst Brammell has clearly been present at a previous encounter with this young man, he stands back to place Giffen in the key role of negotiator. Recognising the young working-class man, Roy has referred to him as Maxwell which Giffen then continues to do, assuming that this is his name and that familiarity will help facilitate his safe removal from the roof edge. Maxwell, consumed by bitter self-denigration and convinced of his own worthlessness, challenges Giffen to confirm his own self-assessment that he is a waste of time:

> Maxwell: Say it. I'm a waste of time.
>
> (No reply)
>
> Maxwell: Say what you're thinking.
>
> Giffen: Get down off the wall.
>
> Maxwell: I want to hear it from you.
>
> (No reply)
>
> Maxwell: Tell me. Tell me – and I'll get down.
>
> (Beat. Giffen looks at him, weighing it up. He takes the risk, calls his bluff. He speaks quietly, calmly)
>
> Giffen: You're a waste of time.
>
> (Maxwell nods, saying nothing for a beat. It's what he wants to hear. He's gratified – glorified almost)
>
> Maxwell: You're fucking right.
>
> Giffen: Now get down off the wall.

Within one charged moment of Giffen uttering these words, Maxwell spins and hurls himself to his death below. In the shock and trauma of the aftermath of this suicide, Giffen turns to Roy for reassurance:

> Giffen: (In disbelief) I had him. Didn't I? I thought I had him.

(Roy, more swiftly recovered, kicks Giffen while he's down)

Roy: You dropped him.

Brammell's cold and calculating unwillingness to offer any support to the man whom he views as both Poole's replacement and the harbinger of modernisation, powerfully conveys the depth and intensity of the feelings involved. It transpires, later in the episode, that the young man's name was not Maxwell but that he had been given this sobriquet by Poole who had talked him down on the previous occasion with a cup of coffee. Brammell's failure to disclose this information to Giffen, and thereby indirectly reinforcing a false sense of familiarity between the sergeant and the young man, takes on a deeply disturbing significance. In this incident, we witness a depth and degree of deliberate deception that might, in other circumstances, be characterised as criminal in its intent.

Brammell knows that in the circumstances of the young man's suicide, Giffen could face serious disciplinary consequences at any Coroner's inquiry. Both he and Giffen know that the only way that this outcome can be avoided is if it proves impossible to establish the victim's identity. Ever the professional, Giffen embarks upon the grimly tedious task of working through the files of 'Missing Persons.' Against what are seemingly insurmountable odds, we witness him finally finding a match for the dead man. Shot in the dimly lit silence of the basement, this environment communicates a strong sense of Giffen's literal and metaphorical isolation. When, after a pause, he screws up the documentation and dispatches it to the waste paper bin, he becomes actively implicated in the web of intrigue and hidden agenda that defines the lives of so many of the police officers at Stanton.

In terms of exploring some of those conflicts in the wider context of the first series, I am going to proceed by examining some of the other principal characters in further detail.

PC Danny Rylance

PC Danny Rylance is developed in such a way in the first series that his character evolves from the cocky, sexually promiscuous man of the opening episodes through into a traumatised, tragic victim of his both his own guilt and the fury which erupts on Skeetsmoor at the end of Episode Eight. In the opening episode, we first encounter Rylance boasting about both his heavy drinking and his success with women. Significantly however, we also view him seeking to curb and contain Roy's efforts to pursue his personal vendetta against Graves. In Episode Two, an incident occurs which defines the predominant sense of the character as an irresponsible sexual predator. Seeing a young woman, Lisa Willocks, rummaging through a public re-cycling container, he engages her in conversation about her predicament. It transpires that she has dropped her car and house keys while putting some things into the recycling bin. Throughout this initial encounter there is a strong subliminal sense of latent sexual opportunism on Danny's part. This becomes increasingly evident and mutual when the two characters are back at Lisa's flat, where Danny has broken in so that she can retrieve her set of spare keys:

Danny: What do you do then?

Lisa: Telesales....

Danny: You're very persuasive I'd say.

   (He takes the tea off her)

Danny: Wasted though, aren't you – on the phone. Should have you working face to face, someone with your looks.

Lisa: You've embarrassed me now...

Danny: Shift a lot of kitchens then, do you? Or it's not one of those sex lines is it?

Lisa: You're full of questions.

Danny: That's me job.

Lisa: No I don't work on a sex line.

Danny: I believe you.

This encounter develops into a surreally humorous scenario where Lisa, in a dominatrix mode, insists upon Danny enacting a role-play with her where he interrogates her with increasing severity. Culminating in a full sexual encounter between them, it concludes with Lisa insisting, as a means of her achieving full sexual climax, that Danny phone into police HQ. Through its employment of the bizarre and wholly unexpected use of role-play, this sequence again reveals – albeit through some humour – the notion of the enacted role that the uniform brings to its wearer. In so doing, it provides yet another means of fore-grounding the wider and profounder sense of the culturally constructed nature of the police. However, subsequent episodes centring upon Danny's relationship with women reveal the serious and, ultimately, tragic consequences of the colliding of public and private agendas. Once again, Rylance becomes involved with a young woman in the context of her arrest by WPC Draper for being drunk and disorderly. It transpires that the young woman, Jenny, is a student who invites Danny in for coffee after he has escorted her home from the police station. The relationship quickly develops and Rylance begins to invest a degree of seriousness and commitment in it which reveals, perhaps, his underlying insecurity and needs. It becomes fairly clear by Episode Five that Jenny does not reciprocate Danny's perception of their relationship and, in this context, he begins to pursue her and threaten her when she makes it clear she wants the relationship to end. This scenario unfolds against another narrative in which Rylance is called out to deal with a case in which a young girl, Lindsey, has not returned to her father, after a visit to her mother from whom he is estranged. Rylance, traumatised by his sense of rejection by Jenny, threatens violence to her and her flat mate, and ignores his duties, as case officer, to investigate the circumstances of the young girl's disappearance. When he finally arrives at Pauline's – the mother's – house, he finds that she has given her daughter, Lindsey, an overdose of the tablets prescribed for her own depressive illness. Realising that had he given his proper time and attention to the case this situation might have been avoided, he runs out to his car to try and rush the unconscious girl to hospital. However, in a spiraling litany of tragic ineptitude and circumstance, his police car will not start. Desperate, but driven by the adrenaline of the situation, he sends out a message for assistance while running with the prostrate Lindsey through the streets which are by now full of boisterous and aggressive football fans. Although the paramedics and police support arrive, it is too late and the episode ends in a bleakly disturbing tableau of the young girl's death against a snarling backdrop of chanting, abusive football supporters:

> (Paramedic shocks Lindsey. Danny does not respond to the thud)

> Paramedic 2 (OOV): Clear.

> (Paramedic shocks Lindsey again. Jaz looks at the Paramedic who shakes his head and they stop working on Lindsey. A gradual chorus of "ALL COPPERS ARE WANKERS" builds up and a break away group of football fans start walking away from the group, building the chant as they go)

> Jaz: (To Danny) Come on mate.

> (On Danny's face, where all traces of life have left his eyes. It's clear these events will haunt him for the rest of his days)

The culmination of this harrowing narrative is inextricably caught up with events involving WPC Natalie Metcalf, whose own complex narrative strand involves the characters of PC Mike Thompson and the plainclothes Detective Sergeant Wakefield.

WPC Natalie Metcalf

WPC Natalie Metcalf represents an interesting and effective counter-balance to the character of Mel Draper. An established officer, she is a character who has been hardened through her experience and is also caught up in a problematic relationship with the character of Wakefield, an arrogant and ruthlessly pragmatic CID officer. The complex and damaging dynamics of this personal relationship ultimate lead her – and her partner on the beat, PC Mike Thompson – into corruption with dangerous consequences.

In some respects, Natalie shares some similarities in outlook with Roy Brammell. Like him, she recognises a need and subsequent justification for taking matters into her own hands in order to execute 'justice.' Accordingly, when she and Mike are called out to deal with a gang of aggressive youths who are tormenting the Worley family, she soon finds herself employing 'direct' methods to deal with the situation. We discover that the father, Bob Worley, has been imprisoned for raping a local woman and some of the locals, amongst them the youths, are now terrorising Trish Worley, her family, and especially her son, Roderick. Trish has called for the police after he has been beaten up and robbed as he went to do some local shopping for her. The camera-point-of-view tracks around the cramped, squalid interior of the council house, intensifying the overpowering sense of internal and material entrapment. Thompson's insensitive criticism of Trish and the squalor communicates once more, a predominant reactionary and judgmental viewpoint exhibited often in other characters such as Roy. The following scene from Episode Two presents a disturbing and uncomfortable collusion of personal judgment legitimised by the authority encoded within Mike by his uniform:

Mike: Tell me this Trish. Do you never get the urge to clear up a bit?

Trish: Hey?

Mike: Tidy up this shithole. Bit of spring cleaning now and then.

Trish: They only mess it up again.

    (Natalie looks at Mike to shut him up. He obliges reluctantly)

Natalie: Heard from Bob?

    (Trish closes her eyes: it's not even a shake of the head)

Mike: What about the girl – she still living around here?

    (This time it's the nod that's almost imperceptible. Mike surveys the bombsite living room in disgust)

Mike: You don't do yourselves any favours, you lot, do you – living like pigs.

    (A tear or two slips down Trish's frozen, immobile face. She makes no move to wipe them away, no move to do anything. The kids look at Mike now. Seeing he's gone too far, he makes for the door before he says anything worse)

Mike's harsh criticism of Trish amounts to an unwarranted, intrusive value-judgment upon her life. In line with the prevailing simplistic value system, the complex kaleidoscope of deprivation, unemployment and criminal behaviour is reduced to a level of individualised 'fault.' Later on in this episode, Metcalf comes upon the same gang of youths beating up Roderick and intervenes to save him. When they arrive back at his house, Trish's frustration and anger excludes any sense of relief at seeing her son safely home or expressing thanks to the police. Rather, she cuffs Roderick and sends him indoors, leading Lewis Skillett, the gang leader, to observe "Wouldn't let a woman slap me about." Natalie's own feelings of frustration at the gang's bullying and oppressive behaviour is provoked beyond containment by Lewis' cocky, sexist taunt. She automatically pinions him against the side of the police van and roughly questions him. Discovering that he is the son of Brian Skillett, a notorious local criminal, she pursues her prey with added determination. Deftly spinning him around with his arm trapped behind his back – despite Mike's attempts to defuse the situation – she whips her baton out and asks the now frightened boy "What if I started hitting you with this, Lewis – what would you do then?" At this climactic point, there is a moment of marvelously earthed humour, when a passing old woman – rather than question Natalie's actions – says: "Why don't you break his fucking skull and do us all a favour?" In one brief, charged exchange, this uncompromising expression of what constitutes a commonly-felt sense of disempowerment on the estate, affirms both Metcalf's aggressive implementation of justice and, by subtle implication, the corresponding actions of Brammell in his dealings with Nico and Graves. In a social and economic environment which is determined by major issues such as long-term unemployment, alongside continually diminishing resources to repair and maintain public housing stock, there presides a wholly understandable, instinctive desire to see summary justice executed. When even nominally democratic and institutionalised agencies fail to engage with the depressing persistence of social deprivation and inequality, Natalie's actions take on an aura of tangible, proven effectiveness. Of course this legitimisation of direct action is only one remove from the vigilante bullies of Lewis and his gang and threatens to eradicate any wider sense of impartial law enforcement. This reactionary position also contains within its modus operandi the opportunity for personal vendettas to be pursued. It is precisely such a motivation for personal revenge that drives Natalie on to pursue her own agenda against Brian Skillet. On returning Lewis home to his father, she realises that Brian Skillet is the man responsible for assaulting her and breaking her arm when she worked as a clerical officer in the DHSS offices. Challenging him on this and forcing an apology from him, she nevertheless charges him with a minor offence related to his car, which he is in the process of repairing. Mike warns her of the dangers involved in her actions and this warning is dramatically demonstrated when, at the end of the episode, the police are called out to the Worley's house again, this time to see it consumed in flames with the gang looting possessions from it. Brian Skillet stands and smiles at Natalie at his own choreographed act of revenge against her earlier actions. She becomes more and more obsessed at retrieving the initiative in this battle of personal animosity and seeks any opportunity to prosecute Skillet. Ultimately, in Episode Seven, she corruptly manufactures a warrant for his arrest on the false assumption that he has failed to attend a court hearing under a previous ruling. A highly charged and heated exchange occurs when Metcalf arrives at Skillet's house to arrest him. Skillet vociferously defends his innocence, stating – truthfully, as we eventually discover – that the matter has already been dealt with. Metcalf's own personal motivation for vengeance is transparent in her needlessly violent language and actions:

> (Natalie drags him out of the car. His foot gets caught in the seat belt and he falls on the floor, part-way out of the car)

> Natalie: Are you threatening me? Are you threatening me? Eh?… 'Cause that's just about your limit isn't it? Eh? Hitting women. That's how much of a tough guy you are. Give your missus a good slap now and again do you? Eh?… Well take a good look at who's locking you up. You don't look like such a big man now. You look like exactly what you are: a useless piece of shit. Go on, make threats, resist arrest. It'll go on your charge sheet.

When Natalie discovers later in this episode that Skillet was telling the truth and that he is the victim of wrongful arrest, she is advised by Standish, the duty officer, to release him and "Prepare to eat shit." The scene then explodes into a torrent of action and panic as, on opening Skillet's cell, Metcalf discovers him prostrate on the floor, clearly critically ill. The Police Surgeon arrives but it is too late, as Natalie already realises. The consequences of her actions are wide reaching and devastating. As news of his death reaches his family and the estate, there is widespread unrest and preparation amongst his family and friends for violent reprisal at what they mistakenly imagine to be his death caused by police brutality. In Episode Eight, the last of the first series, the mood evoked is one of a growing apprehension of violent unrest on the estate, especially in the context of the impending funeral. It is into this potential maelstrom of bitter grief, anger and violence that Danny enters in the final, moving climax to the series. Traumatised by the guilt and responsibility that he feels for Lindsey's death, he has undergone a bereavement counselling session where he has had to face Lindsey's father, tortured by his anger and bewilderment at his daughter's death. On a journey that carries with it all of the associations of a tragic miscreant seeking repentance, reconciliation and justice, Danny drives up to where the Skillet family and supporters are gathered on the estate. The sense of terrible foreboding is almost tangible, with people at the pub where the Wake is taking place, shouting abuse at him as he moves towards them. Skillet's brother, Pete, tries to intervene and save Danny from the imminent violence. There is an awful pathos in the vulnerable openness that now characterises the traumatised Danny:

> Danny: I'm offering me condolences…. See what it is? It's us and them, isn't it? Always us and them. Everybody at everybody's throat. I tell you what, people tried being civil to each other now and then we'd all be better off.

(Pete Skillet's not untouched by this sentiment. He takes Danny's arm, turns him back towards his car)

Pete Skillet: Go on, lad, get off. You're not wanted.

Danny: I know what you're feeling.

Pete Skillet: Maybe you do, but you'll be feeling a pint glass in your face if you don't get yourself gone.

Danny: I know what you're feeling. I've just come to say that. We're not animals you know. We have feelings.

However, it is too late for reconciliation and despite Pete Skillet's attempts to save Danny, violence breaks out and he disappears under a sickening mass beating of fists, boots and billiard cues. As he drowns beneath their blows, the police reinforcements arrive and, aided by a thunderstorm that suddenly erupts over the scene, they are slowly able to regain order. At the conclusion to the episode, the seeds of a grudging rapprochement and respect between Brammell and Giffen is expressed in their mutual acknowledgment of the rain that has probably saved Danny's life and helped them restore order:

(Roy's gaze breaks off from the departing ambulance, finds Giffen looking towards him, giving homage)

Giffen: PC Rain.

(Roy nods, can't help laughing)

Roy: Best bobby in the fucking world.

DC Alan Wakefield

This character, played with chilling effectiveness by the actor David Crellin, is the most transparently corrupt and ruthlessly self-seeking character across both series. Unlike the character of Roy Brammell, we are offered no mediating, benign perspective upon his constant quest for self-promoting power and status. The principle narratives incorporating Wakefield in Series One necessarily involve Natalie, and by implication, Mike. It's soon revealed that Wakefield and Metcalfe are involved in a personal, intimate relationship outside of their work, sharing a flat with Natalie defined in the problematic dynamics of the relationship as a needy, quasi-passive subject. Wakefield is as arrogantly manipulative in his private life as in his public role as a plainclothes detective. Equally, he is as contemptuous of the uniformed branch as he is of the criminals that cross his path. So it is against this background that he exploits his relationship with Natalie to force her – and Mike her team partner – into a scheme to arrest Stokes, a local big-time drugs dealer. In order to secure a positive identification, Wakefield places pressure upon Natalie to be present, with Mike, in a police car keeping surveillance upon Stokes' home. However, the plan misfires and the two officers narrowly escape serious injury when Stokes, or one of his accomplices, fires at the car. Although neither police officer could identify Stokes, Wakefield pressurises Natalie to commit perjury along with Mike to ensure a positive identification. This scenario is further complicated by evidence of Mike's own sexual attraction to Natalie, even though he is weeks away from marriage. The subtext of jealousy, sexual desire and moral panic infuse what are some of the most powerful scenes in the series. Much against his principles, Mike – driven by a longing for Natalie and her approval – commits himself to the false identification. With a dark, foreboding inevitability, Mike and his newly-wed partner Colleen begin to receive threatening phone calls, culminating in their house being violently trashed, their living room walls disfigured with red spray paint graffiti. In the following scene from Episode Six, the dialogue between the two characters expertly conveys the complex mesh of pragmatism, guilt and unrequited desire that permeates their public roles and duties:

> Mike: Right. (Beat) I – I'm going to talk about this whether you want to or not.
>
> Nat: Don't try to be forceful, Mike, it's not you.
>
> Mike: Don't take the piss. (Beat) When I i.d.'d Stokes, I didn't have a scooby who he was. All I knew was nail the scrote in the red shirt. Now, in my book, that brings us down to Stokes' level.
>
> Nat: (Dismissive) Crap. Stokes is a drug dealing-murdering bastard – is that the level we're at? You're talking crap, Mike.
>
> Mike: No, it's not crap. Everyday in this job you hear lies and lies and lies –
>
> Nat: Any lies?
>
> Mike: (Ignoring this) – and now I'm supposed to stand up in court and do the same. That's not why I joined –
>
> Nat: Oh that's funny. Under 'Reasons for joining,' I wrote 'Lying in court'…

Mike then goes on to tell Natalie about the telephone threats that he and Colleen are receiving to which he receives no sympathy:

> Nat: …Are you saying you're too scared to testify?

Mike: Course I'm not saying that.

Nat: Well, Mike, in case you've forgotten: the first rule of policing is you stand by your mates. And the second rule is you never forget rule one.

In her efforts to ensure that Mike will stay on board, Natalie attempts to persuade Mike of the realpolitik that ultimately drives their lives and actions as police officers. In so doing, she communicates a powerfully oblique challenge to viewers in terms of their own closed, self-interested expectations of the police:

Nat: Mike, one thing I learned when I was with Social Work – everybody's a fascist when his or her home's threatened. People don't want a clean police force, they want results.

Mike: You're so fucking wise, you know that? You're so fucking wise.

Nat: Tell me this: does Stokes deserve to go to jail? (Beat) Would that be justice?

Mike: (Reluctant) Yes.

Nat: Well, on this occasion, justice needs some help. Is that too complex for you?

(Nat has got to him. He stares ahead for a few seconds)

Mike: (Quietly) Yeah, well it wouldn't be that simple if you weren't screwing Wakefield.

Nat: Ah, now we're really getting down to what this is all about. Alan's career'll be over if you don't come through for him and here you are giving me all this I'm-so-moral crap.

Mike: No.

Nat: But you and I know what's really going on: you'd like to see Alan fucked because you fancy the knickers off me.

The brutal and cynical directness with which Natalie attacks Mike's motives for not testifying against Stokes correlates with her own desperate need to rationalise her own role, not only in the framing of Stokes, but as crucially in her private relationship with Wakefield. In maintaining her own raison d'être within her private and public spheres, she must necessarily attack Mike where she knows him to be most vulnerable. Significantly, this Achilles' heel invokes Mike's potency both in terms of his commitment to his fellow officers, as well as his unfulfilled sexual longing for her. Therefore, with cruel manipulation, Natalie is able to simultaneously provoke Mike's sense of professionalism as a paradigm of his own emotional impotence and guilt, in the face of his confused feelings of arousal and jealousy. In its own very powerful way, this exchange between the two characters conveys a microcosm of the strategic and ethical confusion, within the macrocosm of the policing of our society at the end of the twentieth century. In the process, dilemmas central to public expectations and the political rhetoric of law enforcement within the nascent crisis of millennial capitalism are foregrounded. Such dilemmas concern the ethical implications of the means and ownership of wealth and resources, within which may be read equivalence in the ethics of ownership and power in the construction and dynamics of personal relationships.

'The Cops' – Series Two

These irreconcilable conflicts and tensions escalate into the second series with the compelling power and dark, relentless inevitability of a Jacobean tragedy. Yeats' observation that "the centre cannot hold" is an appropriate and evocative image of the ways in which the centrifugal forces of public and private scenarios, threaten to fragment the fragile sense of cohesive identity and purpose within the Stanton police force. In a sense the second series tends to be less incident-based than the opening series in which the characters and issues are initially delineated. While there are unquestionably serious and traumatic incidents in the second series, I believe that they exist in order to frame and facilitate the more fundamental concerns of character exploration, development and inter-action. In this important sense, the second series serves to fulfil Garnett's stated aim of "dealing with human beings who are more than their uniform." In so doing the narrative and ideological axis moves to bring into the centre of this fictive world specific characters and groups from the marginalised domains of class and ethnicity. Clearly, it would be inappropriate to attempt to discuss the second series in complete, chronological detail. Therefore, as in my section dealing with the first series, I intend to focus upon some specific narratives and scenarios, which, I believe, illustrate some of the principal issues arising out of the second series.

> Jo Warren: Can't go on like this can we? It's our community y'know, it's not up to someone else to change this, it's up to us....

> (Episode Five)

The above quotation is taken from the moving scene in Episode Five at the funeral service for a young, thirteen year old girl, Debbie Sharpe, who has died of a drugs overdose. This desperate call for community action, provoked by this tragedy, fuels a central narrative and thematic struggle in Series Two. Jo's plea is heeded and a group, composed almost exclusively of working-class women from Skeetsmoor estate, join together to take action against the drug dealers known to be responsible for her death. Nevertheless, this surge of community identity, anger and action does not ultimately lead to the justice the women seek. As they struggle with their ongoing attempts to assert themselves in the context of structural disempowerment, their frustration leads irrevocably into violent direct action. Caught up in the centre of this maelstrom is the character of WPC Mel Draper who has, by the start of the second series, been moved onto Skeetsmoor as a Community Liaison Officer. The tensions endemic to the moral ambiguity surrounding Mel from the first series are skilfully developed throughout the second series. An essential component within this strategic narrative and ideological device is the new character of Darrill Stone, a Community Worker on Skeetsmoor. As the series unfolds, Mel's initially troubled professional relationship with Stone develops into an intimate relationship. The dialectical tensions which were thus established in the opening sequence of Episode One, discussed earlier in this chapter, are developed to a climactic point of Mel's discovery of Darrill exploiting their relationship for his own strategic, political ends. In the events leading up to Debbie's funeral, a special police Support Unit waits in the vicinity of the funeral in expectation of violent unrest arising from the angered mourners. The arrogant machismo of these Special Officers is evidenced in their flirtation with WPC Amanda Kennett, a new young black graduate recruit, and their peremptory, dismissive contempt at Debbie's death:

Amanda: Where you from?

Support Unit PC: (Like it was Chicago) Burton on Ribble

Amanda: I heard it's rough there.

Support Unit PC: It is when we're around...

   (He lingers by Amanda knowing this infuriates Mike)

Support Unit PC: Was it you found her body then?

Amanda: No. She was just a young girl you know.

Support Unit PC: Junkie though weren't she?

Amanda: Yeah.

Support Unit PC: Hardly surprising she's dead then eh?

   (Mike watches Amanda watch the Support Unit PC as he struts back toward the van with what looks like admiration)

Jo Warren, the councillor from the estate, views Draper's presence at the service with surprise and the following dialogue communicates the tensions between the estate and the police. Intrinsically, Mel's own feelings and principles are torn between herself as a young woman in empathy with these women and her role as a Community WPC. Significantly, the fleece that she wears in her role as a 'plain-clothes' officer is worn on top of her uniform – a visual metaphor of the overlapping identities with which she struggles:

> (Sheenagh notices Mel)

> Jo Warren: This is...

> Sheenagh: Yeah I know who you are. Here to keep tabs on us are you?

> Mel: It wasn't our decision, it was the Court who let him out.

> Sheenagh: Lads up here see that happen and they think "fuck it, I'll do the same. Police won't touch me."

> Mel: We can only work inside the Law.

> Jo Warren: (Darkly) Maybe that's the problem.

> Sheenagh: (Dismissive to Mel) Oh there's always a bloody excuse. Different if it were one of your own.

Mel is torn between her profound and growing sense of solidarity as a woman with other women, and her struggle to exercise help and influence within the constraints of her role as a police officer. As her relationship with Darrill extends into the private arena of her own emotional needs and sexual desire, her attempts to retain professional integrity with personal commitment becoming increasingly perilous. Towards the opening of Episode Five, the camera offers a mid-to-close range shot of a couple 'giggling together under the duvet in a darkened room.' Initially out of view, we hear their voices and then see Mel and Darrill together in bed. They're engaged in an animated talk about their navels, arguing over differences. Darrill patiently explains to Mel the changes that had taken place in terms of the practice of tying the umbilical cord at birth. Within the context of a humorous and inconsequential lovers' pillow talk, Darrill nevertheless seeks to make a wider, political point:

> Darrill: Yours was clipped, like a little crocodile clip... anyone born after about 1974 had a plastic clip snapped on their umbilical...

> Mel: Oh yeah...

> Darrill: Before that midwife just tied a knot. I mean any time between the dawn of man and 1974 a knot was all was needed...

> Mel: So, quicker isn't it?

Darrill: It's a tag isn't it? You're still wet from womb and they find a way to mark you... An ancient skill lost to make way for another plastic product...

(Mel grins, fascinated)

Mel: You're mad, you!

Darrill: How am I?

Mel: Everything's politics, you should be on a bloody soapbox!

Darrill: Everything is politics...

The impact of Darrill's political activities and strategies lead ultimately to the sudden and traumatic end of the relationship later in the series. A premonition of the impossible contradictions the couple face is neatly conveyed in the closing moments of this scene, focusing on Debbie Sharpe's funeral later that same day:

Darrill: Wants me to go to that funeral today. I was going anyway.

Mel: (Remembers) That's Debbie Sharpe isn't it?

Darrill: You know her?

(Mel sits on the bed, her sunny mood gone)

Mel: Sort of... yeah I did...

(Darrill moves closer to her)

Darrill: You going to go?

(Mel frowns, her mood altered)

Mel: No, I can't. I'm on shift.

(She rises and grabs her shirt)

Darrill: Yeah, I better shift myself an' all.

Stone's role as a Community Worker on the estate places this character in a problematic but significant ideological position in the second series. A white, working-class male, this character has grown up on Skeetsmoor and therefore both knows and is known by the local community. He is viewed with serious mistrust and suspicion by many of the older people on the estate. His work role necessitates close proximity to the young people, many of whom are either actively involved in, or on the margins of, criminality. This proximity, expressed visually through his similarity in dress code and appearance to the young offenders he works alongside, is further reinforced through aspects of his work such as providing free, clean syringes on a 'need' basis to counteract the critical health risks involved in addicts sharing used needles. He is, simultaneously, a constituent by birth and upbringing of the estate, whilst also – by personal lifestyle and political action – an ally and supporter of a youth sub-culture delineated by long term unemployment, drug abuse and the criminal hedonism of joy riding. Therefore it is unclear from the viewpoint of either the police or the older working-class residents either what his function is, or what his motives are. The character of Darrill Stone shares some similar territory in this respect to Mel Draper in that they both transgress the comfortable binary positions of law/license, order/disorder and transgression/surveillance. This deeply troubling ambiguity defies ideological closure, whilst simultaneously facilitating oppositional exposure of the contradictions inherent within the private and public domain of the urban location as a site of struggle. Mel and Darrill are constantly caught between moments of tender affection and expressions of commitment, against the continuing tensions that they encounter in their public roles. One example of this is a story line narrative in which a young fourteen-year-old girl, Becky Jennings, is in a sexual relationship with an older man, Trevor Walsh. Mel is the officer on the case and, after completing a police check on Walsh, discovers that he has a previous conviction for sexual assault. However, when Mel goes to enlist Darrill's advice and perspective upon the issue, his pragmatism provokes an uneasy exchange between them. Stone bringing their own relationship into the equation exacerbates this:

Mel: You don't know the Walsh family do you, live on the corner of Salisbury Road?

Darrill: Know of them, why?

Mel: The youngest brother, Trevor, 's seeing a fourteen-year-old girl.

Darrill: (Shrugs) So?

Mel: He's 20. We had an anonymous call.

Darrill: Sounds a bit dodgy.

Mel: Yeah but still...

Darrill: But still what? There's more of an age gap between us.

Mel: It's not the age gap, Darrill, it's the young girl's age. It's against the law.

Darrill: If you're gonna start locking up kids for under age sex you'd better draft in the army.

Mel: What's the matter? Got a little girl of your own stashed away somewhere?

Darrill: I'm looking at her.

Mel: Bastard.

(Mel gets back in the car, happy having seen Darrill)

The campaign begun by the Skeetsmoor women gathers pace and, after the funeral, a deputation from the group arrive at the police station, demanding to see Chief Inspector Newland. Giffen, seeking to defuse the potential unrest, effects a meeting between a spokeswoman for the group and Newland, whose principal motivation appears to be avoiding unwelcome publicity in the local press. The women provide Mel with information about the two Davenport brothers, the younger of whom, Craig was responsible for supplying Debbie with the drugs that caused her overdose. In return for his providing information to arrest and convict Terry Reynolds, a feared and violent drugs dealer, the police offer Craig a deal. However, when he fails to turn up at the court to testify against Reynolds, the police are left without sufficient evidence to pursue their prosecution. Thrown into a desperate search for Craig motivated by their need for him as a witness, and their accompanying fear for his safety, they also arrest his older brother Rosco, for acting as a drug courier for the Caffrey brothers. As he leads the police to Craig's secret hide, he responds to police criticism of distributing drugs as a means of making money in order to get out of Skeetsmoor, by asserting: "It's the only job there is these days. You'd do the same if you were in my shoes." Before either brother can provide testimony against either Reynolds or the Caffreys, PC Dean Wishart discovers the savagely beaten body of their mother left slumped against the back door of her council house. In this climate of escalating community anger and action and the internecine drug war being fought between Reynolds and the Caffreys, the police appear to be powerless against this latent crucible of frustration and violence. Within the police station itself, this incendiary atmosphere culminates in a highly charged encounter between Giffen and Draper. At the heart of the conflict and Giffen's angry impatience with the young WPC, is her failure to separate her convictions and empathy as a young woman from the rigorous demands of policing expected and enacted by Giffen. Having failed to alert Giffen to the planned candle-lit vigil commemorating Debbie Sharpe, Giffen explodes at what he sees to be her naive inaction:

Mel: It's only a candle-light procession, it's a woman's thing, it won't be violent.

Giffen: That's a demo as far as I can see. The place is a powder keg at the moment!

Mel: These people aren't criminals! If it were happening in Shepton…

Giffen: It's not Shepton though, it's Skeetsmoor...

Mel: They just want to grieve the death of a child, why can't we leave them in peace?

Giffen: It's time you started doing the job you're paid to do.

Mel: I'm trying to...

Giffen: Well make up your mind whose side you're on.

Mel: I didn't think it was a question of sides...

Giffen: Well wake up then.

This dialogue encapsulates issues at the heart of both the series as a whole and also within the character of WPC Mel Draper. In the context of what I believe to be such a consistently excellent series, demonstrated in acting, writing, directing and editing of a tellingly sustained quality, it might seem inappropriate to focus as I have upon narratives and issues centring upon this one character. Clearly, the piece is ensemble in form, style and its own ideological purpose. Nevertheless I believe that the character of Mel Draper, played with a focused, pained sensitivity by Katy Cavanagh, along with that of Roy Brammell, played by John Henshaw with an immense, uncluttered sense of his character's humanity and desperate flaws, are perhaps the two principal carriers of the pieces 'moral ambiguity.' I shall be discussing the development and thematic journey of Brammell in the following section.

Mel lets Darrill know that Reynolds's case has had to be postponed, a chain of events is unleashed which finally compromises her professional integrity and brings her relationship with him to a sudden and desperately unhappy end. Reynolds's house is vandalised by spray paint by women from the action group and Darrill is called out in the early hours of the morning to try and intervene. Mel, roused from sleep by the noise and commotion, follows him to the scene where, unbeknown, Reynolds videos the events.

The following day, Mel, as Community Police Officer, is required by Giffen to study the video in the light of a charge that Reynolds wants to bring against the perpetrators. In a moment of crucial internal conflict, Mel is forced to irrevocably undermine her latent empathy and support with the women. She names the perpetrators from the video. Thus ensuring their arrest, Mel has – as Giffen had threatened she must – positioned herself on a side in the wider struggle. Having placed herself beyond the tenuous ground of shared concern and action with the women, her sense of alienation, confusion and failure is finally confirmed on learning that Darrill had used the information she had made available to him to fuel and provoke the attack. Knowing, and wanting, the women to attack Reynolds's house to fuel a climate of anarchy in which Newland might, at last, support his proposals for community action on the estate, Darrill has irreversibly compromised his relationship with Mel, betraying her trust in the process. When he endeavours to rationalise his actions to her with "Sometimes you have to make things happen, Mel…. You have to do these things to get things done," she is left angry and disillusioned. Her final words to him, "I never realised what a smug bastard you are," Draper has moved beyond the point of recall in both her private and public lives. When, having booked a holiday abroad to recuperate and take stock of her life, she is refused leave by Giffen, her final actions are transparently inevitable. Arriving at a party to celebrate Natalie's promotion as Sergeant, she lingers half way down the steps into the basement restaurant. Viewing the scenes of rather desperate, drunken bonhomie, she turns, retraces her steps and the camera cuts to a rear view long shot of Mel running through the midnight airport concourse to take her literal and metaphorical flight away into an uncertain future.

> Roy: See what's on this badge? It's a crown not a fucking chapati
>
> (Episode Ten)

In this section I intend to deal with issues of race, racism and ethnicity and in order to explore those issues, I will be centring upon the characters of PC Roy Brammell, PC Jaz Chundhara, WPC Amanda Kennett and also on some specific scenarios and narratives related to the second series.

> Maybe we were over sensitive [in the treatment of issues of race and ethnicity] in the first series to avoid clichés. Once you get into stories of colour, racial stories and sexual harassment as well, it's not easy to avoid the clichéd predictable ways of telling those stories, taking also a politically respectable liberal position but a dramatically empty one… It's unhelpful politics and bad drama. In the second series we're grasping that nettle more and I hope – other people must be the judge – in ways that will be unpredictable and not ways that will be knee-jerk politically correct.

This observation made by Tony Garnett in our interview during the shooting of the second series provides a useful frame for the discussion in this section. In Series Two, the complex issues of both racism and the representations of characters of colour are explored with the same uncompromising honesty and integrity that characterises the series as a whole. The unwillingness and caution to simply replicate characterisations that meet the requirements of a white liberal agenda results in a wholly more compelling, dramatic and convincing investigation of these themes in both series. The character newly introduced in Series Two, Amanda Kennett, is a young, attractive, Afro-Caribbean fast track graduate officer. Significantly, as the narratives centred upon her unfold, the viewer discovers that Chief Inspector Newland is specifically grooming her. In terms of his white liberal, modernising management strategy, this positions her metaphorically as a 'trophy,' equivalent to the one he has received for his golfing achievements, boasting of both with no sense of self-critical irony. The character of Amanda is a hugely problematic and controversial fictive construction. Resisting the more obvious opportunity to present an unambiguously positive role model in terms of the media representation of racial character-types, the programme makers seek to

43

construct a more complex combination of ambition, self-assertion and resistance to the reactionary attitudes and rites of passage within the established police culture.

WPC Amanda Kennett

Described by Newland as "Young, black, female… a flagship recruit," Kennett arrives at Stanton to replace Danny Rylance who is obliged to leave the force following further investigations into the death of the young girl Lindsey Wilcox. Her arrival at Stanton and presence within the series proves to be explosive, resisting the comfortable categorisation of either reactionary or liberal positions. She is first viewed with Wakefield who, in this second series, has been returned to plain-clothes duties in the light of the breakdown of the Stokes case. Inevitably, Wakefield is as flirtatiously manipulative with her as he is with all women that he encounters. She appears to be attracted to his crass arrogance and Natalie – with a subtext of lingering jealousy – finds the conversation turning to Wakefield as they drive a detainee to Stanton police station.

Kennett: You're in the middle of your Sergeant's…

Natalie: Sergeant Wakefield tell you that?

Kennett: He said you're a good officer. (Beat) Role model.

(Despite herself, Natalie is warmed by Wakefield's compliment. She immediately becomes suspicious)

Kennett: He knows I want to get ahead. Said I should pick your brains.

Natalie: Oh, he did, did he?

Kennett: I think he meant it as a compliment.

(Natalie is still suspicious)

Kennett: I was wondering if you had any tips?

Natalie: You're a graduate?

Kennett: Psychology.

Natalie: Psychology? Forget it. Forget everything they taught you at university. It's worse than useless.

(Kennett laughs politely. She's heard that before)

Kennett: I was wondering how to play the politics. You had that death in custody but they're still letting you do your –

Natalie: (Sharp) We've got a prisoner in the car.

Kennett: I'm sorry.

Natalie: And even if we hadn't what makes you think I'm going to stand for that kind of garbage?

Kennett: If I got it wrong, I'm sorry.

When Natalie, seething with anger at the insensitive presumption inherent in Kennett's behaviour and tone, reprimands her, Kennett – though naivety or a deliberate rebuttal to Natalie's reproof – answers by saying "Thanks. It's good to hear the other side." Any potential sense of support that Amanda might have received from another female officer is undermined by an underlying resonance of arrogant resistance to both the reprimand and, by consequence, to the hierarchical relations of status and deference. However in the following Episode Four, when Metcalf meets Kennett again, it is in the context of Wakefield having driven over to Stanton police station. The potential for duplicity motivating Kennett's character is glimpsed in the contrast between her observing to Metcalf that "Alan kindly offered me a lift" to her comment as Wakefield leaves:

Kennett: What a creep.

Natalie: (Indignant) Thought you two were best buddies?

Kennett: (Dismissive) No.

She then proceeds immediately to view Mike entering the station, commenting "now him…" to which Metcalf warns, "He's married." Kennett observes wistfully that "All the good ones usually are." Later on in the series, Amanda and Mike are paired as a team and there remains an underlying sexual flirtation within their professional relationship. This is most clearly seen in two incidents, one from Episode Five and the other in Episode Six. Most tellingly however is a later scene in Episode Six when Amanda exposes Mike to blame and possible formal discipline following a parking incident that flares up into a racist scenario.

In Episode Five Amanda and Mike are on patrol together in the early hours of the morning, parked in a small retail estate. Amanda makes a clear flirtatious pass at Mike, which ends with a sense of inconclusive and confused agendas:

Amanda: Nice to be out with someone my own age…

(Amanda grins to herself, lays her head back in the seat, comfortable with Mike. It's that confessional hour)

Amanda: I've always had this fantasy of making love in a Police Car...

Mike: Yeah?

Amanda: You know, with the sirens blaring and the blue lights flashing...

(Mike casts a surreptitious glance at Amanda who is looking dreamily out the windscreen. He reaches over, very, very cautiously along the dash and slowly presses the switch, which operates the blue lights. Amanda sees the pool of blue light splash the ground before her and looks round sharply at Mike)

Wondering at what Amanda's reaction might be, there is a tacit sense of relief when Amanda reaches across and turns the blue light off. Nevertheless, in Episode Six, Mike and Amanda – despite being uniformed and on duty – take unauthorised time off for Mike to view a single flat in the aftermath of his marriage to Colleen breaking up. Mike lies on the bed and shuts his eyes, remarking that it's very comfy. Amanda's response is similarly provocative, asking Mike "Wanna try it out do you?" to which Mike replies "Come on then." There follows a short scene charged with the ambiguity and excitement of underlying sexual frisson, defused only when Mike asserts that he was "only joking." These two incidents have an additional significance in terms of what proves to be one of the major incidents of the second series, when Amanda – having had a practical joke played upon her – then accuses Giffen of sexual misconduct when she takes her complaint to him. Before proceeding to analyse that later incident, it's important to examine the later scene in Episode Six when she attempts to issue a parking ticket to an older, disabled man: Mr Kerin. Although displaying his orange disabled card and explaining that he is waiting for his wife, Kennett informs him that he is not allowed to park in that place. What should have been a minor incident flares into an unpleasant and explosive mix of violent misconduct and racial abuse. Clearly and understandably angered by Kerin's shout of "Get back to the jungle where you belong," she attempts to drag him out of his car, provoking another racist tirade of "Get off you fucking black bitch." As he strikes out at her, she steps back and sprays him with CS gas. This scenario is framed and constructed in such a way that specific viewing positions are challenged and exposed. Prospective readings of this incident, stipulated by gender and racial concerns, are disrupted by both a recognition that Kennett has handled a minor parking offence in an unnecessarily confrontational way, with the latent and then virulent racial prejudice that the incident unleashes. The use of the CS gas propels the action into a major incident with Giffen arriving on the scene to ascertain what has happened, with neither he or Metcalfe able to assimilate Kennett's actions. On the defensive, Kennett then implicates Mike who, as the senior officer in the team, should have been there to prevent this happening. When Natalie questions Mike's absence, Amanda replies that he is "Messing around with two little tarts." Her uncompromising comment is made in full and deliberate hearing of Giffen who instructs her to return to the station. When Metcalf reproaches Kennett for implicating Mike "You don't do it, Amanda, not in front of a Sergeant," her response remains characteristically defiant: "You shouldn't have asked me where he was then should you."

There remains a residual cluster of unresolved questions surrounding Amanda Kennett's behaviour and actions. A fundamental ambiguity seems to mark much of her behaviour. For example, her willing compliance with Mike in their ambivalent flirtations and apparent friendship and esprit de corps is then suddenly betrayed through her comments to Natalie before Giffen. Her acidic terseness is further complicated by the growing realisation that Mike, in purporting to deal with an indecent exposure to two young woman, is exploiting the opportunity to flirt with one of the victims. The character's actions and motives appear to oscillate between a proper and commendable sense of self-assertion, with a failure to respect the conventions of loyalty expected by the police officers to each other. However, this failure to commit herself to that comradeship of unquestioning loyalty provokes consideration of the legitimacy and implications of that loyalty. As one sees throughout both series, its presiding characteristic seems located in an essentially reactionary, masculine code of duty and pragmatic honour. Roy Brammell's framing of Vince Graves, Mike's ultimately unwilling participation in perjury with Natalie, and Jaz and Mel's agreement to protect each other over their inept failure to arrest a house thief, are all expressions of loyal commitment to the cause and rationale of policing. These contradictions inherent within the code of loyalty are, I believe, linked directly to the wider paradoxes of policing within a contemporary urban environment. They are inescapably related to the constructed myth of the force: i.e. a constructed, iconic image of·coherent, dispassionate law enforcement, executed by trained professionals with an uncompromising and consistent fairness. However, the reality of the diminishing levels of resourcing of policing in urban areas and the scale of criminal activity in relation to chronic poverty and unemployment undermine the efficacy of that myth. Finally, the exposure of institutionalised racism through the tragic cases of Stephen Lawrence and Ricky Reels, place even more pressure upon serving officers to seek recourse in a lexicon of 'loyalty' to redress growing public criticism of their role. It is in this context that I want to complete this discussion of the character of Amanda Kennett with an incident that strikes right at the heart of these issues.

Arriving at the 'Snack Shack' café in a run down, industrial estate, Natalie, Mike, Dean and Roy are implicated in a practical joke played upon Amanda, which seriously backfires. Kennett views Natalie carrying out an exercise with cuffs in preparation for her forthcoming Sergeant's exams. Taking an interest in the exercise and, predictably, offering an opinion to Metcalf about the procedure, Natalie makes as if to demonstrate a point relating to hand cuffing a suspect by taking Kennett's own arms behind her back. Culminating in Amanda being handcuffed to the railings, the others gladly participate in this effectively humiliating practical joke, walking away to have their 'Big Boys' breakfast in the café, leaving her stranded outside. Through a deft interplay of her voice out of shot and mid range shots lingering on her face pouting at her humiliation, the scene continues with the dialogue between Mike and Natalie in particular suggesting the residual sub-text of the tensions and jealousies in their relationship:

Natalie: Go on, Mike. Rescue your little princess.

Mike: You're the one's worried. You do it.

Natalie: Yeah, watch me.

Roy: (To Mike) I thought you liked her. (It's a wind up)

Kennett: (o.s.) Mike! (Her tone annoys Mike)

Mike: (To Roy) How'd you fancy being stuck in a car with that, day in day out.

Natalie: Giffen told me he thought you might learn something from her.

    (Mike falls for it)

Mike: He what!?

    (Natalie laughs. Roy and Wishaw smile)

Natalie: You're too easy.

Metcalf is then called away to an incident that parallels the wider issues of compromise and pragmatic self-interest masquerading as loyalty. Briefly, she finds herself called to an incident which has ramifications beyond the obvious. A group of older and middle-aged men are at a club. It transpires that one of them, Frank Northam, is a former police inspector who, with a tone of patronising authority, informs Metcalf that he wants a senior male officer to deal with the incident in which their wallets have allegedly been stolen. She is confronted by the patronising middle-aged man, Northam, who refuses her entry into the club.

When Natalie realises that she's not going to gain entrance, she reluctantly radios for Giffen who, in the ensuing scene, arrives to give her unqualified support for handling the case. It becomes clear that there is another agenda concerning the woman – a Stripper hired for the previous evening's Stag Night – which necessitates covert handling from a male officer prepared to be complicit in the incident. Giffen however, is not prepared to do so and apprehends that the men have engaged in a brutal gang-rape of the woman, dismissed casually by Northam as, "I'd had a bit to drink… wasn't the only one got carried away. You see why I want this handling carefully? She's threatening all sorts back there." Giffen is not going to be diverted from the lawful execution of investigating the incident and a scuffle ensues in which Northam hits Giffen in his attempt to do his duty. When he is being placed in custody at the station,

Northam comes across Roy whom he mistakenly thinks might help him and the others out. Significantly however, we notice that the code of loyalty does not encompass, from even Brammell's viewpoint, a violent sexual attack upon a woman: "Don't (He reins in his anger and disappointment) – don't judge me by your standards." The tangled web of assumed and mistaken assumptions about the perimeters of this corrupt, 'Old Boy's Network' is exacerbated by Inspector Stowe seeking to pressurise Giffen while, simultaneously, Newland supports Giffen's actions:

Newland: Hear it was Frank Northam.

Giffen: Stanton old boy.

Newland: Oh, I know Frank well. (Beat) No favours.

Giffen: Sir.

(Newland smiles)

Returning to the narrative centring upon Kennett. The practical joke gets badly out of hand when two young men appear outside the café, unable to believe what they see: a young WPC hand-cuffed to railings. Her colleagues are all aware that the 'joke' has gone too far with Roy warning them that, "If she spills her guts, the whole thing lasted thirty seconds tops. Those lads – that didn't happen. Just so we're all singing the same song." Back at the station canteen, the situation isn't helped by the crude sexist banter engaged in around their break. When Kennett, understandably irritated and offended, accuses them of being 'dirty minded little school boys' Wishaw responds with his usual rash impetus with "We're dirty minded? You're the one who wants to have sex in a car with the sirens going." Mike cannot believe that Dean has disclosed the locker room gossip and boasting he has clearly been engaging in. The others try to pacify Kennett by asserting that she's now 'one of the lads' and that they were only 'having a laugh.' The climactic point is reached when Roy seeks to pour oil on troubled waters with a rather puerile, sexually laden offer to her, suggesting that she might like to cuff him to some railings the next day. Kennett's aggressive response crosses the boundary of the scale's code:

Kennett: Cuffs wouldn't go round your wrists you fat slob.

(She's crossed the line. The scale waits to see how Roy will react. Roy fixes her with his eyes)

Roy: Don't really think you should start a slagging match, love. There's a few things I could say about your appearance you might not appreciate. (Beat) Don't get out of your depth.

The latent racist and sexist menace in Brammell's response has itself, perhaps, contravened the unspoken camaraderie of the station, catapulting the situation into a trajectory of accusations and critical disciplinary procedures. These threaten to engulf Giffen, the other officers involved in the original incident and, by implication therefore, Metcalf's promotion to Sergeant. When Kennett immediately goes to Giffen to make a formal complaint after Brammell's outburst, she believes that Giffen is not taking the situation sufficiently seriously. Furthermore, when he tries to hand Amanda her radio, which has become dislodged in her distress, she reads his behaviour as a sexual assault. When she demands and threatens a visit to Maggie Hayes, the newly appointed Personnel Officer, Giffen stands his ground and warns her of the serious implications of making a malicious complaint against another officer:

Kennett: Maybe... I've had a terrible day... maybe you didn't...

(Giffen says nothing)

Kennett: ...but this happens all the time if you're a woman.

Giffen: A malicious complaint against another officer is a sacking offence.

Without entering into an unnecessarily detailed exposition of this plot narrative, it is sufficient to say that Amanda Kennett is communicated increasingly as a character liable to disrupt, challenge and undermine the complex web of institutionalised codes of loyalty and conduct. Through this narrative strategy, the character also threatens the professional livelihoods of those officers involved in the original incident. With Giffen assuring Kennett that he will formally investigate the hand-cuffing incident, she then finds herself visiting an Asian family – the Ifrazs – in the context of alleged bullying and victimisation. The following telling piece of dialogue illustrates the dilemmas and difficulties inherent in the two women finding some shared territory to define themselves as women in the implicit, reactionary masculinity of the force:

Natalie: First few months in, I was arsey as hell. Thought they were a right bunch of wankers.

Kennett: Then you realised, you were right.

Natalie: Yeah, some of them are, but most of them are okay.

Kennett: I thought you were all right.

Natalie: Is that why you didn't name me to Giffen?

Kennett: These practical jokes are a way for insecure little boys to keep control –

Natalie: You've got it all worked out haven't you?

Kennett: Women in this job should stick together.

Natalie: So what am I? A collaborator?

Kennett: (Regret) I expected better of you.

   (Beat. Natalie doesn't know how to react. Kennett's honesty has wrong-footed her)

Natalie: (Bluster) Yeah, well that's me, just one big let down.

The collision between Amanda's efforts to establish some ideological shared ground on the basis of their shared gender identity, is undermined and resisted by Natalie's commitment to a pragmatic acceptance of a culture within which she must survive if she is to achieve her promotion. In this instance, there is therefore a compelling example of how individuals, marginalised by gender or ethnicity within a given constructed group, embrace the dominant values – effectively denying their specific identity in order to be accepted and survive within the group. Kennett, as a graduate newcomer, and as an ambitious young black recruit, will not co-operate with – or be assimilated by – those group strategies and expectations. While, as Natalie asserts to her, she rather self-righteously neglects to ever think about her own faults, the character's experience of the police force confirms the likely difficulties inherent in adjusting to, and internalising, its strategies of loyalty, deference and pragmatism. When the incident to which they have been called escalates as racial tensions and prejudices provoke allegations of death threats, Giffen arrives on the scene to assist. With Kennett deeply unhappy at Giffen's handling of the disciplinary enquiry, she begins to publicly denounce him on the street outside the Ifraz's home. Sensing the potential professional and operational embarrassment in the situation, Giffen orders her into his police car. After Giffen gets in beside her, she launches herself out of it, refusing Giffen's order to return. A later scene in the episode confirms that she has accused Giffen once again of sexual misconduct but has this time, gone straight to Newland. In the cataclysmic fallout from this second accusation, the chain of events involving the practical joke and her initial allegations spiral into a regional – and potentially national – controversy, which Newland realises he must suppress for his own career's sake. Giffen, convinced of his own innocence, wants the accusations dealt with openly, but Newland, observing to him that, "These sorts of complaints tend to leave their taint on everyone. Doesn't do anyone's promotion prospects any favours," initiates a series of behind-the-scenes manoeuvres in order to stage-manage a resolution. Kennett is transferred whilst Giffen resumes his duties having been suspended while the investigation took place. He is unhappy that he wasn't presented with the opportunity to prove his innocence but Newland's final, smug retort is "Swings and roundabouts, Ed." It has become evident that not only are constructs such as 'justice' problematic in terms of the policing of society, but equally so in terms of the police force's own, flawed attempts to regulate itself.

PC Jaz Chundhara, PC Roy Brammell, Karim Ifraz

In the opening stages of this chapter, I discussed the dilemmas that PC Jaz Chundhara faced in the first series, especially in relation to Newland's managerial, pseudo-liberal agenda regarding the policing of ethnic communities. In the second series, we discover Jaz still intent upon promotion although the character is required to navigate a less than easy course through the internal politics at Stanton police station. Furthermore, his own illicit 'moonlighting' – having a second, job through the night as a taxi driver – utterly contravenes police regulations, threatening him with dismissal if discovered. After an incident in which a motorist's car has been hit by a taxicab, Roy Brammell is called in, as the officer on the case, only to discover that Jaz was the driver concerned. The formal execution of the law is once more compromised as Roy seeks to protect a fellow officer from a disclosure, which will end his career. A deal is brokered by which the taxi firm owner will pay the motorist direct compensation, to be paid in cash by Jaz to the firm.

Chundhara's instinct for self-preservation and promotion is further facilitated when, as an officer investigating Terry Reynolds's house in the circumstances surrounding Debbie Sharpe's death, it is he who finds the stash of heroin essential to justify Giffen's initiative in organising the raid. Displaying his characteristic sense of self-promotion, he boasts to the others in the locker room at the end of that day, "Giffen singled me out" to which egotism Mel responds by placing the day's events into a grimmer context: "A thirteen-year-old girl died today." When Giffen looks in to say "Well done everyone" the point is reaffirmed once more about the ideological and operational principle of the police working collectively as a team. Nevertheless, news of Chundhara's achievements and ambition are clearly communicated as a plain clothes detective approaches Jaz and indicates that there is an imminent opening for him. It is with predictable and depressing inevitability that, on being promoted into CID mid-way through the second series, Jaz is initiated into the culture of the CID – seen most chillingly in the arrogant self-interest of Wakefield. This happens when in accepting a financial payment as thanks from a young Asian factory owner he betrays his own professionalism as a police officer. This payment has been made after Jaz has successfully – and unofficially – dealt in incidents involving the former white lover of the factory owner's deceased father. Family honour and cultural values have been sustained and protected but at a traumatic emotional cost to Annie – the grieving lover – and at an equally significant cost to Jaz's integrity.

However, of all of the narrative developments involving Jaz in series two, the character's involvement in a deeply shocking scenario centring upon Brammell and a young Asian man called Karim Ifraz is perhaps the most telling. This is essentially because of the nature of a terribly savage beating that Karim suffers at the hands of two white working-class men on Skeetsmoor estate, and Roy Brammell's ultimate responsibility for manufacturing the incident. It is also particularly important in terms of the insight that the scenario provides into the cultural and ethnic tensions and pressures that are brought to bear upon Jaz.

The Ifraz family is introduced in the earlier incident involving Metcalf, Kennett and Giffen. Karim is the older brother of Sahid who, on hearsay alone, has been accused of selling drugs to certain young teenagers. However, as Kennett observes when she accompanies Brammell on a visit to the Ifraz house:

> Kennett: I don't think it's a very good idea coming round here on the strength of tittle-tattle – not when they've been complaining about our lack of response... It's going to look like we're harassing them isn't it.

> Roy: We are harassing them. If this lad Sahid's giving drugs to little girls, he wants harassing.

> Kennett: Little white girls.

> Roy: Don't care what colour they are love.

Kennett's attempts to constrain Brammell's usual no-nonsense, direct approach is vindicated when Roy is confronted by Sahid's older brother, Karim who is not prepared to co-operate with what he construes – quite correctly – as Brammell's attempts to enter their house and interview his younger brother with no proper, proven grounds. It is out of Karim's legitimate self-assertion on behalf of his brother, family and community that the circumstances leading to his beating unfold. At the grim heart of these events is, essentially, Karim daring to confront and question Roy's authority. By implication, in terms of Roy's world-view, any resistance or implied humiliation that he encounters is effectively a display of crucial disrespect for the police force itself. Karim has previously telephoned the police to complain about the force's lack of response to their allegations of racial harassment from their white neighbours, the Nuttalls. Karim insists upon taking the epaulette numbers from Brammell and warns him that he will report the police officer's intrusive behaviour to the station sergeant:

> (Roy shoves up close to Karim, prodding him with his finger)

> Roy: Think you're clever you don't you?

> Karim: Hard not to, stood next to you.

> Roy: Keep it coming, keep it coming.

> (Nuttall has come out again to watch)

> Karim: There you are Mr Nuttall. Shouldn't have worried about that injunction. Got this lot doing your dirty work for you.

> Nuttall: He hangs round that youth club – Sahid. Open arms to Pakis – Won't have my lad.

(Roy turns back to Karim)

Roy: Bit of co-operation goes a long way.

(Karim straightens his jacket)

Karim: Peas in a pod, you two.

From Karim's perspective, Brammell and Nuttall represent the same face of hostile, racist intrusion into his family and community's lives. Within this situation, the police are perceived effectively to be an instrument of other, latently oppressive agendas. When Roy, intent on settling a score with Karim and achieving his aim of getting access to Sahid, arrives at the Skeetsmoor Youth Club, an ugly encounter erupts. Roy, with the actively unwilling and concerned Amanda, arrives at the Youth Club where Karim is due to give a talk to the members about their rights in relation to police stop and search, and similar issues. Darrill has organised the event and Mel is also present in her role as Community Officer. Karim remarks to Roy that "Yesterday we complain we're getting no support with our neighbours. Today you're harassing me and me brother. Bit of a coincidence that." When Mel tries to intervene to calm things down, Karim observes to her "You might be trying something different, but all your mates – they just want business as usual." The confrontation escalates when Roy tries to force his way into the room to get Sahid. When provoking Roy in ridiculing his status and intelligence as a policeman, Karim says "There's a line across that doorway. You'd see it if you had an IQ to match your belt size," Brammell goes to grab him and there is a scuffle between the two with Darrill intervening. Roy knows that he has been publicly humiliated and makes a very unwilling tactical withdrawal, lacking the real support of either Kennett or Draper.

When, shortly afterwards, he discovers that there has been a general identification of an indecent exposure suspect as having 'darkish skin,' Roy realises a means of exacting a terrible vengeance upon Karim. The daughter of a local publican and associate, Phil Hughes, was a victim of this indecent exposure. Aware of Hughes' anger about the incident, Brammell gives him Karim's name, inviting Hughes to exact a brutal and lawless revenge. In the final scene of Episode Eight, the camera frames – through revealing Roy, alone in the police van, observing with quiet satisfaction – the vicious beating in the far to mid-distance. Allowing the two assailants sufficient time to carry out their appalling attack, he eventually drives over, ensuring the two men can escape. The bloody, badly beaten figure lying prostrate is glimpsed as Karim. Members of Karim's family and the wider Indian community determine to discover the perpetrators, convinced that the incident represents the most vicious form of racially motivated violence. A sequence of events leads them to realise that a police officer is behind the attack. The family and community leaders try to bring the officer responsible to a formal, police arrest and investigation approach Jaz. Jaz is caught between his commitment to the code of honour and justice within the Indian community, in conflict with his commitment to the code of loyalty amongst his police colleagues. This latter consideration carries with it a particularly personal connotation for Jaz, as it is Roy who protected him from disclosure and dismissal in the taxicab incident. When he endeavours to approach Brammell about his role and motivation in framing Karim for the beating, Roy responds angrily by showing Jaz his police badge and telling him that, on its crest, "It's a crown, not a fucking chapati." This sudden, virulent expression of Brammell's latent racial prejudice is both shocking and explosive. Having tried to warn Roy of the consequences of his actions, Jaz now knows that Roy must face a violent retribution from those British-Indian men seeking justice. Running simultaneously with this narrative in Episode Ten, the final episode of Series Two, is the discovery that Roy's wife, Ellen, has to undergo life-saving surgery after the diagnosis of breast cancer. For the first and only time in the series, the audience views Roy in a position of desperate emotional vulnerability, traumatised by his sense of helplessness and loss. In the final scenes of the second series, Roy arrives back at his family home late at night, leaving his wife in a critical condition in hospital. Out of the shadows, Karim's family and community leaders emerge to surely exact a violent retribution for Karim's savage beating. In a sequence charged with latent fear and the anticipation of Roy's personal suffering being brutally compounded, the camera focuses upon him, the voices of his Nemesis heard principally out of shot. They question him with quiet insistence about what he has done and why. Roy acknowledges, by his own values and strategies, the summary justice about to be enacted like some apocalyptic scene from a Greek tragedy. He shouts defiantly and desperately at his interlocutors, "He should have shown me some respect… I've given my life for this country." The scene and series end with the men, perhaps in pity, possibly out of an alternative and more developed sense of moral justice, walking quietly away. Brammell is left alone: an aura of complex pathos, vulnerability and bewildered defiance emanating from him in the arc light of the suburban street lamps. In one profound sense, a cycle of primitive, pragmatic vengeance has been defused and made redundant. Nevertheless, the final searing image of the complex, contradictory signifiers that define Roy Brammell evoke a sense of troubling and problematic closure.

> Yes, the cops are repressive and indulge in the arbitrary use of power…. They get depressed at their own impotence…. They are lost in the consequences of economic and political cruelty and failure, plus those tragic events in people's lives that are beyond human intervention.

I want to use the sentiments expressed above by Tony Garnett to bring this chapter on 'The Cops' to a close. They are taken from some 'Notes on Cops' that he distributed to the entire production team and crew (dated 29 November 1998). In the second series, along with the characters and narratives that I have dealt with in some detail in the second half of this chapter, two other characters reach a point of closure, signified by the discharge of PC Danny Rylance and the resignation of PC Mike Thomson. In both cases, Garnett's observations concerning aspects of the problems and issues surrounding contemporary policing are foregrounded.

For Danny, the aftermath of Lindsey's death remains with him and leads ultimately to his discharge, with pension, from the force. Although desperate to remain in the police, a counselling session with a psychiatrist, Dr Boylan, leads him to a final, painful admission of the roots of his guilty feelings:

Dr Boylan: It wasn't just the death, was it? You'd dealt with deaths before?

Danny: (Bitter) When I should've been saving Lindsey I was wasting time trying to save a relationship that was a joke in the first place. I thought we had something….

Dr Boylan: You were with a girlfriend…. When you should've been on duty.

Danny: Yes.

Dr Boylan: You felt guilty.

Danny: I AM GUILTY! (Beat) I am guilty.

On the basis of this cathartic disclosure, Boylan is unable to do anything else other than to recommend Danny's discharge from the force. This represents the final, depressing stage in the narrative development and journey of this character when, with bleak irony, it is Danny's ultimate vulnerability and disclosure that proves to be self-condemnatory. With a degree of abject pathos associated ultimately with Roy Brammell, Danny Rylance still arrives for that evening's pub quiz. However, he knows that his dismissal places him beyond the frame of those personal loyalties and social interactions and walks off into the night, to an uncertain future.

In relation to the character of Mike Thomson, his decision to resign comes in Episode Eight out of a spiraling sense of failure and compromise in both his personal and professional life. As his short-lived marriage to Colleen collapses, his loneliness and frustration lead him to make an unacceptable and misguided pass at a young single mother. She has been a victim/witness of indecent exposure and Thomson visits her at her home that evening on the pretext that the perpetrator has been found. The young woman is rightly angry at Mike's inappropriate and clumsy advances. The final straw for Mike is the formal enquiry launched into the handcuffing of Amanda Kennett. As the police officers involved await formal interview from a senior officer from outside Stanton, Mike is consigned to the menial and thankless task of being duty officer on the cells. Here, as he has to try and deal with, amongst others, an incontinent drunk and down-and-out, Kenny, Thomson exclaims to Brammell "It was supposed to be a sodding prank for God's sake. A bit of fun." Later, in one of the penultimate scenes of Episode Eight, Mike is called by Kenny to come and give him assistance. On opening the cell door, Mike witnesses the gruesome sight of Kenny having defecated in his white custody boiler suit:

(Mike's heart sinks)

Kenny: I couldn't get it off quickly enough – with it being all in one.

(Mike says nothing)

Kenny: Get us a fresh one? And help us get cleaned up?

(Mike stares at him wordlessly)

Kenny: Come on lad. Have a heart.

(Mike lingers another beat – then turns on his heel and goes)

Without pausing, Mike storms off to where a nervous Wishaw is being interviewed by Bradley, the senior officer. Thomson storms into the interview room and takes full responsibility for the Kennett incident:

Mike: I did it.

Bradley: You are?

Mike: (Hardly hearing) So you can write that in your note book. (Catching up) Mike Thomson. She deserved it. It had nothing to do with him or any of the other lads. And you don't need to sack me cause I'm sick of this job. You can keep it.

Steve Jackson, the actor who plays Mike with such an understated and focused sense of the character observed:

Mike is repressed, and all his emotions are internal. The trick is to play the subtext... so that the audience have to guess what he's thinking and feeling. In the dramatic sense, Mike can't stay the same.... Now he has become more cynical about life in the police. Police officers aren't cynical – they've gone beyond that.... They have to be like that, or it would bring them down. To begin with, younger officers take it more seriously. Then they realise that if they carry on like that, they'll soon have a nervous breakdown.[4]

The first series won a BAFTA award for Best Drama Series and received unambiguous critical praise. A.A. Gill wrote in *The Sunday Times*: "It's the British version of a Steve Bochco police-procedural... if that sounds like praise, then it's meant to be. It's gritty, it talks the talk and walks the walk. And it's very well made, shot and edited with an inquisitive verité."

The first series was also notable for the controversy it caused within the police. The Greater Manchester and Lancashire Police forces, who had actively co-operated with the making of the first series, withdrew their support and help for the second series.

Whilst 'The Cops' unquestionably reveals the complex narratives of human beings caught within the contradictions of their private lives in public uniforms, it is not in any sense simplisitically critical of the police. As I stated in my introduction to this chapter, I believe that the series, through its stylish and richly textured performative aesthetic, exhibits ideological anxieties and concerns about the rationale, means and legitimacy of policing the urban wastelands of contemporary British society. In so doing, it inevitably – and properly – exposes the hypocritical simplistic rationale of Home Office rhetoric about 'zero tolerance' policing methods and 'three hits and you're out' prison sentencing of repeat offenders. However, the series also exposes the growing indeterminancy of left-field ideological positions in relation to both the broader issues of cultural and political analysis, and to the problems of what constitutes the law, its transgression and punishment at the close of the twentieth century. I shall return to a final, brief review of 'The Cops' in my final chapter but wish to conclude this opening study with some final observations from Tony Garnett:

> The band aid is not responsible for the wound, just because it's used as a cover-up… we see the wider circumstances – which some of the cops don't see or won't see – which make people behave the way they do and become what they are. Yes, we share the frustrations of the police, asked to solve problems which in reality are beyond their remit or competence… we see the products of despair and give tangible life to the dry phrase 'cycles of deprivation'…. Our stance is sympathetic detachment, our righteous anger is in check lest it becomes self-righteous, and our task is to ask those questions for which there are no ready answers.[5]

Notes

1. Anne Power and Katherine Mumford (1999) *The slow death of great cities? Urban abandonment or urban renaissance*, York Publishing Services for The Joseph Rowntree Foundation.
2. Notes prepared and distributed to the production team of 'The Cops' by Tony Garnett, dated 29 January 1998, who generously provided me with a copy for my research and preparation.
3. Hendon College is a specialist Police Officer Training College, located in Hendon on the northern outskirts of London. It has traditionally been associated with the highest standards in police training.
4. The actor Steve Jackson, talking about his character PC Mike Thompson in Press Release Material distributed to journalists and researchers by BBC Drama/World Productions, for the opening series of 'The Cops.'
5. Garnett, *ibid.*

2   The City as a Site of Redemptive Struggle
Tony Marchant's 'Holding On'

Tony Marchant's eight episode series, 'Holding On,' was screened in the autumn of 1997 on BBC2. It went on to win a BAFTA for Best Drama Serial Award 1998 and two Royal Television Society 1998 awards for Best Drama Serial and Best Writer. It is a powerfully compelling drama, set in contemporary London in what was to be a transitional period between the last vestiges of a Conservative administration with the election, in May 1997, of Tony Blair's 'New Labour.' The drama's structure might be described as kaleidoscopic, with a cluster of eight principal characters functioning in relation to a central narrative concerning the character of Shaun, an obsessive tax inspector with the Inland Revenue. In November 1997, I had the privilege to interview Tony Marchant and the following quote comes from a transcript of that interview, as do all other direct quotes from him unless otherwise indicated.

> Shaun's narrative is the absolute spine of the story…. There is something about him that is constructed more than any of the other characters. Shaun represents someone who is utterly contemporary – the moral crisis precipitated by the realisation that what we thought we believed in is built on very shaky ground.

The choice of a kaleidoscopic multi-narrative structure was a central decision on Marchant's part in his preparation and researching of his material. As he stated in an interview for *The Guardian* in September 1997, "I looked again at works that all shared multiple storylines and… characters – Dickens's Our *Mutual Friend*, Tom Wolfe's *Bonfire of the Vanities*, John Sayles's film 'City of Hope' and Robert Altman's 'Short Cuts'."

It is Altman's film, an evocative portrait of lives in contemporary Los Angeles, which the viewer glimpses showing at a cinema towards the end of Episode One. This becomes the grimly ironic backdrop for the murder of Sally, a victim of an attack by Alan, a paranoid schizophrenic. Having been arrested by the police, his release onto the streets of the capital reflects one of many similar, actual tragedies caused through the Tory government's policy of 'Care in the Community.' As the series unfolds its rich and complex interweaving of individual lives in the context of contemporary city life, there emerges a relationship between Shaun and Alan that is at the very heart of the drama's relentlessly driving momentum. I believe that Marchant's drama is engaged in a struggle to define London in terms of three pairs of binary, interactive signifiers: Enclosure/Disclosure, Private/Public, and Personal/Political. These operate in dialectical interaction with each other, and serve to construct a prismatic signing of the city, in which individual subjects are inextricably constrained and defined by the city as a site of redemptive struggle. This geo-ideological landscape is characterised by a moral and ideological anxiety and indeterminacy which it shares with certain fundamental concerns in 'The Cops.' Given the socio-cultural and political context in which the series was conceived and produced, that sense of uncertain boundaries is understandable, as Marchant observes:

> It's very hard these days to know what your political responsibilities are… the irony is that you have a public-school educated, middle-class Prime Minister, who won the election because he managed to convince enough of Middle-England to vote for him. That is depressing because you realise that there are huge numbers of people excluded from those considerations and that we still seem to be in the midst of a Thatcherite revolution, because I think Blair's conservatism is a manifestation of that Thatcherite revolution.

It is within this ideological landscape of the manufacturing of image over substance and rhetoric over policy, that Marchant presents us with the interconnected narratives of the personal and the political, the private and the public, and the disclosure of hidden agendas working throughout them all. It is a construction of London that takes the viewer from the high-rise blocks of council flats of the inner city to the purpose-built apartments of the New Labour bourgeoisie. The micro-locations within the macro-frame encompass the worlds of multi-national capitalism, the metropolitan obsession with chic food as status-symbol and sexual sublimation, along with the daily demands and personal tragedies of ordinary citizens who are simply 'Holding On' in the maelstrom of London life. As stated in the introduction to this chapter, the central character within this quasi-Dickensian world is Shaun, whose work as an investigator carries with it a latently symbolic significance. The character is simultaneously investigated and exposed by Marchant's authorial strategy, even as Shaun seeks to expose corruption within the financial institutions of the City. As Marchant expressed so cogently: "He is the hunter who becomes hunted by his own private demons." With a seemingly tragic inevitability reminiscent of the classic Oedipal narratives, Shaun's crusade to expose serious financial corruption centring on the Maxwell-esque Werner is subsequently undermined and deconstructed as Shaun's own problematic past is revealed.

In terms of my exploration of 'Holding On,' I intend to analyse central characters and issues across each of the eight episodes on a thematic basis. This is principally because the inter-relatedness of the character and narrative strands is such that any other chronological approach might prove unwieldy and prone to repetition. In the discussion of each character-narrative cluster, I shall endeavour to focus upon issues and themes relating to specific characters and their relationships with each other. This analysis will conclude with an overview of my principle concerns and considerations.

Shaun and Gary

> People do have different lives within one existence. It's axiomatic that there is conflict
> because you can't reconcile them all.
>
> (Tony Marchant)

One of the very opening images of the series is framed from the camera point of view
of an underground train hurtling out of the darkness, simultaneously penetrating and
revealing the dimly lit station it is about to enter. With an inexorable and subliminal
effectiveness, this image is constructed to be read in the context of Nick Bicat's
haunting soundtrack of discordant alienation. David Snodin, the Producer of the series,
remarked of the soundtrack:

> He [Bicat] was very concerned to make the music 'connective' in the sense that by
> choosing a different theme for each 'theme' (rather than the character), he could help us
> make the movement from one story to another more seamless. The basis for everything
> he wrote was a 'Jungle' beat which comes out of the black characters [Chris and Marcus]
> because they have a 'Jungle' FM station, but it also goes through every body else's theme
> as well. It's absolutely brilliant and there's quite a lot of it for a television drama. [1]

This opening image inter-cuts – in a montage style visual grammar – with an image of
the character Gary Rickey who, in keeping with his self-aggrandising self-regard, is
viewing himself in a full-length mirror. Being fitted for a suit, the white chalk markings
on the material communicate a marvelous visual metaphor of the delineated
construction of this extraordinary character. A bulimic restaurant critic working for the
quality broadsheets, he is the only character empowered by Marchant to speak directly
to the viewing audience. As Marchant observed:

> There was the idea that there was always the possibility for him to be a narrator, a
> Chorus, and that was something I liked the idea of because I could use his restaurant
> reviews to comment on other things. It was Adrian [Shergold – the director of 'Holding
> On'] who suggested that some of his dialogue should be addressed to the audience.

There is a most effective and bitingly satirical example of Gary's direct address to the
camera/viewer in the opening scene of Episode Three where he is seated at a dinner
engagement with other food critics. The sequence opens with Gary holding forth as an
out of vision commentator, addressing Nelson – a fellow critic – about the problems
surrounding the popularising of the elite food sub-culture:

> Gary: Fucking meritocratic eating – I can't stand it. Coming in here is like buying your
> clothes from Gap. This lot wanking on about gastronomic innovation. Who for? Losers

61

from St. Albans coming up to town for a night out? Come in here before they go and see *Phantom of the Opera*? You could serve them a prawn cocktail and they'd go home happy. I don't want to see a load of sweaty chefs running about through plate glass. Chefs should be downstairs, not in my eyeline. Unless they're called Nico or Marco.

The complete vacuity of his upper-class sexual partner, Jemma, contributes to the sense of self-indulgent, mindless bourgeois hedonism. She is eating out at the same restaurant with her new employer, Hilary, another principal character, discussed in more detail in a subsequent section. Jemma's assessment of the restaurant's qualities is suitably and superbly superficial:

Jemma: It's brilliant isn't it? It's so big and gorgeous and the waiters are dreamy. Apparently their uniforms are designed by Jaspar. Oh Gary let me introduce you to the brilliant boss of mine that I've just got myself.

It transpires that Gary was formerly represented by Hilary's PR agency but has clearly left under unhappy circumstances. Marchant's positioning of the vacuous and intellectually challenged Jemma as a new recruit to Hilary's agency exposes, with a wonderfully acerbic sense of social satire, the triumph of class and presentation over competence and integrity. The following short extract also illustrates Gary's combative means of social survival within this cosmopolitan world of competitive, aggressive festishised consumption:

Gary: Hello Hilary.

Hilary: Hello Gary.

Jemma: You know each other? God, what a small world!

Gary: Teensy weensy. So Jemma's one of your PR poppets is she?

Hilary: And you're her.... What? Fellah? Well, well.

Gary: I hear you're representing corporate chairmen these days. Wouldn't they be better off with a probation officer?

Hilary: Perhaps you could recommend one of your old ones.

Gary: My readers love hearing how I dragged myself up from the gutter.

Hilary: I didn't realise that particular project was finished.

Gary: You don't realise a lot of things Hilary. That's why I moved to another agency.

Jemma: You used to be a client of Hilary's? I don't believe it! God we're all so... connected. Spooky!

Jemma's parting line is an ironically self-reflective comment by Marchant, on the suspension of disbelief required at certain plot moments to accept the narrative contrivance of particular characters meeting with one another. Furthermore, he is bringing to the fore a serious ideological concern that he holds as the author of 'Holding On': namely, of the existential inter-connectedness of human lives – a direct rebuff to Thatcher's infamous assertion that "There is no such thing as society." This passage is also another example of the conflicts arising from personal agendas of ambition and sexual desire and the shifting but immanent territory of class-consciousness. The savage interplay and dialectical tension between Gary's class origins and socially gendered masculinity, and his acquired status as food critic, place these conflicts of class, status and gender into sharp relief. This sequence closes with Gary having to rush to the toilets to be sick – an increasingly familiar and disturbing occurrence for him in terms of his bulimia. From this incident, in which a genuinely concerned Jemma follows him anxiously on his escape route, Gary's illness is given a 'public' context as she hears him being violently sick in the toilets. Predictably, Gary finishes his relationship with her later in the episode with the same ravenous determination that has propelled him into media celebrity status. It is another scorchingly effective example of Marchant's facility for a textured dialogue that plays against itself in its inherent stylistic contradictions. In doing so, the dialogue absolutely communicates the fundamental contradiction within the character of Gary Rickey, whilst simultaneously exposing the chasm of class that separates Gary from Jemma:

> (Sat on the edge of Gary's bed after she's obviously just been making love with him, Jemma is crying. Gary is next to her, rationalising and explaining to her with barely disguised insincerity)

Gary: Relationships are like seasons. We've had our spring, now autumn has come. Leaves fall from the trees and feelings... well they drop off too don't they?

Jemma: I thought you really liked me!

Gary: I do. I've been very happy. I just feel like it's time for me to... for my tree to be bare. (Beat) I want to be on my own.

Jemma: But why did you have to tell me after you bonked me!

Gary: Don't say bonk, it's so naff.

Jemma: Who cares? (Beat) It's because I saw you being ill isn't it? Ever since then....

Gary: I think you'd better get dressed,

Jemma: I saw that look on your face. I heard the sound you made in the toilet. I heard you crying in there and you can't forgive me for that can you?!

Gary: Don't be ridiculous.

Jemma: You want to get rid of me because of what I know about you!

Gary: That's nothing to do with it! Nothing right?! You're a soufflé that didn't rise, a sauce that failed to inspire, a main course I could only get halfway through. That's why I'm throwing you out! That's all!

This final equation of Jemma with and as food is a telling signing of the commodification of both food and the female person. Within the London that Marchant constructs, themes of excess, consumption and this reified commodification are prevalent and persuasive.

The character of Gary works as a constantly disruptive and unsettling iconic sign, signaling wickedly funny satire on both the metropolitan, bourgeois restaurant culture and, stylistically, the relationship between the viewer and their reading of the drama's meaning(s). Although Marchant denied that his intention in using the device had ever carried with it Brechtian associations, I feel nevertheless that Gary's direct address to camera inevitably – and creatively – unsettles the interpretative space, foregrounding the meta-narrative in the 'quotation marks' of referentiality. Gary is the very embodiment of the voyeuristic, crudely pragmatic ethos of the metropolitan media, proclaiming: "Culture? I eat it. Art? I want it on my plate" With an outrageous sense of the infallibility of his critique, Gary Rickey is essential to the savage, Swiftian satire that runs parallel with the drama's other, serious concerns. His casual denunciation of contemporary London life conveys a darkly aggressive, predatory environment: "If you live in London, it's helpful if you enjoy tearing flesh apart with your bare hands and consuming it."

However, beneath the surface of Gary's bravado, there remains a hidden and profoundly undermining insecurity. This centres upon a conflict of class and identity with, we discover, Gary having sought to disown his working class roots in the former Thatcher stronghold and heartland of London's Essex estuary belt. Destined by his parent's misguided sense of local loyalty and humour, he was christened Billy Rickey, after his place of birth, Billericay. The dysfunctional behaviour that this self-initiated split has caused also has significant ideological connotations:

Gary is someone who has re-invented himself in a fit of pique, dismayed and ashamed of his roots and his class and so has turned upon them. [However] he has done this not by assuming the identity of the wellborn, but by being what he always was, a terrible, terrible snob but unmistakably working class and very right wing.

(Marchant)

– *City as a Site of Redemptive Struggle: 'Holding On'* –

Despite his efforts to jettison and silence Jemma's realisation of his condition, his bulimia results in increasingly confrontational and unpredictable social behaviour. Inevitably, Gary loses his well-paid job as a restaurant critic and retreats into a solitary world of alcohol and self-pitying depression. He is offered the opportunity of returning to his previous role as a tabloid football correspondent, which he desperately tries to resist. For Gary, as we discover later in the series, football is inextricably bound up with his class background and origins. Also, in terms of his own inverted class prejudice which also colours his fashion sense, Gary perceives the social climate of the football reporter's sub-culture as "being surrounded by people who wear man-made fibres." It is only through the friendship of a young Asian woman, Karen – an up-and-coming Asian football reporter – that Gary begins the slow journey back to self-acceptance and sanity. There is a particular narrative sequence in the final episode where Karen quietly but determinedly insists that Gary recites a catechism of who he actually is and what he actually likes. She realises that an essential part of his therapy and healing is for Gary to articulate what he has so consistently denied – the authenticity of his own actual class background and tastes. Once again, Marchant uses this as an opportunity to characterise Gary with the same caustically resilient humour that has, in a sense, served as a survival strategy for him throughout his illness:

Gary: My first name's really Billy. My Mum and Dad thought it would be funny if they called me Billy Rickey. Because it's where we come from. That's why I had to change my name to Gary.

Karen: I like egg and chips.

Gary: I like egg and chips. (Beat) My Dad never forgave me for not getting through the West Ham trials. That's what he wanted me to be you see – a footballer. I got my own back on him though. I got a load of 'O' levels instead. In Billericay, an 'O' level meant you were a Renaissance man.

Karen: You hate your parents don't you?

Gary: They're so working class. I wanted my head turned... away from all that. So I became the posh paper's enfant terrible. Hating what it was that made me. But I can't keep down fillet of grey mullet with chives either.

Karen: Come on – I'll make you a nice green salad.

In terms of the aesthetic and thematic concerns within the series, Gary's character may be viewed as a binary and complementary aspect of the construction, treatment and function of Shaun's character. Both characters have – albeit for very different reasons – denied their class and family origins and for both characters, this denial carries with it long-term, traumatic consequences. Stylistically, as I have already discussed, Gary is defined in performative values and dialogue that is richly stylised and non-naturalistic, played with wonderful brio by Phil Daniels. By comparison, David Morrissey's portrayal of Shaun expresses with breathtaking intensity a character whose seeming solidity conceals volcanic conflicts of guilt and desire. Metaphorically, both characters signal the serious consequences of psychological denial.

In a sequence taken from Episode Four, there is an excellent example of Marchant's use of Gary to disclose the inherent contradictions and hypocrisy of a governing culture in which, to use Marchant's own words: "Everyone's busy marketing their finer feelings… it's just a brand, a copyright." The sequence also presents a useful example of the way in which the episodic structuring of the narrative enables different characters and story lines to interact. The scene is a restaurant where Gary is entertaining a New Labour apparatchik, Bridget, who agonises over the 'ethical' implications of her expensive meal – albeit one which she will not have to pay for as his guest:

Bridget: I always feel so guilty when I'm eating food like this.

Gary: Could have fooled me.

Bridget: No, you know… knowing there are people sleeping in doorways and somewhere in Africa….

Gary: Yeah well it can present a bit of a moral conundrum being a food critic post 'Live Aid,' post-eighties excess. That's why you have to demand value for money. Large portions. You know the restaurant community's response to Third World starvation? Put more offal on the menu. Homelessness? 800 seat gaffs. Soup kitchen aesthetic. All major credit cards accepted.

Bridget: I can't tell whether that means you approve or not.

Gary: I don't know. Everything's bollocks.

Bridget: You're amoral.

Gary: So's that bleedin' Labour party think tank you work for. The electronic tagging of claimants? Do me a favour.

Bridget: Well I think we have to make sure they really are available for work. Rights *and* responsibilities.

Gary: I'm going to get my knob out. In the toilet.

Gary's dismissive evasion of his guest's over-stated and self-important soundbite is confirmed visually through a sardonic smile to the viewer via the camera.

Simultaneously, this generates a relationship of knowing complicity with the viewer between Gary's covert contempt for the woman's vacuous ethical posturing.

Meanwhile, within the same restaurant, Shaun is dining with a young travel agent clerk, Tina, with whom he is about to embark upon a serious but doomed affair. This scene conveys a sense of the emotional vulnerability within Shaun, usually displaced by an overriding, arrogant self-certainty. Feeling trapped within the everyday, domestic demands and constraints of his marriage and family life, he yearns for the supposed stimulation of an imagined alternative life of personal and sexual freedom. Using a shot that appears casually random, the viewer catches Shaun and Gary passing one another in the restaurant, as an economic, visual narrative device, cutting then to Shaun's conversation with Tina:

Shaun: Like, at the moment, I'm investigating some guy for fraud. He's already admitted his guilt but I've discovered there's even more than meets the eye. One deception piled on top of another. (Beat) I'm married Tina.

Tina: Thought so.

Shaun: I'm married, I've got two kids, I'm fed up with my job and I'm trying to climb out of the rut I've found myself in.

Tina: Is that why we're here?

Shaun: Yeah, well, I wouldn't come to a restaurant like this normally.

Tina: Me neither.

Shaun: But why shouldn't we? I mean why shouldn't we do things we wouldn't have dreamt of normally?

Tina: Am I something, you know, you wouldn't...?

(She's embarrassed)

Shaun: Yes you are.

(Pause. She is flattered and affected by this)

Tina: I'm glad you've come clean.

Shaun: Down with deception eh?

The bitterly ironic subtext of Shaun's final line foregrounds once again the binary signifiers of public and private disclosure and accountability that characterises both

Shaun's narrative journey and the series as a whole. The scene then cuts to an interior shot of Gary escorting Bridget back to his flat, clearly expectant of sexual favours. I want to quote from this short scene because again it provides an excellent example of the structural interweaving of narrative and ideological concerns. Even as Shaun, the moral crusader of public fiscal accountability and justice, is shown to be subject to traumatic moral compromise, this theme of a careering post-modernist ethical location is explored with excoriating wit:

> Bridget: Rationing's been a dirty word in the party for too long. That's why our think tank published a paper on means tested access to the NHS – "In Sickness and in Wealth."
>
> Gary: You were giving it the anguished conscience in the restaurant – "how can I eat my rib-eye of beef while our social fabric falls apart?"
>
> Bridget: I suppose it's just something I feel I should say.
>
> (Gary smiles, pleased to hear this. He wants to tell her something but is a little hesitant)
>
> Gary: Shall I tell you something? You're not the only one who puts up a bit of a front.
>
> Bridget: Really?
>
> Gary: We all have our secrets don't we? Our... cupboards.
>
> Bridget: You mean, the difference between our political beliefs and our personal choice?

Moments later, panning up from the taxi in which Gary and his guest drive away, the camera point of view translate into a framing of Zahid and Helen. Zahid is from a British-Indian family and is a hard working, ambitious young professional. He is first introduced in Episode One as Shaun's junior assistant working on the Werner case. Frustrated and suspicious that Shaun's uncompromising ambition is inhibiting his own potential for promotion, Zahid ultimately becomes the agent of the disclosure of Shaun's public and private deception, to be discussed in the ensuing part of this section. Helen is a young white, middle class woman also working at the Inland Revenue. At this point in the narrative development – Episode Four – she and Zahid are seeking to navigate their relationship through the pressures faced by them both from values and expectations located in his family's ethnicity. In a scene in which they have just made love, the themes of inter-connected lives and ideological concerns of personal and public probity are now transposed to this evolving intimate relationship. Helen is understandably keen to try and meet Zahid's family and is frustrated at her lover's evident reluctance to talk about them:

Helen: Look forward to meeting your family one day.

Zahid: What for?

Helen: Sorry?

Zahid: What's the point?

(Helen a little taken aback by his sudden defensiveness, prickliness)

Helen: I don't know…. I'm assuming if that's all right that if we… carry on you'd want me to. What's wrong with that?

Zahid: Nothing.

(He doesn't elaborate)

Helen: Shaun's not the only one who goes in and out of focus is he?

When Helen, frustrated, tells him that he can't live two lives, Zahid retorts angrily: "That's bollocks, I've been living two, three lives all my life." The conflicts inherent within this pained outburst reflect abiding tensions of integrity, loyalty, commitment and ambition, which reappear throughout 'Holding On.' They are tensions resulting inescapably from the city as an ideological location, in which a constant clamour is enacted between the demands, for example, of ethnicity, ambition and desire. I shall explore the relationship between Helen and Zahid in a subsequent section in this chapter.

This five or six minute sequence that I have examined provides one amongst many other examples of how the series merges the disparate narratives and subtexts. Returning to the character of Shaun, his subtext of guilt and frustrated desire for escape communicates a potent sense of those private dilemmas carrying inevitable consequences in the theatre of public affairs. As Marchant once more observes of this character: "He represents the schism between his public beliefs and his private morality."

Shaun's desire and determination to see justice done in the case of the powerful businessman, Werner, is relentlessly obsessive. Through an exacting commitment to expose a massive financial fraud that Werner is perpetuating, Shaun succeeds in enlisting his line manager's support in accessing crucial evidence that implicates Werner's covert, corrupt agenda. A dawn raid is visited upon Werner at his home, led by Shaun with an unswerving zeal. However, having previously always acted in strict accordance to protocol and procedure, Shaun agrees to an illicit meeting with the businessman. The encounter is defined by enclosure in terms of its literal and metaphorical secrecy, whilst simultaneously encoding the public and personal issues of disclosure. It is significant that these wholly uncharacteristic actions are symptomatic of increasingly dysfunctional behaviour on the part of Shaun. His seeing a newspaper report of Sally's murder has precipitated this behaviour first exhibited through his fleeing in panic from a crowded underground train. Traumatised by the circumstances of her death, his guilt – without obvious location or cause at this stage in Episode Two – begins to fragment both his public and private persona. He begins calculatedly to embrace the temptations of financial corruption that he has previously resisted with unflinching, moral probity. Simultaneously, he embarks upon the first tentative stages of his affair with Tina. In a scene signed in muted light, Shaun journeys from a position of cold confrontation to what, after this scene's closure, will become a point of no return in terms of his own compromised integrity. Climbing the stairs into Werner's apartment, Shaun announces that "I'm here for disclosures" employing that term in its financial sense. However, what prove to be called into account and disclosure are not Werner's financial dealings, but Shaun's own problematic past and compromised present. Indeed, Marchant structures the scene with a quietly devastating formalism that turns the ideological and ethical balance: a skilful transposition of roles in which the interrogated becomes the interrogator and vice versa. Werner discloses that his personal experience of discrimination and prejudice has determined both his own political expediency and pragmatic self-interest. His bitter experience of marginalisation by the Tory establishment is defined in the context of both his nationality and ethnicity: he is a Hungarian Jew. Shaun's self righteous indignation is partially checked by Werner's admission and this immanent awareness of the humanity of his opponent is consolidated, when Werner relates his profound sense of loss following his wife's death from cancer. In recounting this tragic loss, he also exposes the corruption of class prejudice and privilege inherent within British society:

> Werner: Mind you, you know, I thought it was a good idea to get to know the royal patrons of those charities. I mean, to be well thought of by people like that. But you know you have to make money discretely in this country. And if you give it away, well, it has to be almost an act of embarrassment. I made a big mistake. I made the mistake of being pleased to do it. You know, wealth – it can insulate you from many things but it can never insulate you from the men who go to the right schools with the other men and who then marry the other men's sisters.

Nevertheless, it is with some strategic manoeuvring borne out of his own struggle to succeed and survive that he observes to Shaun that "Wealth can insulate you from many things." Sensing that he has identified Shaun's Achilles' Heel, he deftly suggests to his interlocutor that his public role and raison d'être is not welcomed and supported by society at large:

> Werner: I mean, d'you think I'm cheating you, is that it? D'you think I'm not playing cricket? D'you think it's a case of moral turpitude? Well, nobody else does, do they?
>
> Shaun: Really?

> Werner: Well, the general public don't, do they? They think you're fair game. You're the taxman, the bogeyman. Everyone would get away with it if they could. They don't give a damn what you say about me at all. Where's the harm in it? Don't people tell that to you all the time?

> Shaun: Only the ones who don't understand how this country pays for itself.

> Werner: Has anybody actually ever thanked you for uncovering a tax fraud?

> Shaun: I didn't come here for this.

Werner is played by David Calder with a wonderful mix of menacing bravado, the quiet assurance of the powerful whilst retaining a glimpse of the human dimension to this character. Shaun's growing response of angry uncertainty about why he has come to Werner's house at all, is exacerbated as Werner pursues his prey by next challenging him to consider his own motivations: "Envy? Spite? Because you can't insulate yourself in the same way I can, you must tear my insulation away?" When Shaun prepares to leave at this point, Werner then asks him where he lives, noting that in South London there are a number of burglaries. Shaun's house has, in fact, been burgled following on the start of the Werner case. A sinister subtext of threat and intimidation now discloses itself and Werner moves in for a metaphorical 'kill.' Marchant develops the motif of disclosure and insulation with a mastery of the complex dynamics at work within this encounter:

> Werner: Look at me, I live in Notting Hill Gate but I hardly even notice. Like I told you, wealth can insulate you from many things. You really notice where you live, don't you? All the time, I could insulate you, you know.

Even as Shaun endeavours to stand his moral ground and challenges Werner's attempt to bribe him, Werner plays the ace card when he suddenly asks Shaun why he changed his name. Marchant uses this opportunity to finally place an interpretative focus and frame upon the dialectical mutuality of personal and public disclosure and fraudulence:

> Werner: You investigate me. I thought I should reciprocate. (Beat) In 1980 you changed your name. Why?

> Shaun: Look... that's got nothing to do with you, okay?!

> Werner: You mean you don't want to make a disclosure?

> Shaun: Well, I haven't committed fraud have I?

> Werner: Haven't you?

Shaun's response is to display the same mix of anger and bewilderment exhibited when he fled the train. Promising Werner that the authorities will prosecute, he runs out into the quiet streets of Ladbrooke Grove. It is clear that Marchant's intention is not to underestimate or nullify the extent and significance of the corruption confronted and exposed by Shaun. However, it is equally true that the dramatist is making a fundamental point about how Sean's own secret, compromised past crucially undermines the execution of his public role:

> The series is set in 1996, but it's really a look at the nineties from the time when no one took the blame for anything to now, when people are becoming accountable. Shaun is chasing the fat cats, making them face up to their responsibilities, but the irony is he also has some facing up to do. His corruption isn't simply about taking bribes, but something that began long ago. Personal demons.
>
> (Radio Times, 4–10 October, 1997)

It is an axiomatic lynch pin of both Shaun's narrative and, in an important respect, the series as a whole, that he must and turn and acknowledge his own past – the 'demons' of past actions and events – and through that process find a form of redemption. Whilst he resists Werner's strategy of complicity and runs out into the dark London streets, he later negotiates a bribe with one of the businessman's associates. From this point on in the series, his public and private roles and integrity are irrevocably damaged. Having compromised his relationship with his wife Vicki, he ultimately flees from his commitment to Tina as the authorities – alerted by Zahid – close in on him. Having made a serious emotional commitment to him, a distraught Tina makes an unsuccessful suicide attempt as Shaun endures a Dante-esque descent into a personal hell – the subterranean underclass of London. Living with an anger and desolation that makes him hugely vulnerable on the harsh streets of the city, he is beaten up in a pub after confronting a group of men at a bar. Bloodied and traumatised by guilt he finally arrives at the end of Episode Seven at the house belonging to Annie, the mother of the murderer, Alan. His redemptive journey has finally brought him face to face with the woman who, we now realise, is also his own mother. Although this closure of Shaun's narrative is potentially and perilously melodramatic, the quality of the writing, the depth of the characterisation and some compelling performances, succeed in achieving moments of unsentimental pathos and pain. The following sequence communicates most effectively the tightrope balance between the volcanic emotional layers beneath the surface and a mother and son seeking to articulate a reconciliation:

Shaun: I couldn't handle it Mum. When Alan started getting worse and we finally got the diagnosis I just thought I'm his brother and Mum's gonna be looking to me now. All that responsibility all down to you. Phone calls from the police, having to go down and get him. Find somewhere else for him to stay and then making sure he took his drugs, talking to his Social Worker and I just thought I don't want it. I just don't want any of it!

Annie: When you disappeared it was worse than you being dead. All that grief you left me with and no forwarding address. You were cruel to him walking out like that, crueller to me. Such a bastard.

Shaun: If I'd stayed you'd have hated me more for not being able to cope with you.

Annie: I'd never hate you. You just broke my heart that's all.

Shaun breaks down into uncontrollable tears and finally names the Furies that have been pursuing him since he first learnt of Sally's death:

Shaun: Oh God! It was me wasn't it? It was me that killed that girl?

Annie: D'you want to see Alan? (He looks at her, nodding)

It is only as he continues to confronting his own past and disowned responsibilities to his brother, that the possibility of a painful, but ultimately affirming, reconciliation can be envisaged with Annie, Alan and – eventually – Vicki.

In a moving visit to see Alan who is serving a life sentence for the murder, Annie warns Shaun that Alan isn't able to express or acknowledge his terrible actions "He has to keep it in…. You'd know about that wouldn't you?" In the ensuing scene between the two brothers, there begins the careful negotiation of their relationship, a darkly ironic humour tempering their shared guilt and pain:

Alan: Mum didn't have much luck did she? One son who went away and another one who had to be sent away.

Shaun: I'm sorry I lost contact.

Alan: You make it sound like an accident.

Shaun: I'm sorry I ran out.

Alan: That's better.

As Annie discovers the daughter-in-law and grandchildren that she never knew, she is able slowly and sensitively to persuade Vicki to try and rebuild a marriage relationship shattered by the betrayal of trust: "Sean wants another chance and Alan's giving it to him." The emotional minefield of possible reconciliation is problematic as Vicki clearly feels the pain of Shaun's relationship with Tina and the traumatic revelation of his secret past. Nevertheless, with a strong and growing relationship between the two women, a space is slowly and painfully defined in which there is at least the possibility of a life for Shaun and Vicki beyond his own court case and possible imprisonment.

Florrie, Janet, Chris and Marcus

Our message is that a black life is not expendable.... We refuse to be guilty of the crime of being black.

(Episode Seven)

In this section, I want to explore the interrelationships within an Afro-Caribbean family and also wider issues of race, identity and racial violence. The Robertson family consists of Florrie, the middle aged mother who is a Nurse, and her two children – both in their early twenties – Chris and Janet. Chris's closest friend is Marcus and their passion for Jungle music and a dream of running their own illegal FM radio station, Massive FM, binds them in a deep friendship of mutual solidarity. When these characters are viewed initially in early episodes, Chris is working, unwillingly, as a commis chef in one of the fashionable restaurants frequented by Gary and the food fashion clientele. The fact that Chris, like so many other young black men, is obliged to do menial work, is a telling factor in the character's construction. Feeling exploited and frustrated, he explodes to his employer, an arrogantly patronising chef, "I ain't no fucking slave, man!" and angrily walks away from his job. For Chris, in the kitchen he is not himself but "everybody's"; whilst when he is mixing music, "I'm my own man." Lying to his mother in telling her that he would like a loan to study for qualifications to further his career, he and Marcus use the money to buy and install their own underground radio station in the block of flats where they live. Whereas the son, whom she loves uncritically, is deceiving Florrie, her relationship with her daughter, Janet, is much more obviously problematic. Viewing Janet as irresponsible and disinterested, a complex subtext of sibling jealousy and parent–daughter tensions is established which erupts to the surface of their lives in the context of two critical events. The first incident centres upon Janet who, fuelled by anger about her mother's adulation for Chris, informs the authorities about the location of Massive FM. This results in the equipment being taken away and leaves Florrie sadly bewildered at her son's deception, whilst Janet experiences a bitter revenge coloured by guilty reflection about the motives for her actions. Neither of these confused and unresolved feelings can be dealt with, when, in the context of the second, tragic, event, Chris is murdered at the hands of Bernard, a white working class taxi cab driver. To employ the metaphor of the kaleidoscope once more, individual events, characters, and their public and private actions, exist in synchrony with each other yet again. This brings us to another fundamental constituent of Tony Marchant's agenda within 'Holding On,' the interconnectedness of both his fictive characters' lives and, by implication, our own:

The abiding theme of 'Holding On' is about how we construct a society, and that's really about recognising mutuality and reciprocity, connectedness and the realisation that we don't go on our personal journeys in complete isolation or in a vacuum.

[Marchant]

That sense of connection is explored and expressed through both aesthetic and structural narrative means. Underlying the separate narratives and thematic concerns is therefore Marchant's own desire to signal moral coherence. That ideological position embodies a left-field critique of institutionalised corruption and oppression, with recognition of personal responsibility more usually located in a reactionary frame. This searching for a moral centre carries with it clear difficulties in terms of an associative notion of community that is subject both to liberal idealism and reactionary, social atomic viewpoints. Between those dialectical demarcations of collective social commitment to one another, and the primacy of the individual as an agent of moral responsibility, resides a site of ideological struggle and shifting positions.

These considerations are nowhere more prevalent and symptomatic than in those characters and narratives centring upon race and, specifically, the murder of Chris. Following the narrative sequence referred to in the previous section linking Shaun and Gary in the restaurant, the visual text transfers to Chris on what proves to be his fatal journey to try and retrieve his job. His cab driver, Bernard, has been portrayed earlier . A lonely middle-aged man whose passion is building and sailing model boats – has been shown enduring a final, customary humiliation at the hands of his wife and brother. It has been clear that they are having an ongoing and transparent sexual affair with little or no attempt to conceal it from him. Earlier, in Episode One, it is Bernard who has also witnessed the tragic stabbing of Sally. However, with a sense of moral impotence and an evasion of the commitment to others articulated by Marchant, he drives away from the scene, secure only in the self-sufficient world of his taxicab.

When Chris enters his cab, it is clear that he has reached a point where he can no longer internalise his anger as the impotent victim of emotional and psychological bullying. His excessive and irrational reaction to Chris smoking in his cab, and subsequently forcing him out of the car, finally culminates in Bernard, his self-pity transformed into rage, beating Chris to death on the pavement next to where he has stopped the cab. Moments later, the camera cuts to Werner escaping the city and the country in his private helicopter. The final, potent image is of a panoramic, bird's eye view of the city and river below, Werner escaping to Switzerland and immunity. The demi-god ascending from the site of struggle had earlier told Shaun that "Wealth can insulate you against many things." As he disappears into the heavens, his wealth is, indeed, his transcendence.

Following on the tragedy of Chris's death, his mother embarks upon a campaign for justice. Bernard has received a derisory two-year prison sentence for the crime. This follows Bernard, whether in shock, denial or some perversely misperceived sense of celebrity after years of anonymity, reinventing the actual circumstances of the murder. In so doing, he presents himself as a kind of hero caught in tragic circumstances. His construction of Chris as an aggressive, threatening presence within the cab reinforces with a bleak familiarity, the dominant white reactionary stereotypes of young Afro - Caribbean men. With deeply depressing resonance, his testimony bears strong similarity to evidence given in the context of the Macpherson Inquiry into the death of Stephen Lawrence. Bernard's wife, attracted herself by her husband's new found role as "decent white working class man-as-hero," promises him her support – albeit short lived. The racial stereotyping implicit both in Bernard's testimony and also the judicial system that sentences him collides with the traumatic impact of the tragedy on the family and their community.

Florrie's narrative journey intersects with Claire, Sally's older sister, when Claire is assigned as a volunteer support worker for her as part of a scheme called 'Action for Victims.' However, it soon transpires that Claire has still not recovered sufficiently from her own traumatic loss to give Florrie the measured, objective support that she will need through the trial and its aftermath. In order to launch a campaign to challenge the racism and injustice inherent within the judge's sentencing of Bernard, she is advised to approach a black lawyer John Eylot. He confirms the dual victim status enacted upon her dead son:

> Eylot: Your son was attacked twice. First by Bernard Hotton, then by the Criminal Justice system. I'd like to act for you.

Through the campaign, in seeking to find justice for Chris, characters discover and earn a new understanding of themselves and each other. These personal journeys of grief, pain and self-realisation are inseparable from their fresh understanding of, and involvement in, wider political issues of race and justice. Nevertheless, these are not easy journeys or resolutions, and complications of trust, betrayal and sexual desire have to be reconnoitred. Across the eight episodes of 'Holding On,' boundaries of race, ethnicity, familial loyalty, class and desire are challenged and confronted, reflecting a struggle for the personal and the public city. For Janet and Marcus, an intimate relationship grows out of their despair, with Janet finding a new sense of purpose and focus by helping Marcus through the early stages of bereavement. Believing initially that he is incapable of carrying on with either his life or Massive FM, Janet helps him to find a way of articulating his anger and grief: principally by encouraging him to restart Massive FM. In her grief, Florrie blames first herself and then Marcus for her son's death. Sensing that she failed to understand her son's real needs, she blames herself for trying to define his life in terms of her own expectations for him. Consequently, she feels partially responsible that Chris was unable to be honest and open about Massive FM. Equally – and paradoxically – she blames Marcus as a bad influence upon Chris, seeing his friend as the dominant influence in the setting up of the radio station.

As Marcus slowly begins to find a new sense of purpose through re-launching his music and in a deepening relationship with Janet, he also begins to compromise the authenticity of that music. Commercial and entrepreneurial success threatens to undermine the non-commercial, creative ethos of the original Massive FM project. When tackled on this by Janet, angry that Chris's ideals will be lost along with his life, Marcus responds "I'm giving people what they want, can't you see the change in me?" With cutting irony, it is of course only too clear that Marcus has changed. His growing achievement of mainstream success signals a crucial undermining of alternative ideals and values. The strain that this issue places upon their relationship is compounded as John Eylot becomes increasingly and actively involved in their campaign to secure a posthumous justice for Chris. It also presents a moral dilemma for Florrie when Eylot seeks to convince her that the heart of the campaign must focus upon race, thus requiring that Chris's murder must have racial overtones.

Eylot: The defence demonised him and the judge went along with it.

Florrie: That man would have gone for anyone. He didn't attack Chris because he was black.

Eylot: That's not the point Florrie. We're talking about the leniency of the sentence. If you want to make the Attorney General listen you have to embarrass him. You need a campaign which focuses on the rights of a victim being sold short because he was black.

Florrie: I'm just not sure I want to turn this into a race thing.

Eylot: You can't just act on the grounds the sentence was 'unfair.' You tell them they should be reassuring the black community that a black life is every bit – every bit as valuable as a white's. When Roland Adams was murdered, the police said it was territorial.

Stating that "When I buried Chris I didn't want what happened to him to be buried too," Florrie agrees to Eylot's strategy. Further tensions arise between Janet and Marcus when she approaches him to use Massive FM to support the campaign:

Marcus: You're better off going to like Station FM or someone. They do community stuff.

Janet: I've come to you! You were Chris' best friend Marcus! And you've got a community you play out to!

Marcus: Music! Music right!

Janet: You telling me you can't find time for this?

Marcus: Look I got a lot of people to satisfy. Listeners want their dedications, the labels want their power plays....

Janet: I'm asking you to remember Chris that's all.

Marcus: If I don't satisfy people Janet, they'll just check somewhere else on the dial you know what I'm saying?

Janet: You think you're Mister Entrepreneur now don't you?

Marcus: I think I'm serious.

Janet: You're scared of anything serious! You hid in your room when Chris died – you're doing it all over again!

Within to this web of tension and tangled loyalties and desire re-enters John Eylot. High-profiled, able and charismatic, the seeds of latent and mutual sexual attraction are soon sown between Janet and the lawyer. Marcus is alert to these sub-currents which threaten to destabilise his hard-won sense of purpose and equilibrium. At a campaigning candlelit vigil. Eylot makes a rousing speech, intervening to speak when Florrie is overcome by her grief:

> Eylot: The derisory sentence handed out to his killer, his white killer adds great insult to great injury. We owe it to his memory to ensure that his death is not taken lightly. Chris may have been cheated of his life but he should not be cheated of justice. This campaign will intensify to ensure that the person who denied Chris his future is adequately punished, that the criminal justice system recognises its duty to act in the interests of all the community. Our message is that a black life is not expendable. We refuse to be guilty for the crime of being black.

Later that evening, with emotions running high and Janet attracted to Eylot's commitment to the campaign and his mature self-assurance, he and Janet engage in a casual sexual encounter with Janet subsequently feeling angry, confused and used. The following day, motivated perhaps by his own mixed feelings of guilt, Eylot goes to see Marcus and offer his thanks for him eventually agreeing to use Massive FM to promote the campaign. Marcus, however, is sceptical of Eylot's motives – both in relation to himself and Janet, and also to the campaign. Once again in this series, the complexities of personal agendas and insecurities slip through into matters of public and political discourse. Later that day, an angry and jealous Marcus confronts Janet:

> Marcus: He thinks we're on the same mission.
>
> Janet: What's wrong with that?
>
> Marcus: I'm doing it for my friend. He just wants to make a name for himself.
>
> Janet: That's not fair. He believes in this campaign.
>
> Marcus: He just likes campaigns. He's got a political mind, yeah. But his heart... forget about it.... And what about the rest of it? Him doing his Jesse Jackson number.
>
> Janet: Have you got any idea how nervous he was doing that?
>
> Marcus: No. You obviously do though, innit?
>
> Janet: Look, let's forget about it. I don't want to talk about John Eylot.
>
> Marcus: Vouched for him enough already yeah? What happened last night?

(Janet looks up. She feels very guilty and needs to express it)

Janet: I liked the idea of it. I liked the idea of him. But afterwards... I just wanted to get away as soon as I could.

It soon becomes clear that Marcus is devastated by Janet's betrayal of their relationship and he scores some crack cocaine, preparing to anaesthetise his pain through its use.

In a climactic final scene in Episode Eight, Florrie goes up onto the roofs of the high rise flats where they live to try and talk down a distraught Marcus. Imprisoned by both his sense of Janet's betrayal and the lingering aftermath of Chris's death, he sees his only salvation and release through a cocaine-charged leap from the roof edge "I'm going to fly over London town... Seven Sisters Road and Tottenham Court Road, watch me go!" In a highly charged scene of his desperate grief and Florrie's equally desperate desire to bring Marcus down, the acceptance and love that she demonstrates to him completes a cycle of grief, bitterness and, ultimately, reconciliation. This fragile closure signals, perhaps, to a future of tentative optimism, in which Chris's life and tragic death might be signed in the transformed relationships of those who live on. Once again, there are no easy solutions or promises made, but the web of personal and political struggle suggests a future in which these characters might find, through a tolerant acceptance of their own fractured humanity, a way forward.

Lloyd and Hilary

Hilary: I just can't get my bearings as far as you're concerned. I really wish we could get back together. Listen to me, fantasy world again, it's all I'm good for.

(Dialogue with Lloyd, Episode Seven)

In terms of the series' wider thematic and ideological concerns, the character of Hilary exhibits the principal characteristics of the wider political culture in which the characters exist. Ambivalent, image-conscious, torn between diametric positions of gender, class, sexuality and a reactionary pragmatism, she becomes engaged in a difficult relationship with Lloyd. Lloyd is black, working class and works as a Security Guard at the private apartments where she lives. Hilary is a successful public relations agent, employed by Werner, amongst others. With calculating and cutting irony, she observes to Werner and his financial consultant, Lake:

In the eighties it was my job to get people into the papers. Now it's my job to keep them out. No more promoting good stories just managing bad ones.... The main perception has to be that you've become the victim of the Inland Revenue not the subject of a raid. Why are the Revenue threatening the jobs of all your workers? Why are they behaving so spitefully and arbitrarily? Blame becomes something the Revenue has to defend itself from. That's the approach we take.

That latent sense of the framing and manufacturing of news is a dominant phenomenon within contemporary British political culture. Hilary is effectively a stage manager of the public's perception both of what is significant in news terms and also, by implication, of what is appropriate and necessary for the mediated public gaze. In a decade in which the concept and function of the 'Spin Doctor' has become a byword for deception and control and the execution of covert ideological agendas, Hilary is constructed as similarly manipulative and oblique in the strategies of her private relationships. This presents worrying implications in terms of democratic public accountability, and also in the indeterminate codes and boundaries of personal relationships within a post-modern location. The beginning of the couple's personal encounter follows a criminal attack upon Hilary as she arrives home late at night. Subsequently, she begins to receive menacing telephone calls and, besieged by paranoia and fear, asks for assistance from Security. Lloyd arrives at her apartment and deals with the threatening calls. The next day, Hilary makes a pass at Lloyd:

> Hilary: Well as a mark of gratitude I could buy you a beer or something. One night… anytime.

> Lloyd: There's no need for that.

> Hilary: Well, it wouldn't be just gratitude.

> (Pause. She's having to work hard. She's not nearly so smooth as in her job)

> Hilary: It would be interest as well. I mean I'd be interested in… well, seeing you… away from those gates and your patrol.

> Lloyd: I don't think that'd be a good idea.

From the outset, when Hilary first makes this sexual pass at Lloyd, he expresses concern and serious reservations about the implications of their relationship, expressed most cogently and directly in his acknowledgment to her that "I work for you." For someone used to managing and directing others, Hilary cannot at first see any contradictions between them in terms of class and race. When Lloyd comes to her apartment on the pretext of apologising for his earlier rejection of her interest, Hilary senses her opportunity and makes a strategic use of the ambivalent irony on the notion of security:

> Hilary: I didn't ask you out because I wanted some kind of bodyguard. In fact, I think you're the one whose scared, aren't you?

> (This has a playful tone but she means it. He's honest enough to admit:)

> Lloyd: Bit.

> Hilary: Don't worry. You're perfectly safe with me.

Their relationship enters into intimacy with increasing intensity with Hilary paying for a meal for them at an expensive hotel and booking, without consulting Lloyd, a room for the night. The tensions between Lloyd's job and their relationship is increasingly precarious and comes to a head when, having spent the night together at her apartment, Hilary asks Lloyd to kiss her goodbye as she leaves for work and he is about to start his morning shift. When she playfully challenges him to compromise his job by kissing her in the car park, he responds by reminding her that her livelihood is not implicated or threatened in the same way. Nevertheless, it is a sign of the seriousness of their relationship that he does then kiss her, effectively handing in his notice. It is also significant that as a young Afro-Caribbean man in contemporary London, one of the few opportunities open to him is to work in the Private Security sector – an expanding but very poorly paid area. Even as they fall into a full and passionate consummation of their mutual sexual desire, it's not long before Lloyd accuses her of using him as a sexual status symbol. The climactic moment for this crisis in their relationship is at a dinner party, which Hilary holds for some white, upper-middle class professional friends.

When the conversation turns to Lloyd's occupation, Hilary intervenes by saying that he is a 'Security Consultant.' Placing him thus in an impossible position, an embarrassed Lloyd is obliged to try and sustain the deception, knowing that Hilary is ashamed that he is a Security Guard. After the guests have left, sensing that his colour and ethnicity constitute an erotic post-colonial trophy, he angrily confronts her motives as wanting "A black guy good in bed. Don't patronise me." Throughout the precarious and troubled navigation of their relationship, Hilary tries to compensate for her own confused agenda by seeking to purchase Lloyd's affections and commitment through material means. Expensive meals, rooms booked in luxury hotels and the gift of a designer shirt, all denote someone whose strategies seek to control and define the other through the display and exchange of material excess. Beneath the radical rhetoric of Hilary's viewpoint – the transgressing of racial and class boundaries – resides a far more problematic ideological position. Individual sensibilities and fundamental issues of dignity and self-determination are not transmutable into sound bites. Nevertheless, Hilary seeks to use the same unreflective pragmatism that defines her working-mode to determine and delineate the dynamics and perimeters of her relationship with Lloyd. At the disastrous dinner party, one of her dinner guests refers to Lloyd – in his absence – with a patronising lack of candour, as "her Denzil Washington," Lloyd's angry refusal to be compromised and demeaned by her hypocrisy leads to him leaving her. She is genuinely shaken and disorientated at this expression of his own sense of self-determination and self-respect. After the trauma of this episode, a compromise seems suddenly possible in the couple's agreement to meet one another in a geographical 'middle-ground' location. This notion of delineating a spatial location of a centre that might accommodate the conflicts of class, ethnicity, gender and sexual desire, is clearly wishful thinking on Hilary's part. Trying to negotiate an ideological middle of the road position can only have one inevitable consequence – one or other of them will become casualties of the traffic of reactionary, predatory discourse. Consequently, the painful boundaries of sexual desire and insecurity, compounded by those of race and class, force Lloyd to finally bring the relationship to a close. The embarrassment that Lloyd had experienced at the party is repaid to Hilary when she arrives at a south London pub where Lloyd is playing pool, with some black friends. This represents alien territory to Hilary and she experiences the marginalisation and 'invisibility' which Lloyd will live with on a daily basis because of his racial identity. In Hilary's case, it is her code and demeanour of white, female middle-class sensibility that positions her in this location. The lingering and powerful anger and humiliation that Lloyd clearly still feels is now re-enacted with Hilary as the demeaned subject:

> Lloyd: If you're looking for a nice black boy, go to Gambia for your holidays, buy them a t-shirt and they'll walk down the beach with you. They're easily pleased and they know their place. Should suit you.
>
> (She's being humiliated but she knew she might be. She came to tell him something privately but is now going to tell him anyway)
>
> Hilary: If an MP gets caught coming out of his researcher's flat at four in the morning I'm the kind of person they employ to mop up after them. I'll have him and his wife at a press call by breakfast arm-in-arm. I'm making a right mess of this though aren't I? I just can't get my bearings at all as far as you're concerned, not when it's starting to become something proper anyway. I really wish... listen to me, fantasy world again. All I'm good for. I'm sorry Lloyd.

Towards the closure of the final episode, the camera locates Hilary in the shifting frame of a taxi speeding through busy London streets. This location conveys the continuing certainties of her public persona with her own inward confusion and insecurity. She articulates a depressed and resigned personal worldview that "Nothing changes." In terms of the apparent fluidity of the concepts of policy and presentation in contemporary political life, and the absence of any effective radical opposition to the neutralising centre-right location of New Labour, Hilary's assessment that "Nothing changes" seems depressingly appropriate.

Claire, Sally, Brenda and Annie

> Claire: I didn't do enough for Sally when she was here.
>
> (Episode Eight)

These sentiments convey the journey of grief, anger and loss that underscores the character of Claire, the older sister of Sally, who was so tragically murdered at the closure of Episode One. At the opening of the series Claire is characterised as an attractive, sexually active young woman, who enjoys a lifestyle of pragmatic self-interest mixed in with hedonistic pleasures that defined upwardly mobile women and men from Thatcher's 1980s onwards. Sally is rather protectively critical of her elder sister's way of life and the tensions between the two women are exhibited by Sally's traumatic experience of sexual harassment at work as an office clerk. In the opening sequence of Episode One located in the underground train, the camera frames Sally in oblique close-up. She is furtively examining a Polaroid photograph of a man's penis that has been anonymously sent to her at her workplace. The latent sense of claustrophobic vulnerability that the young woman feels is heightened by an angled shot, from her point of view, glimpsing the alienating indifference of middle-aged male passengers standing around her on the overcrowded train. Through this camera point of view, there is a potent sense of a reflected, displaced male gaze upon a female subject. This is powerfully developed as an iconic, aesthetic sign in the narrative dealing with her experience of intrusion and harassment. When Sally is released into the supposed, relative liberty of the streets and daylight, however, her attempts to enlist her sister's interest and support are painfully misplaced. Claire's response to her sister's stumbling attempts to tell her about the obscene photograph and the wider frame of harassment, is to jokingly assert that her sister must be the "only woman given a penis and couldn't get any pleasure from it." Her sense of humour, borne out of surviving in the city as a young woman, serves only to upset and alienate Sally. Newly arrived in London, she is not prepared for its corrosive impact upon either personal space or sensibilities.

This conflict of perspective and expectation is explored further as we see the two women negotiating a route through London as a post-modern, pleasured location in which they encounter Wild West-themed bars, parties and, invariably, sex. There is a subliminal, connotative use of music once again in the setting of the party where Sally angrily resists the unwanted attentions of a man, only to return to find her sister in an erotic embrace with a total stranger. This whole sequence is played to a backdrop of the Manic Street Preachers' album title track 'Design for Life' which features the lyric, "We don't talk about love/ We only want to get drunk." Even as this song seeks to offer a critique of unthinking, materialistic hedonism, its use as a musical signature for this scene is poignant and potent. In terms of Claire's attempts to design her own life in terms of casual sexual encounters and the constant liberating anaesthetic of alcohol, her apparently impregnable, confident self-sufficiency is only challenged by Sally's sudden death. Determined to deal with and confront her anonymous harasser, Sally discovers – by chance – that he is her manager in the Education Authority offices where she is working. A sequence of events unfolds in which she eventually, through the support and actions of UNISON – the union at her workplace – is able to bring a disciplinary procedure against him. However, this is not easily achieved and requires her courage and determination to persuade another woman, who had been an earlier victim of his sexual overtures, to agree to testify against him.

Stylistically, the director Adrian Shergold makes subtle use of the mirror in both its literal and metaphorical terms. On several different occasions within this narrative, the viewer sees Sally, as the female subject of the voyeuristic male gaze, fixed within the mirror. Equally powerfully, the camera frames Sally seated, from behind and across her shoulder, suddenly capturing the interrogating stare of her oppressor within her open cosmetic mirror. The geo-ideological spatial relationships of the intruding male presence, resisted by the female subject, whom he strives to define as passive and receptive, are communicated with a quietly compelling ideological critique.

After her hard struggle and eventual victory in the case, Sally invites Claire to come out with her for a celebration drink. However, sibling tensions resurface between them and Sally goes out alone for what proves to be her last, fatal journey. Bored at drinking alone in a bar, she goes into a public call box to telephone her sister in a spirit of reconciliation. Her telephone conversation is brutally interrupted when Alan bursts in upon her, wielding a knife with which he savagely attacks her as he screams "Why are you talking to the Devil?" In this devastating sequence of motiveless and appalling violence, the camera focuses upon the ashen, disbelieving face of his victim. With the telephone left dangling as she slumps to the floor, there is a chillingly poignant image of panic and confusion, as Claire desperately tries to restore an active communication with a sister with whom contact has always been impeded by affectionate antagonism. From this moment on, the character of Claire undergoes a complex redemptive journey, which is similar in ideological significance to that endured by Shaun. Experiencing all of the inevitable emotions of shock, denial, anger and guilt, there is a very moving scene where she has to identify Sally's body in the morgue, saying to the police officers, "No, no that's not my sister." After the arrival of her parents in London, she unintentionally compounds their grief by referring to her dead sister in the quasi-formal language of the authorities as 'the body." Both of these instances convey an endemic psychological disengagement from her own overwhelming sense of loss and displaced responsibility for the circumstances of her sister's death. At Alan's trial, there is a painful and angry encounter between the parents and Annie, Alan's mother, provoked in part by Claire's request to sit with her. This has followed Claire, initially driven by anger, confronting Annie and blaming her for Alan's murderous actions. However, a totally unexpected and moving relationship develops between the two women, united in grief and a profound desire to see a formal inquiry mounted into the circumstances of Alan's initial release onto the streets and into the wider community. This process of reconciliation that eventually leads them into securing a public enquiry into Sally's death and the circumstances that led to Alan's release from psychiatric care, begins with a poignant visit to Annie's home immediately after Alan's trial:

> Claire: I came to apologise for for what I did at the committal. The way I... as if you were fair game or something.

> Annie: Well I'm not.

> Claire: No. (Beat) I've come across London to see you.

> (Annie doesn't respond)

> Claire: Can I come in?

Reluctantly, Annie allows Claire into her home and the two women begin a slow and painful negotiation of their shared territory of grief and loss. Claire articulates the sense of displaced guilt that so often accompanies the sudden and violent loss of a loved one:

> Claire: If I hadn't been so churlish that night she wouldn't have run out. I was always trying to put her in her place. She wasn't going to have that anymore. She went out on her own, ended up on some street on her own because of me. I thought you could be unscathed by everything. She showed me that you can't be. By dying.

Later in the series, as the two women continue to campaign for justice, Annie skilfully and sensitively asks Claire about her past and how both of their lives have been traumatically and permanently changed:

> Annie: What was your life like before all this?

> Claire: What do you mean?

> Annie: Well. Was it good? Was it fun?

> Claire: Yeah.

> Annie: I've lived with Alan's illness for fifteen years now, I wouldn't know how to go back to whatever life I had before, but you do.

> Claire: She was my sister.

> Annie: You won't stop being related to her. Leave me to keep an eye on the enquiry – I can do that now.

> Claire: I was always going on to her about how people should just take off when they feel like it. You know. Not get dragged down by responsibility. Look at me now!

> Annie: That's something else you can do for her. Live some of her life for her, instead of her death, hey?

Through their tenacious courage and determination for justice, a formal inquiry is granted. After its findings have led to as denunciation of the system that forced Alan onto the street, Annie observes "I suppose justice does come eventually. But not when you need it." Alongside her growing friendship with Annie, Claire initially tries to submerge and smother her loss through reverting to systematic, meaningless sex with Kurt, the young man that she'd picked up previously at the party. In an emotionally gruelling and shocking scene, the camera frames her from above in a soul-less, mechanistic sexual encounter with Kurt, she shouting, "This is what I need. You on me, you over me, making me feel it right inside me. Let's do everything. I want to," and eventually crying out, "I'm not dead! I'm not fucking dead." In another development which shows her seeking to build an alternative, more purposeful future for herself, she trains as a volunteer counsellor and support worker for 'Action for Victims' – a group established to offer support to the grieving families of those murdered through crimes of violence. As I observed in my earlier discussion of Florrie, it transpires that she is the first person to whom Claire is attached at the time of Bernard's trial and the investigations into Chris's death. However, it soon becomes clear that in trying to sublimate her own grieving through throwing herself into this work, she is – with tragic irony – less able to support Florrie than she might comfort Claire. Florrie observes in a phrase potent with both poetic economy and political comment "Courts like silence." In the context of a grief so deep that it defies articulation, Claire says to her "I don't know anything anymore, which way is up. " Another important stage in Claire's journey from self-centred self-interest to a deeper maturity and understanding of herself and issues of justice, lies in her decision to re-let Sally's former room. This decision brings her into contact with Brenda, a working class woman who, it is eventually discovered, has run away from her abusive husband. What begins as an unlikely friendship between the two women eventually grows into one of mutual admiration and respect. For Brenda, who has come from ordinary working class life in the West Country, London represents a new opportunity for her, "As far as I'm concerned, life doesn't begin at forty, it begun at Victoria." Brenda is constructed as an intriguing mix of naive enthusiasm for life in the city with an experience of sterile getting on and 'coping' that stands in stark contrast to Claire's earlier modus operandi of the 'pleasure principle'.

> Brenda: I thought I was good at coping. When I had the three jobs I still found time to feed the kids and wash their clothes. I coped. When he spent most of his time out fishing I coped. Just before I left I was telling him I'd be back with the shopping in between my cleaning job and my waitressing one. Out of the blue, he just smacked me one. He'd never done that before. Couldn't work out what made him, then it dawned on me – he didn't like the way I just kept going…. That's when I did the runner. Stupid coping for them all the time. Thought I'd come here and cope for myself for a change. (Beat) It's harder than you think though.

However, as with all relationships in this series, their ultimate affirmation of each other has first to traverse issues surrounding their differing experiences as women. Claire's reaction to her older housemate conveys her underlying prejudiced assumptions about Brenda's age and class. Having to juggle two or three menial jobs in order to survive in the city, Brenda's cheerful if sometimes clumsy attempts at establishing a friendship with Claire falter. Nevertheless, when Claire discovers, to her horror and shock, that her encounter with Kurt has left her pregnant, it is Brenda whose life experience and uncompromising openness allows her to give Claire the support and advice that she needs. With Claire uncertain as to whether keep the baby or have an abortion, it is Brenda who is there to listen to her anxieties and fears.

Significantly, when Claire arranges to meet with Kurt to tell him that he is the prospective father of her child to be, the encounter finally confirms for her the extent to which she and her life have changed. Even as she tries to talk seriously with him, he responds with smug disdain "I liked your old self – you didn't give a toss about anything."

Earlier in the same episode, Claire is able to repay Brenda's loyal commitment to her by intervening to protect her from the unwanted attentions of an aggressive man. Wearing a blonde wig and trying to re-invent herself into a younger, 'fashionable' woman, Brenda has arrived home in the early hours of the morning, terrified. Her social naivety has led to her accepting a taxi ride home with a stranger who has tried to pick her up that evening. Claire is able to intervene and send the man away, but then she explodes into anger with Brenda as the circumstances of Sally's death return to haunt her. Shouting at her "Things happen here" and awash with displaced anger and worry over Brenda's vulnerability, she is finally able to talk to Brenda about Sally and her death. In the quiet after the storm, the two women share previously hidden aspects of their lives, with Brenda describing the physical abuse she received from her husband "He didn't like the way I just kept going." Through sharing their respective pain and bewilderment, their relationship moves into a new area of mutual trust, support and respect. But, just as Claire comes to rely upon having Brenda in her life and believes that her friend is developing the confidence to live an independent life, the two women receive a visit from Brenda's husband. After much reflection and uncertainty, Brenda decides to leave London and return to her husband. Whilst he has made assurances that he will reform his behaviour, Brenda leaves without any real confidence, convinced merely that 'where she belongs' is with her husband and children. Annie and Brenda represent two working class women for whom commitment and identification with the personal demands and responsibilities of domestic life carry prior consideration. In terms of the construction and development of Claire's character, it is only as she is able to accept the moral gravitational pull of responsibility and concern for others that she is shown to mature. The potential problem associated with the delineation of the two other women is of idealising their self-effacing endurance as an unconditional virtue – a latent signing of affective moral solidity within the construction of the working class mother/wife. Similarly the way in which Claire's journey is navigated strongly implies that the acceptance of personal responsibility is of greater social and ethical value than the more problematic domain of the individual as self-validating agent of choice and identity. Again, these tensions clearly relate back to Marchant's view of the need for the moral coherence of both the mutual reciprocity of our concerns for each other, alongside the need for the individual needing to confront responsibilities for their own actions. Bearing in mind his critique of Blairite ideology and its execution, this moral debate is framed in terms surprisingly close to the Communitarianism that the Prime Minister and New Labour have espoused.

Helen and Zahid

> Zahid: (To his father, Shahid) When you do business you don't rely on your ethnic base
> any more. You can't. So what do you do? You sell frozen curries to the white
> community. I know it came from Hafiz but you could always be open-minded where
> money's concerned, couldn't you? Why can't you do the same for me?!

In this short section, I want to return to the characters of Zahid and Helen who I
discussed briefly earlier in this chapter. The construction of these characters and their
relationship to each other is of significant interest highlighting as it does the tensions
within Zahid's family background, and the difficulties of negotiating an intimate
relationship across a territory of cultural, ethnic and familial expectations.

These tensions are nowhere more evident than in the scene at a Muslim wedding
reception where it becomes apparent that Helen is meeting Zahid's family for the first
time. Zahid's family – principally his father, Shahid and brother, Hafiz – run a very
successful Indian food manufacturing company. Subsequently, they are necessarily
positioned as wanting to see business and commerce secured and advocated. Even
though it is expressed in the context of a humorous attack upon his brother, Hafiz
nevertheless places a question mark about Zahid's actions in relation to the Werner
case:

> Hafiz: A poor refugee comes over here from Hungary in 1956, fleeing the communists and
> builds up his own business. He creates thousands of jobs, gives generously to charity
> and what do Zahid and his friends at the Inland Revenue do? They make him flee all
> over again.

Meanwhile, Helen has taken the initiative of going and sitting next to Shahid at the
meal table. She approaches this situation with all of the well-intentioned openness and
tolerance associated with a white, middle-class liberal position. However, this cannot
prepare her for the quiet anger and prejudice that she encounters:

> Helen: This food's delicious isn't it? (Beat) I'm a friend of Zahid's Mr Ahmad. Actually, I'm
> his…
>
> Shahid: (Interrupting) I know what you are. He's my shame and you're his.
>
> Helen: I beg your pardon?
>
> Zahid: Helen… just leave it.
>
> (Shahid turning on Zahid)

Shahid: (In Urdu) You want to humiliate me all over again? It's not enough you turn your back on your family's business but you have to parade your whore?

Helen: What's he saying? What did he say?!

The scene continues with a cut to the hotel corridor where Zahid accuses his father of hypocrisy and double standards in engaging with the white community in terms of his business interests, whilst retaining a separatist stance in terms of his son's relationship with Helen:

Shahid: I sell to the white community. You're selling yourself to them.

Zahid: I'm my own man there Dad. I'm my own man!

Zahid then has to pursue Helen who is leving the building angry, confused and humiliated. She accuses Zahid of having taken her to the reception as "a badge you were wearing" – "Zahid's white girlfriend," and when Zahid retorts with, "Look I've been fighting my Father for years," Helen turns angrily once more and challenges him with "What am I – your latest move?" For Zahid, the pressures generated within his own familial and ethnic background must needs be kept separate from both his work and his relationship with Helen. Nevertheless, it's clearly very difficult to maintain this precarious juggling act of divided loyalties and ambitions. Confused and emotionally exhausted himself, he seeks to reassure Helen that "I want you. I want you to come first." In an earlier scene, Zahid has called in to see his brother at the family factory and they exchange ironic observations about the post-modern discourse of multiculturalism with the reactionary, hard-headed business sense that drives the firm's success:

Hafiz: I just love picturing it you know – Tracy and Wayne popping it in the microwave, sitting down in front of Jim Davidson..

Zahid: (Wry) There's multiculturalism for you.

Hafiz: Multiculturalism my arse, it's market penetration.

Later on in the series, a crisis hits the family business when Shahid arrives to tell Zahid that Hafiz has been extorting money from the business accounts to pay off gambling debts. Again, Helen tries to intervene when Shahid exerts moral pressure upon Zahid to return to the family business to sort out the affair. She is desperately concerned that his own independent life and career in the Revenue will be jeopardised, especially when he has recently been temporarily promoted into the disgraced Shaun's position. A compromise is eventually reached where, in return for returning to sort out and take over the running of the family business, Zahid exacts of his father a proper acceptance and respect of himself and his relationship with Helen. He presents these terms and conditions to his father who, perhaps challenged by his earlier heated exchanges with his son, and also needing his support, begins a slow journey of personal, cultural assimilation and tolerance:

> Shahid: These terms and conditions – are they negotiable?
>
> Zahid: No, you need me here – I come on my own terms. (Beat) Our terms. (Beat) We're going to live together.
>
> Shahid: What is your religion?
>
> Helen: I'm a Charlton supporter.
>
> Shahid: An optimist.
>
> Helen: Doggedly.
>
> Shahid: I have my own way to see things too.
>
> Zahid: Yeah, you wave your stick till it hits something. Sorry Dad.
>
> (Zahid knows he has been cruel)
>
> Shahid: No, it's true. (Beat, slyly) And Helen, she's saying she's going to respect what makes me 'tick.'
>
> Zahid: But this time you're going to be different aren't you?

In the final sequence of 'Holding On,' Tony Marchant uses a voice-over commentary from Gary Rickey who is in the process of rebuilding his life through the support of Karen. Through a carefully constructed visual narrative, offsetting Gary's travelogue of the benefits and pleasures of living in London, a thought-provoking, reflective mode is established. This final sequence acts as a kind of montage of events, themes and characters, which constitute the fictional construct of London that the serial evokes. The style of Gary's commentary is framed in the same register as his restaurant reviews, unsettling the basis on which the viewer is to receive and interpret his assessment of life in contemporary London. I want to quote from what is an excellent piece of writing and will return to this final speech in my final considerations in my concluding chapter:

> Gary: (Voice Over) Leave town and after a bit you just can't wait to get back again, in the thick of it. London casts that sort of spell. There's nowhere like it for meeting old friends, and making new ones. The possibilities just multiply every time you walk down the street....

(As Helen leaves the Revenue building, a car horn attracts her attention. It's Zahid at the wheel of his new Mercedes. He's smiling broadly. She looks embarrassed, almost disapproving, like she's not sure what she's seeing anymore. She approaches the car and almost reluctantly, gets in)

Gary: There's still that frightening division between the haves and the have nots and I certainly wouldn't dream of waving my gold card at people who live in Newham. Well not anymore. Anyway, in the world of work, job insecurities have become a way of life and you can throw your year planner away because you might not be needing it. What's round the corner these days is usually a nasty shock.

The montage ranges from Bernard, released from prison and consumed by despair, committing suicide by throwing himself into the Thames. We also view Shaun arriving at court supported by Vicki and viewed through a media scrum of flashing cameras and reporters that had previously accompanied Shaun's investigation of Werner. Other images cut and move between an increasingly successful Zahid with a slightly apprehensive Helen, to Marcus cutting a new piece of music dedicated to Chris's memory. Finally, the camera point of view swirls high above some London suburbs from which vantage-point, we see Claire and Brenda playing a game of knock-about tennis in a public park. With them is Claire's baby daughter, safe within her pram as the two friends laugh and joke together. The deliberately disjointed collision of Gary's up-beat, pro-active assessment of contemporary London with fragmented images of Bernard's body being dredged from the river, undermines any comfortable or cohesive conclusions. As John Dugdale perceptively observed in an article for *The Guardian* (1 September 1997):

His [Marchant's] London – the "crime-infested, decaying, paranoid capital" of Gary Rickey's monologue – is a merciless pre-millennial waste-land whose citizens appear to live discrete, zoned-off lives but are actually endlessly connected: by sudden acts of violence and their rippling repercussions; by a kind of urban chaos theory…; by parallels between disparate, unsuspecting characters who are… linked by guilt of a trapped desperation.

We are left at the end of this powerful drama with a view of the city and ourselves at the end of the century on the edge of a new millennium, in which those who survive do so at a cost. As Tony Marchant observed in a discussion about the serial in April 1998:

The ending, yes it is a love letter to London in lots of ways, but it's a very qualified one because I couldn't write an unambiguous eulogy. The note in the end is stoic. We'd got around to convincing ourselves in the end that 'Holding On' was a good title for this series (which is not the title I wanted at all) and that's what it's about: it's about people who do, from the beginning of the piece to the end, manage to take over control of their own lives. It's a deeply ironic eulogy… but obviously it is also true to his character in that he is deeply ambiguous despite his redemptive thing at the end.

I believe that 'Holding On' represents one of the most significant pieces of television drama screened on British drama in the last decade of the century. Its struggle with issues arising from an attempt to define a sense of moral and ideological cohesion in the fractured alienation of contemporary London, helps to mark its scale and ambition. There is a tentative but authentic optimism signed at the margins of the character's lives, resisting the cliched assumptions of either the left or reactionary positions. The London that emerges from, and is delineated by 'Holding On' is an geo-ideological landscape in which individual characters and communities engage in a redemptive struggle to sustain and transform their lives. Simultaneously this struggle signals a wider dialectical discourse of resistance to the corrosive strategies of late twentieth century, western capitalism upon the structures and citizens of the contemporary city.

In contrast to 'The Cops,' there is a very strong sense in which 'Holding On' is driven and characterised by a dramatic meta-frame of a centralising, thematic coherence in which all of the characters are ultimately connected. In this respect, one can see perhaps the influence of Marchant's wider engagement with other, essentially, literary works such as Dickens' *Hard Times*. Also in its stylish, almost filmic, performative aesthetic, the ways in which the series mediates the geo-ideological terrain of its city locations and narrative strategies, is distinctively different from the discordant visual grammar of 'The Cops.' With the exception of Shergold's use of the 'fish-eye' lens to accentuate and signal Gary Rickey's stylistic and ideological role, the framing of the visual narrative within 'Holding On' is much more in keeping with mainstream television drama forms. Associated with this is a telling ideological connotation of form as a performative aesthetic across these two series. For all of the latent post-modern boundaries of Marchant's geo-ideological landscape, there is a cool and stylish formalism and aesthetic coherence, which interestingly differentiates the drama's thematic concerns from its narrative and visual methodology. Whereas 'The Cops' seeks to embed its relentless exposure and examination of northern urban life, within the implied authenticity sanctioned by its quasi-documentary aesthetic, 'Holding On' presents a performative aesthetic of the capital which is, by contrast, a landscape of stylised cinéma verité.

Might there be an abiding sense in which the more self-evident radicalism of the ideological critique within 'The Cops' is necessarily reflected in that drama's performative aesthetic? I shall return to these considerations in my conclusion.

In the following chapter, these issues of the relationship between the performative aesthetic and the thematic concerns of the drama are examined in further detail in the context of Armistead Maupin's 'Tales of the City.' In my discussion of that series and its sequel, 'More Tales of the City,' I shall assert that their fictive construction of a pre-AIDS, San Francisco setting, serves as a nostalgic displacement of some of the hopes and anxieties incumbent upon the liberal radicalism associated with that west coast city.

3 The Fabled City
The San Francisco of Armistead Maupin's 'Tales of the City'

In Episode One of the television dramatisation of Armistead Maupin's 'Tales of the City,' the predatory, bisexual Beauchamp Day says to Mary Ann Singleton, whom he's seeking to seduce "We're all babes in the woods.... Your innocence, use it. It's very erotic – to me anyway."

In this award-winning series, Maupin constructs the San Francisco of 1976 as a kind of fabled city, an allegorical location where alternative and multiple identities and desires might be exposed and realised. Within this meta-construct of the city, Maupin offers us a specific microcosm of that world in the narrative location of 28, Barbary Lane, Russian Hill. In this rambling multi-storeyed house, the strange character of Anna Madrigal presides over a community of disparate lodgers navigating their lives through the shifting sign that is delineated as the San Francisco of the period.

Into this world of seemingly endless possibilities for self-discovery, change and transformation, Maupin introduces the character of Mary Ann Singleton as a framing device through which the audience can themselves enter and negotiate a route of interpretation and meaning. Mary Ann is a relatively fixed point of constructed referentiality, an innocent abroad who is, significantly, a character from outside of San Francisco. Furthermore, she is an entrant from the distant, middle-class suburbs of Cleveland – the very embodiment of constructs of normality and morality. Indeed, in the opening episode, having found a room in Mrs Madrigal's house, she observes to Mona – a fellow housemate – of her landlady "We don't have people like that in Cleveland." Mary Ann serves as an intriguingly effective narrative device. In the context of Maupin's San Francisco where ambiguity is such a prescient signifier, Mary Ann is constructed, at least initially, as a singularly uncomplicated character.

Nevertheless, the opening visual sequence of Episode One already communicates the sub-text of latent sexual yearning and desire for change. The camera focuses on a pair of sensual female lips, accompanied by a soundtrack of an ambient, mysterious, romantic musical signature for the series. As the frame opens, we view Mary Ann's thoughtful face. Subsequently, we hear a pre-existent telephone conversation between Mary Ann and her mother: two lines of dialogue, which summarise and preview her subsequent personal journey. When, on hearing from her daughter that she intends to stay in San Francisco, her mother warns her that "You won't be the same", Mary Ann answers with quiet determination "No, I hope not." It is with that sense of understated conviction that the character journeys and evolves through the first series. Crucially, as she does so, she must traverse her sexual virginity within a world of differences and public and private discourses of sexuality and identity.

In examining the ways in which both the first series 'Tales of the City' and its sequel 'More Tales of the City,' convey a sense of the city as an allegory of ambiguity and disclosure, I intend to frame my discussion through character analysis on a thematic, cluster basis. Whilst my principal focus is upon the six-episode first series, my overall discussion and analysis inevitably includes the narrative and thematic development of 'More Tales of the City.'

Anna Madrigal

Anna: I have no objection to anything.

This quotation from Anna Madrigal, spoken in response to Mary Ann in their first encounter in Episode One, expresses the profoundly liberal constructs delineating this central and defining character. This quality of liberalism, so readily associated with the city of San Francisco, is not simply a matter of ideological posturing or positioning. Madrigal is bestowed by Maupin with a mysterious prescience of other character's lives, whilst simultaneously communicating a camp sensibility earthed in the exigencies of everyday life. As the viewer discovers by the end of the first series, this combination of almost transcendent foresight with an empathetic engagement in the daily turmoil of others is perhaps an expression of Madrigal's translated, gendered sexuality. In terms of conventional binary concepts of socially gendered identity and sexuality, Madrigal constitutes both a transgression and transcendence of those fixed entrapments. Therefore empowered with this allegorical and ideological vantage point, Anna Madrigal embodies both the contradiction and assimilation of differentiation and opposites. As she herself puts it in the closing moments of the final episode of 'More Tales of the City,' "My darling daughter, transsexuals can never be sexists!" Furthermore, she may be seen to function as a kind of prismatic lens through which the complex web of discoursed identity and sexuality is mediated throughout the first series. Madrigal's house at 28 Barbary Lane serves as a geoideological location for the interweaving of the personal 'tales'. Like the forest in *A Midsummer Night's Dream* or *As You Like It*, Barbary Lane represents a place where the hidden and suppressed can be revealed, and where alternative, potentially disruptive modes of identity and consciousness can be played out.

Whilst, given the nature of her role, Madrigal encounters and counsels many of the drama's characters and narratives, her principal relationship rests with Edgar Halcyon, the successful businessman, who discovers that he has a fatal illness and has only six months to live. There is a cruelly ironic association to this character's name, 'halcyon' meaning calm and having its derivation from a mythic bird that was believed to bring calm waters at the time of the midwinter solstice. Whilst materially successful and prosperous, his personal and domestic life is characterised by a turmoil of disappointment and regret. In the same respect that Singleton's relationship to the narrative is defined by her role of being the outsider, Halcyon's traumatic experience of his own mortality offers another significant reference point for viewing and interpretation. Innocence and mortality are characterised by their very transience and therefore place issues of identity, desire and meaning into a uniquely experiential context. The initial meeting between Madrigal and Halcyon is on a hilltop overlooking San Francisco and the bay. This setting carefully, almost subliminally, communicates evocative signifiers of San Francisco the city. The camera offers a panoramic sweep of the distant sea, moving into a mid distance horizon of decorative bohemian house-tops. Gradually a mid- to long-shot reveals Halcyon walking with distraught determination up the hill side through a disparate group of San Francisco residents practising Tai Chi. Prior to this meeting between Halcyon and Madrigal, Maupin has humorously raised suspicions of Halcyon's engagement in an illicit affair. Trapped in a loveless marriage to his alcoholic society wife Frannie, he escapes for an evening to what the viewer presumes will be a sexual liaison. This expectation is confirmed when Halcyon arrives at an anonymous house in the suburbs to be greeted by an older woman of fading beauty, Ruby. She escorts him into a garage converted into a scarlet-lit space of candles and incense. Maupin cleverly evokes both the diverse pseudo-spirituality associated with San Francisco, whilst gently satirising its eccentricity. Rather than ameliorative sex, we discover Edgar receiving a form of 'laying on of hands'. Ruby is a faith healer, and Halcyon has gone to her as a last, desperate resort. When Edgar expresses doubts about the efficacy of her spiritual healing, given his own nominal Catholicism, Ruby kindly reassures him that "Jesus loves the Catholics too and Jesus can help you."

Returning to the encounter on the hilltop, the camera angle shows us a glimpse over Anna Madrigal's shoulder as she sits on a bench of a copy of the 'Bhagavad Gita' – the Hindu sacred text. Maupin uses this text and the opening dialogue between the two to defuse any sense of latent fashionable eastern mysticism within Madrigal's character. Edgar sits down next to her and, glancing at the cover of her book, asks, "Is that the answer?", to which Anna answers "What's the question?" When Edgar acknowledges her elliptical answer as the alleged last words of Gertrude Stein, he asks her whether she thinks that those really were Stein's final words. With characteristic, centred pragmatism, Anna seeks to lighten his mood by observing "No one's that clever on their death bed." Slightly heartened, Halcyon asks her what her last words would be, to which she replies with earthy humour "Oh shit?" This unlikely compassion from a stranger provokes tears of liberating relief from Edgar and they proceed to share a sandwich lunch. As their conversation and friendship slowly develops, Maupin empowers Madrigal with a foreknowledge of Edgar's earlier life – principally losing his virginity with a prostitute – that reaffirms her unique role within the narrative. In similar vein she views Mary Ann's arrival at the house as carrying a significance beyond the narrative constraints of everyday life – "You can't wait to bite into that lotus…. You're one of us". It transpires that her mother ran the desert bordello where Edgar had experienced his rite of passage some forty years previously. This sense of omniscient perspective is reinforced in her words to Edgar at the closure of their first meeting, "I thought you could remember who you were then. You don't seem too happy with who you are now." Other implications of this past are fully developed as central story lines in 'More Tales of the City. Principally, we discover that Madrigal is Mona's father and, as s/he reveals to her in the final episode of the second series, his assumed name, as a woman, is an anagram of 'A MAN AND A GIRL.' Earlier, in Episode Three of Series One, in a scene between Madrigal and Mona, she says to her young, emotionally troubled lodger, "You didn't choose Barbary Lane. It chose you." When Mona responds by acknowledging, "It was inevitable that I wind up here," Madrigal reacts with a tone that both sustains the sense of synchronicity with the prosaic – "No, not inevitable. Just – necessary." I believe that there is a strong sense in which the role and function of Anna Madrigal serves as a paradigm of the writer and artist in relation to their work. Like a transsexual, Californian Prospero, Madrigal is inextricably caught up in the complexities and sufferings of the world, and yet contrives to occupy a self-reflexive, post-modern space in which s/he can disrupt and temporarily transcend the narrative confines of that world. Nevertheless, this character is not immune from the suffering of life. Indeed, in a poignant and moving scene with the character Brian Hawkins in the second series, she reflects upon the pain of love and loss:

Anna: It's part of the deal you know?

Brian: What?

Anna: Losing people, wanting them back. It's the price you pay for being alive and – guess what? – age doesn't fix a thing. It doesn't get any easier, just more familiar. So, when the pain comes around again, all you can do is look back at it, straight in the eye and say, "I recognise you, you old bastard."

It is as if Maupin as author is seeking to exorcise the dilemma concerning the multiplicity of fictional possibilities and narratives within his constructed San Francisco, with recognition of the problematic, painful and even darker contingencies of a city struggling to sustain libertarian agendas. In Episode Three, there is a wonderfully evocative moment when, in the mid-distance of an exterior scene at Barbary Lane in which an unlikely friendship is emerging between Brian and Michael, the camera locates Maupin working at a typewriter in one of the rooms. Simultaneously part of and yet separate from his allegorical San Francisco, it is a marvelously unexpected moment: post-modern magic realism meeting an ironic – if problematic – camp sensibility. Similarly, in the second series, there is a wonderfully comic vignette of Maupin appearing as a priest conducting the Eucharist. This cameo role carries a moment of dark humour in the context of the Mary Ann/Burke Andrews storyline: Maupin's priest gazes bewildered as a severed human foot falls into the midst of his Communion service. Within Maupin's writing, there is an evocative and idiosyncratic mix of pathos and wistful sentiment, along with an uncompromising realisation of the ways in which self-interest, denial, ambition and loneliness can corrode and distort individual lives. In many respects, the characters of 'Tales of the City' are caught in the crossfire of this aesthetic and ideological conflict. One of the qualities and strengths of Maupin's writing is that he does not allow that latent longing for an alternative world of sexual freedom and personal self-fulfilment, to dilute a proper and necessary engagement with a city struggling to explore the possibility of that other world.

Through the developing relationship between Anna Madrigal and Edgar Halcyon, Maupin creates and develops a relationship, which is both moving and reflective of the potential impact of radical, libertarian values upon the inhibiting, repressive ideology of prosperous WASP America. This creative collision is often expressed through moments of humour, handled with a superbly light touch by Maupin. For example, in Episode Two, as the two friends grow into lovers, there is a scene in which Edgar is bemused by the fashionably arty café that Anna has chosen for their lunch date. Halcyon who has earlier been described by Mona as "Old money, Republican, show jumps with the Regans," is pleasantly bemused at the bohemian ambience of their surroundings. In the context of his heightened sense of his own mortality, he is embarking with his new friend and lover upon a journey of exhilarating and poignant self-discovery. Moments after the lunch scene, the camera hovers on a kite suspended in the blue sky above a Californian beach – an image of open expansiveness and freedom, life and spontaneity. The camera follows the string of the kite to a group of young people relaxing below. Simultaneously, the initially out-of-vision dialogue between Madrigal and Halcyon is brought into the frame. He is rather shocked to be informed by Anna that flying a kite when stoned is a marvelous experience and is concerned that she will react against his lingering, residual conservatism:

> Edgar: I wish you approved of me.

> Anna: (Taking his arm for the first time) I approve of you. I just want you to climb out of that tough old hide of yours. I want you to see how wonderful you....

As she bargains with the young people, exchanging a joint with the use of the kite for ten minutes, Edgar flying the kite communicates a touching and poignant image of a slowly and belatedly opening out into a San Francisco of spontaneous, unselfconscious pleasure.

Further on in the series, in Episode Four, there is a scene in which Edgar and Anna are viewed in bed together, happy and secure within their relationship. Maupin develops this scene into a conversation between the two in which she talks to him about the alternative folklore that San Francisco corresponds to the ancient, mythical city of Atlantis and that its twentieth century residents are Atlanteans:

> There's a theory that we were all Atlanteans... we all lived in this lovely, enlightened kingdom that sank beneath the sea a long time ago. Now we've come back to this special peninsula on the edge of the continent... because we know, in a secret corner of our minds, that we must return together to the sea.

Madrigal continues this exposition of San Francisco's mythic status by comparing The Transamerica Pyramid – which dominates the skyline of the city – with the notion that an enormous pyramid with a burning beacon was the dominating feature of the lost city. Atlantis was the mid-Atlantic island described by Plato in his dialogue 'Timaeus.' In the Middle Ages, other, similar myths evolved regarding the existence of mystical westerly islands such as Avalon and Lyonesse, both referred to in Arthurian legend. It is significant that these locations were imagined as earthly paradises. In the Renaissance period such constructs evolved and were developed into allegories of a Platonic, ideal government or state. One particular example of this was Bacon's *The New Atlantis* (1626) The association of late twentieth-century San Francisco with the Atlantean myth carries some significant associations. Perhaps one of the principal signifiers in the construct of Atlantis is that of a place of separation and/or at the liminal extremity of the known. Synonymous with its residing beyond the formal and established markings of cartography is a powerful, subliminal signification of the pleasured innocence and liberty of Paradise. The etymological root of Paradise in its ancient, Old Persian meaning, was 'garden.' An important characteristic of 28 Barbary Lane is Mrs Madrigal's garden where she grows, amongst other things, her cannabis plants. The plants in the garden are given names with symbolic significance for Madrigal, such as Dante, Beatrice, and Heathcliff. The connotative associations of San Francisco as a city of mythical location – a garden of pleasured liberty, beyond the limits and prohibitions of the dominant ideology and its repressive categorisation, reiterates my principal assertion of Maupin's intentions in constructing his fictionalised city. Equally significant is that in the Judaic/Christian myth of Paradise as a Garden of Eden, it is its predominant characteristic of libidinous joy that simultaneously appears to provoke a diametric anxiety about the feared consequences of desire expressed beyond limitation or constraint. The etymological root of the word Eden has its origins in the Hebrew for pleasure. It is not possible in the context of this chapter to enter into a detailed psychoanalytic debate of either Freudian theories, or the post-Freudian discourse of Lacan and Kristeva, as they impact upon the symbiotic relationship between pleasure and its alternating expression and repression. Nevertheless, I believe that it is apparent within 'Tales of the City' that the city as an alternative, mythic location of semiotic fluidity and liberated desire, exists in a powerful oppositional dialectic with the dominant ideological discourse of heterosexual phallocentricity, with its denial of pleasured plurality.

Returning to the scene in Episode Four where Anna and Edgar seek to inhabit their own pleasured, if transient, paradise, it is with disturbing significance that their Eden is subject to the malevolent, intrusive gaze of Norman Williams, the dysfunctional tenant who occupies the roof top apartment at Barbary Lane. Socially awkward and exuding a disconcerting cocktail of quiet repression and inarticulate desire for recognition, he is befriended by Mary Ann who empathises for this middle-aged misfit. Agreeing to go out with him socially and quietly impressed by the 'quality time' he shares with Lexy, the young daughter of his married friends, it is she who eventually discovers the dreadful truth underlying the gauche pathos of his social awkwardness.

Mary Ann Singleton

Mona: She's decent – that's her quirk.

(Speaking of Mary Ann to Mrs Madrigal, Episode One)

As I established in my opening section to this chapter, the character of Mary Ann Singleton serves to confront the liberal climate of San Francisco with more conventionally mainstream social and cultural values and expectations. From the moment that she decides, at the beginning of the series, to extend her stay in San Francisco into a permanent residence, her journey navigates a central and essential paradigm through both the novel and its television adaptation. Having broken the news to her parents that she's not coming home to the suburban Middle America of Cleveland, she stays temporarily with an old college friend, Connie Bradshaw, who has been a long term resident in the city. With an enthusiastic commitment to sex and socialising, Connie alerts Mary Ann to the fact that "You're new – this city loosens people up" in response to her friend's shocked reaction to a proposed evening of hedonistic pleasure. Reluctantly, she accompanies Connie to a stereotypical discotheque of the period but feels uncomfortable and alienated by its atmosphere of loud music and predatory sexual manoeuvring. We do, however, get a glimpse of her potential assertiveness and sense of humour when she responds to Connie's disdainful "If you can't deal with your sexuality, you're going to be screwed up good in this town" with a delightfully acerbic "Sounds like a Country and Western number." Surviving the embarrassing, pseudo-mystical overtures of a middle-aged hippie, she determines to find her own place to live and establish her own independence. Being received into the world of Barbary Lane, she then encounters another embarrassing episode in a supermarket, which Connie has explained is a place to meet and pick up men. A marvelously funny insight into the unfamiliar world in which she has chosen to live, she finds herself approached by a good looking man. In the rules of the mating games that are transacted in the supermarket, individuals approach their potential partners with seemingly innocuous questions about shopping, as a means of establishing contact. As Mary Ann converses cheerfully and naively with her handsome fellow shopper, she is oblivious to his stereotypically 'clone' persona and gay sexuality until his partner, Michael appears. Michael – known affectionately as 'Mouse' – transmits a potent image of gay sexuality, a homoerotic mix of an well-exercised body poured into a sleeveless T-shirt emblazoned with the 'Stars and Stripes.' This character, glimpsed briefly in this scene, develops into one of the principal characters in the series. I will discuss his character in more detail in the following section.

From the moment that she moves into her apartment at Barbary Lane, her life begins to change gradually but irretrievably. In a telling dialogue between Mona and Mrs Madrigal, Mona expresses her slight reservations about the newcomer:

Mona: She's been asking a lot about you.

Anna: Have you told her anything?

Mona: I figured that was your business.

Anna: You think she's too green?

Mona: Right now? Yes.

Nevertheless, in keeping with the atmosphere of tolerance and acceptance that characterises the house, Mary Ann is welcomed into its life with Mona helping her to find a job at Edgar Halcyon's firm – Halcyon Communications – where she herself works as a successful advertising copywriter. Furthermore, Mrs Madrigal invites her to dinner where, although the newcomer initially feels out of place amongst the post-Woodstock guests (one of whom played by one of the enduring icons of that festival and period, Country Joe Macdonald and joints-as-hors d'oeuvres) the two women begin to establish a friendship. This emerging relationship propels Mrs Madrigal into a failed attempt at matchmaking, seeking to introduce her young ingenue to Brian Hawkins, another resident of the house. Mary Ann immediately recognises both her landlady's strategy and the aura of unmistakable sexual opportunism exuded by Hawkins. Still recovering from her embarrassment at the supermarket, she is anxious to ascertain his sexual orientation. This established, she tells him in the course of their conversation that she has no secrets. He replies with a worldly wisdom honed from a lifestyle of multiple, casual sexual encounters, "Don't count on it. We all have secrets in this town, you just have to dig a little deeper for them." Immediately after this scene the camera cuts to the following day with Mary Ann flagging up the 'Stars and Stripes' at the offices of Halcyon Associates – an ironic image resonant with the contradictions of unquestioning patriotism alongside the diverse agendas encompassed within San Francisco She soon experiences one of the many personal and private agendas at work within the city when she is the subject of the predatory advances of the handsome but singularly cynical self-seeking Beauchamp Day. I opened this chapter with an extract from the dialogue between these two characters. Having married into wealth and prestige through his wife Dee Dee – Edgar's daughter – Beauchamp is an unmistakably vain, manipulative social climber and sexual adventurer. This is evident in the following short exchange between the two at the offices of Halcyon Associates:

Beauchamp: You think I'm OK, don't you?

Mary Ann: As an Accounts Executive?

Beauchamp: As anything.

He pursues his prey along the office corridors urging her to spend a weekend away with him in the country. When she reminds him of his married status and responsibilities, he responds with angry frustration, "Will you quit being so goddam Middle American for a moment?" When the inevitable weekend away materialises, she still mistakenly believes his assurances that there will be separate beds. In a restaurant whose ambience is as facile and deceptive as Beachamp's own integrity and social persona, he talks of how he worships the magic of her innocence. Mistaken and deluded by a combination of her own sexual and life inexperience, she agrees to sleep with him. This scenario is cleverly and effectively inter-cut in the series with another parallel, problematic sexual liaison between Brian and Connie. Through careful and well-paced editing, the viewer's attention and reception is switched between the two scenes. Both are located and defined by the latent frustration, anger and insecurity of sexual encounters predicated by self-interested opportunism on the part of both men.

In an important sense, this sequence – culminating in a further inter-weaving of a scenario in which the lonely and bereft Dee Dee pays for sex from a Delivery Boy – presents a sobering counterbalance to the authenticity of Edgar and Anna's relationship, based on a consent of mutuality, respect and affection. Like a metaphorical Möbius Strip which paradoxically enables two opposite surfaces to become one, the multiple scenarios of individual choice, sexual experimentation and desire within the narrative simultaneously expose the co-existent counter scenarios of self-deception, loneliness and unconditional self-interest. This is a subject to which I shall return. The issues of commitment and integrity within an ideological environment that sought a transformation from hypocrisy, prejudice and denial into honesty, tolerance and acceptance are clear within both series. Indeed, they are developed in significant ways in 'More Tales.' For example, Dee Dee's decision not to have an abortion, despite her husband's appalling self-centredness – "For Christ's sake, Dee Dee, we're up for the Pacific Union Club this year!" – signals an emerging new consciousness and self-belief. This is expressed in particular in the second series through her growing friendship and eventual lesbian relationship with D'orothea Jackson. Equally, as I discuss later in this chapter, Brian Hawkins is developed and revealed as a character whose apparent shallowness in his relations with women represents the painful consequences of earlier personal and ideological tensions and disappointments. Although a very marginal character in the overall narrative scheme, the lonely and confused Connie Bradshaw reappears briefly as a 'born again' proselytiser for the Scientologist cult. In the opening episode of 'More Tales,' she exudes the chillingly unshakeable optimism of the cult member in approaching a depressed Mona. In response to Connie's formulaic question – "Hi! Would you like a personality test?" – Mona ends any hope of her becoming another 'convert' with a weary "Why? To see if I have one?" None of these narrative developments presuppose, of course, any easy resolution to the problematic questions of commitment and freedom within intimate relationships, whether gay, lesbian or straight. As Mrs Madrigal observes to Mona when seeking to give her comfort and advice about her troubled personal life, "There are all kinds of marriages…. There are lots of things more binding than sex, Mona, and last longer too." Maupin closely echoes these sentiments himself in an interview that he gave to Andrew Billen of the London Evening Standard on the 8 July 1998. Reflecting on the complex aftermath of the ending of his relationship with his long-term lover Terry Anderson, he answered Billen's question, "Their love wasn't just about sex?"

> It wasn't about sex at all. It was about some bond that would be there for ever. It is what we all want, and what we end up with anyway… we wind up as a couple of house cats enjoying our mutual warmth…. I think in one-night stands love has to be involved, or at least kindness.

Kindness and love are the last characteristics that would be associated with Beauchamp Day who finds himself unable, initially, to consummate his sexual appetite with Mary Ann. Despite her warm reassurances, his deflated ego provokes him into a sullen mood reminiscent of a child who cannot have immediate gratification. At the same time, a bemused, post-coital Brian remonstrates with a frustrated and angry Connie, "I'm a liberal, I can feel guilty for weeks", when what Connie wants is not expressions of guilt but a sexual encounter in which she can experience some kindness or love. Despite the belated consummation of their sexual encounter, it is a coldly aloof Day that drives Mary Ann home at the conclusion of the weekend. Having eventually secured what he wanted, she is now an embarrassment to him – a used and unwanted commodity. He deliberately leaves her scarf in the glove compartment of his sports car for Dee Dee to find – an act of premeditated, spite towards both women. Later in the first series, the audience discovers what has been latent throughout, that Beauchamp is bisexual or, depending on interpretation, a gay man in – at least – social, closeted denial. In the second series, embittered and vengeful at his wife's refusal to abort her twins fathered by the American Chinese delivery boy, he takes out a contract to have her so badly beaten that the unborn babies will be brutally terminated. Such is the horrifying strategy of a character consumed by deception and egocentric desire. In keeping with the allegorical, folk tale ethos already established, the villain perishes, consumed in the burning wreck of his·sports car.

Meanwhile, in an earlier stage of the first series and emotionally disorientated and profoundly saddened by his treatment of her, Mary Ann decides to terminate her experimental new life and return to the mundane security of life in Cleveland. However, at the end of Episode Two, it is the unconditional warmth and friendship of Mona and Michael who persuade her to stay. Reassured and heartened by their concern for her, her decision to stay is potentially undermined by a phone call from her mother, which Michael initially answers. Convinced that her daughter has decamped with a San Franciscan lover, she demands to know who the 'strange man' was who answered the phone. Her daughter's answer conveys the rich vein of humour and uncompromising assertiveness that is present in both her self-development and throughout Maupin's writing, "Mother, he's not a strange man, he's a homosexual. I know you've heard of it, they have them on TV now."

Determined to stay in the city and establish a new life for herself, she throws herself into useful volunteer work that takes both her – and the audience – into the underside of the San Franciscan dream – working a telephone shift on the Bay Area Crisis Switchboard. Working alongside a depressive long-term volunteer, Vincent, she strives to support those damaged and bereft lives left beyond the Atlantean idyll of freedom and tolerance. Significantly perhaps, it is in the scene following on from that in which Anna tells Edgar of the Atlantis legend, that there is a superbly filmed and edited sequence of grim counterbalance. Having been questioned on her way to her shift by an old woman as to whether she has "found Jesus yet" Mary Ann finds something far more immediately of this world. Through a most effective audio visual montage of an unanswered telephone ringing and her calling out for Vincent, a single feather drifts down across a mid-range close-up of the switchboard interior. This is then unexpectedly developed through the eerie sound of rope twisting back and forth, cutting to a Hitchcock-like panoramic bird's-eye shot of Vincent hanging. A macabre suicide in which he has used his mother's gift of a macramé tapestry to perform the task, the camera picks up Mary Ann ascending the stair well below. The sudden flash of a police photographer's camera cleverly punctuates her dark discovery, enabling her to reflect with unintentionally morbid humour, "At least he went organically." It is as she seeks to come to terms with Vincent's suicide that Mary Ann begins to recognise and discover other aspects of Brian Hawkins. Arriving back later that evening at Barbary Lane, she and Brian smoke a joint together on the steps of his apartment. He recalls his training as a lawyer and his disillusionment with the legal system as opposed to the liberal/radical causes he sought to support through his work. He is also critical of former legal activists who eventually sold out to the material securities of a fashionable liberal lifestyle: "I thank God I'm not trapped in that pathetic middle-class prison." Even as she and the audience are given an alternative perspective into a character previously perceived in the questionable context of serial sexual conquests, his yearning for the authenticity of lost, compromised ideals remains latent and poignant. In Episode Five, the embryonic friendship between Michael and Brian culminates in an evening where they smoke an enormous amount of cannabis together, after the humorous, mutual realisation that they were both alone in their rooms watching the 'Mary Tyler Moore Show.' The bonding between the two men – one gay, the other straight – is compelling and believable as they both look for an elusive sense of meaning and security through and beyond the pleasure principle:

> Maupin writes in More Tales that try as Michael might to imitate those happy people who "skim along the surface of life exulting in their self sufficiency," "the hunger always showed in his eyes."
>
> (Billen)

In this sequence, the out of vision dialogue between the two men finds a counter-point in a slow panning camera shot, leading the audience's line of vision along an evocative, midnight San Francisco skyline of shimmering lights. Their conversation turns both reflective and philosophical as they share an unsettling prescience of a dislocating change in the ideological climate of America, from which even San Francisco will not be immune. Regretting, with a poignant sense of loss and inevitability, the extinguishing of the light of radicalism and tolerance, they envisage future 'twenty year old Calvinists' defining the ethos of the city. Such a vision, of course, carries with it the emergence of the Republican/Fundamentalist movement, a reactionary caucus of capitalism with an Old Testament, patriarchal God who would punish transgressors with a plague as terrifying as any enacted upon Egypt. Only a brutally implacable, self-righteous Calvinism could construct such a malign ideological reading of a city and country gripped by indiscriminate suffering. For the predestined elect however, it would be with a perverse pleasure that the despised Atlantis would metamorphose, through their gaze, into the city of Sodom, welcomed by them in its destruction of plurality, tolerance – and human lives.

Earlier in this chapter, I referred to Mary Ann's befriending of Norman Williams, an awkward outsider who proves to harbour disturbing secrets which threaten to impact upon the lives of Anna Madrigal and Edgar Halcyon. I want to close this section with a more detailed consideration of the implications of that scenario. The character of Williams communicates a profound sense of unease through both his own shiftless inability to hold eye contact, along with the strange sense of alienated isolation of his roof top apartment. From the moment that the two characters meet, when Mary Ann arrives on the rooftop to retrieve Boris, the household cat, a highly improbable friendship emerges. A combination of Mary Ann's empathy and consideration for the outsider with Norman's barely concealed infatuation with her, she accompanies him when he takes his friend's daughter, Lexy, on social outings. When he remarks to Mary Ann of the outings that, "I wouldn't do it if I didn't like it, you know, 'Rent a Kid'?" she responds by trying to support his low self-esteem with, "You're kind and gentle…. You've got so much to give someone." Some ironic, post-modern signaling is employed when the two go to the cinema together. As they leave the cinema, the camera subtly identifies the title of the film: 'Detective Story' starring Kirk Douglas and Eleanor Parker. This semiotic foretelling of Norman's secret identity also prefigures Mary Ann's own investigation and discovery of the subterranean Norman Williams. The self-reflexivity is signed off with Williams saying to her, "I feel like I'm in a Hammett story, you know, 'The Maltese Falcon'?" He invites her to a Chinese restaurant, which ends disastrously when she becomes the victim of a form of practical joke by the restaurant owner. Williams knows that she will be exposed in this way but reflective of his own myopic social awareness, believes that she will enjoy the experience. When he apologises to her later, her enduring good will and kindness prompt her to tell him, "Do you know what you are? Very old fashioned."

What, in fact, she discovers him to be is a seedily disreputable private detective embarked on blackmailing Edgar and Anna and a paedophile involved in a child pornography racket. Lexy is, in fact, a child engaged by Williams as a participant with him in pornographic films. As these revelations are exposed across the final two episodes of the first series, it is important that Mary Ann is the narrative medium through which this chilling subtext is deconstructed. The character's tenacious goodwill and optimism present the perfect foil to uncover the psychological and moral malignancy of Williams. Under instructions from a client –Mona's mother, Mrs Ramsey – Williams has discovered that Anna Madrigal is in fact a transsexual man who has undergone surgery to find fulfilment in his/her identity as a woman. Williams seeks to blackmail Halcyon, threatening him, his family and, ultimately of course, his relationship with Anna, with the lurid exposure attendant upon sensational tabloid publicity. The couple determine that they will resist the blackmailer's threats. When Mary Ann, who has become increasingly suspicious of Williams, enters his room and finds a box containing child pornography and a folder with Anna Madrigal's name upon it, she arranges to meet him at a museum and art gallery just outside the city. Unaware of her discovery, he arrives as arranged and the ensuing clifftop scenario above the bay below is signed with elements resonating of both melodrama and Hitchcock. Unaware that he has uncovered Madrigal's true identity, she confronts him with his involvement in production of pornographic films and books. Against a windswept backdrop, Williams backs away from her in bitter anger at her accusations and stumbles back over the cliff edge. There is a bleakly comic irony in the circumstances of his death when, as Mary Ann tries to pull him to safety, she grabs hold of his tie. As the viewer had witnessed in an earlier episode, Williams wears a quaintly dated clip-on tie and, as she desperately seeks to pull him to safety, he plunges to his death into the rocks and sea below. The almost gothic signature of William's destiny and death is reminiscent of the fate of so many villains in folk tales.

This sense of the Gothic within both series is humorously highlighted in a brief encounter in the opening episode of 'More Tales.' Blue lit and with mist swirling in the evening air, the camera point of view presents a back view of Brian approaching a house in the near distance. The eerie sound of his footsteps is punctuated by the voice of Mrs Madrigal who welcomes him at the entrance to 28 Barbary Lane. She greets him with a camp "Welcome to Mandalay. I'm Mrs Danvers. I'm sure you'll be very happy here", to which he responds, in similar vein, "Feeling Gothic tonight?" Mrs Danvers and Mandalay are, of course a central character and location from that twentieth century Gothic melodrama: Daphne Du Maurier's *Rebecca*.The contrivance of Mary Ann's discovery and her subsequent burning of the unopened folder concerning Mrs Madrigal do require a willing suspension of disbelief. In one sense, the unmasking of Williams and his dark intentions, along with his subsequent fate, is perhaps the most vulnerable narrative point. Momentarily, the parallel narrative genres of the contemporary mini-series with traditional modes of folk-allegory threaten to unbalance each other. Nevertheless, it is a sign of the generic consistency, and stylistic coherence of the drama, that a certain aesthetic and ideological logic might be said to have been sustained by the conclusion of the first series. This sense of the Gothic within the overall ethos of the stylised allegorical texture of the writing is explored and used with obvious brio by Maupin in 'More Tales of the City.' This is executed in the narrative line that introduces Mary Ann to a new character, Burke Andrews, an amnesiac reporter whom she meets and falls in love with on a cruise. In the attempt to discover why he reacts so disturbingly to both roses and to being on cat-walks, a plot line unfolds with all of the mystery, false clues and thrilling denouement that characterise the Gothic genre in both its most classic and populist forms.

In a final sequence set in the Grace Cathedral in San Francisco, the two lovers revisit the scene of a cannibalistic religious cult, which Burke had been investigating while working as an Associated Press reporter in San Francisco. Referred to earlier in my discussion of Maupin's cameo role as the priest officiating at a Eucharist service, the sequence is written, directed and acted with a marvelous theatrical panache. In the course of the second series, Mary Ann develops a close friendship with Michael and it is through both her relationship with him and Burke that she continues and confirms her journey of growth and self-discovery. In the opening moments of 'More Tales' we see Michael making and delivering a Valentine's Day card to Mary Ann. With the card comes an expectation for Mary Ann to make resolutions – a custom more usually associated with the opening and celebrations of the New Year. In playful response to Michael's insistence, she declares that, "One, I will find Mr Right this year. Two, he will not be married. Three, he will not be gay. Four, he will not be... a child pornographer." Her relationship with Burke is curtailed at the end of the series, when he is invited to work on the *New Yorker* magazine. Nevertheless she has developed as a character through the second series to the point where she can admit to Burke of her earlier prejudiced attitude towards Michael. "I really believed he was wasted, that he had gone wrong somehow. Of course, I told myself I felt sorry for him, but I was really just feeling sorry for myself, I found out all the Mr Rights weren't made for me, and I couldn't handle it." When Burke responds by affirming that her critical self-awareness reflects the fact that people change, she replies, "I didn't. Not for a long time. I used to feel.... I don't know. I guess I thought I could change him." Within the macrocosm of 'Tales of the City' and 'More Tales of the City' the possibility of people changing and the need for change in individual journeys reflects a powerful sense of San Francisco as a city – one which embodies and requires fluidity, transition and flux.

Michael and Mona

Mona: I'm Nancy Drew. You must be the Hardy Boys.
(On delivering breakfast in bed to Michael and Chuck, Episode Two)

If Mary Ann's growing friendship and love for Michael characterises one of the central narratives of 'More Tales,' then it is the deep friendship and affection between Mona Ramsey and Michael that plays an important role within the wider concerns of 'Tales of the City.' In the second series, Mona's journey to find herself and her roots are a crucial narrative strand. Both characters are essential to central narrative developments and also, in terms of their sexual orientations, offer a most effective context for consideration of the exploration and depiction of sexuality within the drama.

Therefore, in this section, in exploring their relationship as characters, I intend to investigate some of the central concerns that Maupin raises about sexual identity and its expression (or repression) within 'Tales of the City.'

Mona is introduced in the early stages of the opening episode as a resident of 28 Barbary Lane. With a very early 1970s hairstyle – a cascading shock of hennaed ringlets – she exudes sexual charisma and uncompromising warmth, albeit undercut by sub-currents of emotional angst and insecurity. The subtext of this conflict between her hedonistic self-assertion and deeper unease is carefully and subtly exposed through the eight episodes of the first series. Michael, affectionately known as 'Mouse', is also introduced within the early episodes as a close friend of Mona, who arrives at Barbary Lane looking for support and sanctuary following the traumatic ending of what he had hoped would become a permanent sexual relationship. It was this couple that Mary Ann had inadvertently come across in her supermarket expedition. When Mouse arrives at Mona's apartment, he interrupts her in the midst of meditation, an interruption she gladly welcomes. As he recounts how his lover has prematurely ended his love affair, he explains his demeanour to Mona with a humorous but telling camp sensibility, "This isn't crying, this is damply pensive." Lamenting the loss of his army recruiting officer lover – "The Marines are looking for a few good men" – Mona shows a characteristic blend of empathy and direct good humour, by reassuring Mouse that "The woods are crawling with jack-booted harmonica players." Nevertheless, there is a potent yearning latent within the pathos of Michael's observation to Mona that the relationship had been, "A first for me – we were at the 'furniture-buying stage.'" Happily acceding to Michael sharing her apartment on a temporary basis, the couple are shown later in the episode on a San Francisco beach where straight and gay men and women relax in their nakedness – albeit in segregated areas. Offering him the choice – "Gay end or straight end?" – Mona lies down to relax with Michael amongst the other gay bathers. However, questions of her own sexual orientation and identity, along with the diverse spectrum of possible expressions within a city such as San Francisco, are conveyed in the following dialogue:

Mona: Do you think I'm a fag hag?

Michael: What?

Mona: I do. I'm sure of it.

Michael: You've been eating funny mushrooms again.

Mona: I don't mind being a fag hag, actually. There are worse things to be.

Michael: You are not a fag hag, Mona.

Mona: Look at the symptoms. I hang around with you don't I? We go boogieing at

Buzzby's and The Endup. I'm practically a fixture at The Palms. Shit, I've drunk so many Blue Moons I feel like I'm turning into Dorothy Lamour.

Michael: Mona....

Mona: Hell, Mouse! I hardly know any straight men anymore.

Michael: You live in San Francisco.

Mona: It isn't that. I don't even like most straight men. Brian Hawkins repulses me. Straight men are boorish and boring and....

Michael: Maybe you've just been exposed to the wrong ones

Mona: Then where the hell are the right ones?... Don't you dare suggest one of those mellowed-out Marin types? Underneath all that hair and patchouli oil beats the heart of a true pig. I've been that route.

At the conclusion to the scene, Michael, having reassured Mona of his love for her, goes on to add that "Sometimes, I wish that were enough." This exchange illustrates once again both the possibilities of choice that a libertarian environment such as pre-1977 San Francisco opened up, but also the enduring dilemmas and uncertainties that the complexities and exigencies of human personality also provided. Equally telling is Mona's assertion that, beneath the supposedly progressive possibilities of bohemian heterosexual male behaviour, depressingly familiar evidence of reactionary, sexist attitudes and behaviour lingered.

Within Episode Two, two significant events occur in the individual narratives of Mona and Michael that have considerable implications for both of them. Mona, who is a successful and respected advertising copywriter, is shown making a formal presentation to a businessman whose product – women's panty hose – is being marketed by Halcyon Communications, for whom she works. The simmering frustration and uncertainty that she feels in her personal life is exacerbated, perhaps, by an equally growing frustration with the compromising of her creative talents demanded by her work. It's therefore with little or no surprise that, when faced with the sexist immovability of the client in response to her proposed advertising campaign – "Under My Clothes I Like to feel Adorable" – she loses her self-control, and with it, her well-paid, secure job. As she and the situation veer out of control, Beauchamp, in his role as Accounts Executive, attempts to reprimand her, to which she retorts with devastating acuity, "Don't patronise me you prick, I'm not married to my job!" When later that evening, Mrs Madrigal is offering her comfort and support, Mona rails at both the way in which marketing and advertising reduces people to consumers-as-statistics, and the cynical values underpinning that process. "Numbers can't know people. People can't know people. I was honest with a client – that's the ultimate 'no-no'."

For Michael, following on a casual but pleasurable sexual encounter with a gay guy called Chuck, life literally collides into another sexual relationship: one which he hopes might prove to be the elusive 'Grail' of stability and mutual commitment. Whilst skating slightly precariously around an indoor ice rink, Michael spots an attractive male. Whether a complete accident or by intention, he collides with the stranger who, with chivalry, helps the prostrate Michael to his feet. Introducing himself as Jon, an embryonic relationship is immediately visible. The following morning, the two men are viewed, naked, in bed together. They are clearly very happy and relaxed with each other. It is this scene of domestic bliss that Mona enters upon, remarking with an arch, richly camp comic sentiment: "Hi! I'm Nancy Drew! You must be the Hardy Boys!" This wry evocation of reactionary, fictional models of wholesome Middle American gender stereotypes is wonderfully ironic and funny. It transpires that Jon is a doctor – a gynaecologist – the very same icon of bourgeois security and respectability that Michael has previously fantasised about in his dream of emotional and material permanence. Nevertheless, even as Mouse seeks reassurance from his new partner of the nature and extent of his feelings towards him, the insecurity within Mona briefly views the new relationship as a threat to her new-found personal and domestic life with her close friend. Within this disorientating web of anxiety and longing, the dialogue that closes the scene is both sharply funny whilst also signaling an underlying fear of failure and disappointment:

Michael: I'd marry you in a second, Mona Ramsey.

Mona: If you were the only boy in the world, and I were the only girl. What else is new?

Michael: Don't worry. I'll screw this up.

Mona: It sounds like you want to.

Michael: Spare me the Jungian analysis.

Mona: Take out the garbage then. If it happens, it happens.

It is, therefore, with what proves to be bitter irony that Michael eventually discovers that the very professional status, class and apparent security that Jon signifies, simultaneously represents the basis on which Jon disowns and then leaves him. Through this narrative strand, Maupin proceeds to expose the monied, bourgeois, 'cultured' gay class within San Francisco to scorching satire and criticism. Like Mary Ann Singleton, Michael Tolliver is a paradigm of a background and values which stand in direct contrast to the eclecticism of San Francisco. Therefore, when he escorts Jon to a fashionable dinner party peopled by gay men defined in terms of their income, high-cultural pretensions and smug insularity, his lack of pretension and basic decency inevitably provokes tensions. The plush penthouse setting for the party is communicated through signifiers of economic status and high culture: the camera shot slowly pans along and frames images of valuable paintings – the home of the Hampton-Giddes. In the novel, *More Tales of the City*, Maupin portrays this elite-sub-culture with blistering, but understated satire:

> For the Hampton-Giddes, the mechanics of party-giving were as intricate as the workings of Arch Giddes' new Silver Shadow Rolls.
> After careful scrutiny, prospective guests were divided onto four lists:
> The A List.
> The B List.
> The A-Gay List.
> The B-Gay List.
> The Hampton-Giddes knew no C people, gay or otherwise. As a rule, the A list was comprised of the Beautiful and the Entrenched, the kind of people who might be asked about their favourite junk-food or slumming spot in Metla Zellerbach's column in the Chronicle. There was, of course, a sprinkling of A-Gays on the A List, but they were expected to behave themselves. An A-Gay who turned campy during after dinner A List charades would find himself banished, posthaste, to the purgatory of the B-Gays. The B-Gays, poor wretches, didn't even get to play charades.
>
> (p. 43)

The out-of-vision dialogue is punctuated with the confident, over-loud laughter of the rich and privileged. As the camera rests upon the guests at the table, the conversation turns to opera and Michael is asked – with patronising expectation of his 'ignorance' of this high-cultural art form – what is his favourite opera? Vulnerable but unwilling to be the victim of their manipulative game playing, he answers "'Tommy'." Michael leans across to Jon and whispers, "Are we having fun yet?" As the dinner party conversation descends into one of the guests observing that in the light of "one hundred and twenty thousand practising homosexuals" in San Francisco, lucrative money stood to be made from selling them medical insurance for the infirmities of their later life. Michael cannot tolerate this expression of gratuitous self-interest and exploitation of other gay men. He asks what will become of those gay men who are poor and financially vulnerable – "Faggots on Food Stamps" – and proceeds to articulate a fantasy of Rest Homes for older gay men. With a barely concealed satire and anger, he imagines that such homes might be called 'The Last Round Up,' where those residents who suffer from cancer of the colon or stomach might wear "Denim colostomy bags." With a parting retort of "What are going to do with the Drag Queens?" Jon drives Michael back to Barbary Lane. As they sit in his elegant sports car outside the house, Mouse breaks the awkward and embarrassing silence with a humorous – if barbed – "So which one was Nancy Reagan?" Apologising to Jon for his behaviour – "One bullshot and I was like Barbara Streisand in 'The Owl and the Pussycat'" – Jon reassures Michael of his love and commitment towards him and they drive away into the night. However, Michael's anxiety that Jon might finish the relationship after the dinner party fiasco proves to be delayed, not avoided. Unemployed, homeless and with Mona having been sacked from her job, he is desperate to make some money. An opportunity presents itself with an open Jockey Shorts dance contest at The End Up gay club. With a first prize of one hundred dollars, the competition simply requires that young gay men dance individually on the stage, in their underwear. Even with Mona there to support him, Michael suddenly develops acute anxiety at the prospect of exposing himself in this way. Nevertheless, to a techno-beat soundtrack with a title that proves to be bitterly ironic, Michael launches himself into the song 'Never Can Say Goodbye.' Dancing with increasingly spontaneous enthusiasm, the crowd roar their approval, only for the camera to slowly identify – from Michael's point-of-view – the stern-faced disapproval of Jon, watching at the back of the heaving mass of bodies. Jon exits, followed by a distraught Michael whose moment of triumph – he wins the prize – is simultaneously his moment of loss. The prejudices of dominant class and economic status appear, at this stage in the meta-narrative, to be stronger than the yearning for, and promises of, love and commitment. In 'More Tales' Michael and Jon are reunited, meeting initially by chance in Acapulco where Jon is attending a medical conference, and where Michael's Carnival Cruise with Mary Ann has temporarily disembarked. I shall discuss the development and treatment of that renewed relationship later.

Following on the bitter disappointment of being left by Jon, which ends Episode Three, Episode Four opens with Michael taking a phone call from his mother. His parents, who are unaware of their son's sexuality, are about to arrive from Florida. As he shows them around the city and its sights, there is a moment of wonderful, almost surreal, comedy centring upon Michael's struggle to keep his homosexuality in the precarious 'safety' of the closet in relation to his parents. The camera shot frames a mid to long distant view of Michael and his parents slowly climbing up one of the city's many steep hills. As they gradually appear in shot, the camera inter-cuts to a group of 'Skating Nuns' shooting down an equally steep hill towards them. Michael's discomfort and his parent's bewilderment is painfully funny as the outrageous 'sisters' shout out to him, "Hey, Toliver, loved your underpants!" Even as his father dismisses them with a contemptuous "Fruits!" his son succeeds in navigating a route through the difficulties of deception and exposure during their visit. In the second series, Michael, contracts a potentially fatal paralysing illness (surely a metaphor for the imminent impact of AIDS?) from which he ultimately enters into remission. It is the context of his own mortality and the rise of a Republican/Fundamentalist anti-homosexual campaign called 'Save Our Children,' that he writes to his parents in order to come out about his homosexuality. Unable to write the letter himself, he dictates it to Mona and the scene is one of the most powerful and moving of the series. Having received a letter from his parents, in which they tell him of their own zealous involvement in the campaign, he struggles to find the right words to convey his homosexuality. In a speech of resounding emotional authenticity and also ardent affirmation of himself and the city of San Francisco, Paul Hopkins plays it with quietly understated, but emotionally resonant, authority and focus:

I wouldn't have written, I guess, if you hadn't told me about your involvement in the Save Our Children campaign. That, more than anything, made it clear that my responsibility was to tell you the truth, that your own child is a homosexual, and that I never needed saving from anything except the cruel and ignorant piety of people like Anita Bryant [the founder of SOC].... I wish someone older than me and wiser than the people in Orlando had taken me aside and said "You're all right kid.... You're not crazy or sick or evil.... Most of all though, you can love and be loved, without hating yourself for it." But no one ever said that to me.... I had to find it out on my own, with the help of the city that has become my home. I know that this may be hard for you to believe, but San Francisco is full of men and women, both straight and gay, who don't consider sexuality in measuring the worth of another human being.... Their attitude is neither patronising nor pitying. And their message is simple: Yes, you are a person. Yes, I like you. Yes it's all right for you to like me too.

I've quoted at length from the letter, which is, in effect and intent, a rallying speech to San Francisco and beyond, because it so clearly espouses the defiant and tolerant liberalism within Maupin's writing and his evocation of San Francisco and its residents at that time. In the tradition of other American writers such as Steinbeck and Miller, Maupin seeks to articulate a reasoned, liberal tolerance that is not predicated upon a specific radicalism or ideology but rather upon a notion of humanitarian decency. In terms of the rising wave of homophobic militancy and the virulent supremacy of Republican politics in the post-1977 period, such a plea for consensual tolerance and acceptance might seem as naively optimistic and futile as Canute trying to turn back the tide. Maupin offers some interesting insights into the issue of coming out and of outing others in this following extract from his interview with Andrew Billen. Maupin had been a close friend to the film star Rock Hudson, a sexually active gay man who nonetheless remained in the closet throughout his life:

When, seven years later, Hudson lay dying from AIDS, surrounded by friends "lying through their teeth about his sexuality", Maupin confirmed to the Press that Doris Day's co-star had been homosexual all along. "You would be a madman if you took it upon yourself to out every hypocritical homosexual on the planet, and a very busy madman, but there are times when it is important to tell the truth. I don't think I need permission from another person before I speak honestly about something that is widely known. Rock appeared with his lover in the social columns of the *Hollywood Reporter*. He cruised with me. While I am completely sympathetic to some poor schoolteacher in Idaho who's worried about losing his or her job, I am not to a movie star who is making millions keeping an illusion afloat that makes it tougher for the teacher in Idaho. I have a real burr up my butt about closet cases.... I suppose because I was one for so long. I consider it the most immoral period of my life.

(Billen)

It is interesting that Maupin's coming out in terms of his relationship with his parents was unintentionally activated by the coming out of his fictional counterpart Michael:

In 1974, in San Francisco he consented to be identified as gay in a list of eligible bachelors in the local paper, confident his parents in Carolina would never see the piece.... "They found out when Michael came out to his parents in More Tales of the City.... They were following the serial in the paper and when they read the letter Michael writes his parents they realised I was talking about myself." And their response? "Exactly the one Michael received. My mother wrote to say it was killing my father and my father wrote to say it was killing my mother, who had cancer at the time."

(Ibid)

The complex themes of identity, denial and deception are further explored in the other principal story line featuring Mona – her relationship with D'orothea Jackson. It is clear, as I've already established in this chapter, that Mona is a young woman caught between conflicting desires and concerns. As the series narratives unfold, the audience discovers that a central and previously missing link in the jigsaw of her troubled persona and anima is the character of D'orothea. Acknowledging the latent subtext within her first name, Mona most clearly had been an intimate 'friend of Dorothy' – her lover when they met on the East Coast in New York. I think that there is also arguably a narrative and thematic significance in that this character is introduced into the narrative in Episode Three through an unexpected encounter with Brian Hawkins. Working as a waiter in a restaurant, he waits upon D'orothea, a very attractive African American woman and, in almost Pavlovian fashion, proceeds to try and find and conversational routes towards her. Ironically, it is she that seeks conversation but not as a means towards a sexual encounter, rather as a means for her to have someone – a stranger – listen to her personal dilemma. After he has finished his shift, she tells him over a drink about how she has returned, a very successful black soul singer, to San Francisco to rediscover a lost love, "I met this person working on a swimsuit campaign for J Walter Thompson and fell in love. My lover came back here." Revealing that her lover was a 'she,' there is a moment of some pathos in a character who is lesbian in denial, off-loading to a white, heterosexual man, torn between sexual adventuring and a longing for something more meaningful than 'sex-as-conquest.'

There is a sense in which both characters embody some central issues and themes within the series. D'orothea telephones Mona and the two women meet up. With a shared need but also a shared recognition of those issues of commitment and trust that had previously undermined their relationship, they attempt to renegotiate a way of being together. It soon transpires that Mona is at least partly attracted to the prospect of material security, especially in the context of her current circumstances. D'orothea wants her to move into her luxurious Pacific Heights house and Mona tries to talk her dilemma through with Michael. Perhaps partly projecting his doubts and conflicts about his own search for security, he is concerned that Mona might make a major decision for the wrong reasons. The strength and depth of Mona's own self-questioning and uncertainty is reflected when she inadvertently hurts Michael in his efforts to support and advise her:

Michael: Nothing is free, Mona, nothing.

Mona: Oh yeah? What about your rent?

Whilst the two are effectively reconciled as Mona apologies profusely to him, a lingering tension remains regarding her tentative, problematic return to D'orothea. Anna Madrigal who clearly enjoys a very close friendship with Mona experiences this tension and emotional anxiety. It is clear from oblique references between the two in early episodes that Mona is aware of Anna's secret past. When Mona decides to leave Barbary Lane in order to move in with D'orothea, her decision leaves Mrs Madrigal quietly devastated:

Anna: Did she ever say anything about me that might make you think she was unhappy here?

Michael: No, Ma'am. She's very fond of you.

Mona believes that an essential part of her and D'orothea's reunion is that her partner opens up about her family and past. Believing that D'orothea is in a different form of denial about her black, working-class roots, Mona urges her to share and celebrate her background. Meeting with little or no response from her, Mona sets out to arrange a meeting at Pacific Heights. She discovers that D'orothea's father works in a bakery and arranges to go and meet him. On arrival, she is clearly slightly shaken to discover that he's white. Whilst he is very reluctant that he and his wife should endure the pain and embarrassment of meeting up with a daughter who has apparently rejected them, he is persuaded by Mona for them to come to Christmas dinner at Pacific Heights. Simultaneously, Mona has discovered that D'orothea is taking tablets, which might indicate that she is suffering from a terminal illness. In the final episode of the first series, the arrival of D'orothea's parents finally reveals the nature of her deception – Mona greets her white parents on their arrival. As D'orothea is finally forced to admit to herself, her lover and her parents, "I'm a fraud. I'm just a white girl from Oakland." Forced, as she saw it, by the commercial considerations within the popular music business, to adopt a black persona in order to achieve success, she reconstructed herself into a young black woman, with the aid of a medication that darkens skin pigmentation.

In a way that might justifiably trouble a sceptical reading of this resolution, there are clearly issues about the 'white-woman-inhabiting-the black-woman' which raise ideological concerns about the construction of racial and ethnic identity. That this narrative allows for a double take on the themes of deception and denial, I do nevertheless feel uncomfortable with its latent – if unconscious – representation of racial identity and difference. In a series that is effectively exclusively white Anglo-Saxon in its geo-ideological setting, the revelation that the African American lesbian character is only so for the purposes of other narrative/thematic concerns is disconcerting. Equally concerning, from my interpretative viewpoint, is that the character of Mona is presented, initially at least, as uncritically accepting of this revelation. If Maupin is arguing somehow on the basis of 'accepting and loving the person beneath the surface,' then this nevertheless might be seen to represent a disingenuous evasion or denial of the biologically and socially encultured issues of racial identity within the inequalities and oppressions of African American history. Along with the rather contrived melodrama of Williams' death, I believe that this proposed resolution of Mona's relationship with D'orothea represents both an ideological and thematic Achilles Heel in what is an otherwise fascinating, intriguing and compelling drama.

Tales and More Tales

> Jon: I just get sick of hearing that bitchy talk about Twinks. It's just a Queen's way of being a male chauvinist pig.
>
> (Episode Five)

> Anna: I'm a liar. I love you with all of my heart but I'm a liar.
>
> (To Edgar, Episode Five)

I've chosen these two quotations to frame the context of this concluding summary of Series One of 'Tales of the City.' In their respective ways, they embody central themes and narrative strategies within the first series. Jon's anger and criticism of the moneyed, bourgeois gay culture in San Francisco displays Maupin's own uncompromising critique of class and privilege within the series. Whilst an audience might view the lonely alcoholism of Frannie Halcyon with some sense of painful pathos, her bizarre transformation in the following series is exposed with scintillating satire. The ideological implications of the sexual politics of the Pinus Club are many and problematic. Essentially, lonely older women from the class who would consitute Hampton-Giddes' A-List, employ the personal and sexual services of young handsome men.

Situated in a surreally Californian quasi-Classical setting, these women are essentially exercising their purchasing power to alleviate their sexual frustration and entry into older age. The young men, who are given mystical – effectively fetishised – names such as Birdsong, are essentially reduced to commodities: Rent Boys in a grotesque Elysian idyll predicated upon the insulating properties of wealth and excess. In 'Tales of the City,' Dee Dee's solitary preoccupation with her weight and appearance replicates in full measure the futility of her meaningless marriage to Beauchamp. The privileged dominant class – both straight and gay – within San Franciscan and Californian society are exposed in all of their vanity and irresponsible excess. In one scene of excruciating cultural hypocrisy and egocentricity, Dee Dee is invited to attend an A-List women's luncheon club where the diners indulge in the fashionable pastime of pseudo-psychological 'sharing' of their 'problems.' On this particular occasion, the theme for the lunch is 'Rapping about Rape,' with the guest speaker a 'token' American Indian woman who has herself been the victim of rape. Edgar Halcyon himself can only be liberated from the crippling self-deception and austere conformity of his class in the context of his sudden awareness of his own mortality. For Dee Dee, her decision to have her baby – the offspring from her desperate 'Rent Boy' liaison – also signals at least a potential resistance to the hypocrisy of the deception and shallow social mirage of her marriage. In a further development to the issues I discussed previously concerning D'orothea, it is with this – now 're-whitened' – character that Dee Dee develops an emancipating friendship which, by the closure of 'More Tales,' has become openly lesbian. However, the seemingly liberating nature of their relationship is critically questioned when we discover that they – with the new-born twins – are leaving to live in what they imagine might be a utopian, radical Christian community: the Reverend Jim Jones' People's Church.

Anna Madrigal's anguished engagement with issues of identity, acceptance, deception and denial is developed and, ultimately, resolved, in 'More Tales of the City.' She tells Brian that she is Mona's father while in a simultaneous narrative, Mona leaves to try and resolve her own inner dilemmas about who she is and where her life is leading. Her profound disorientation and inner turmoil exhibited in her nihilistic use of 'angel dust' – crack cocaine – she meets up with strange old woman, called Mother Mucca, as she is about to leave San Francisco for the desert of Reno and beyond. In yet another improbable narrative that rests upon an acceptance of the benevolent synchronicity of Bettelheim's Freudian interpretation of folk tales, it transpires that Mucca is Madrigal's mother. With Mona agreeing, before this realisation, to work as a receptionist at the 'Blue Lodge' (Mucca's desert brothel where Halcyon had lost his virginity many years before) a growing recognition dawns of the inter-weaving narrative and thematic strands that bind the three women together. However, even as this painful tripartite reconciliation evolves, another malevolent personal agenda still threatens to intrude upon and undermine the relationship between Mona and Anna: Mona's mother and Anna/Andy's ex-wife. Betty Ramsay has tracked down her ex-husband through the auspices of Norman Williams and, embittered by her lingering sense of rejection and desertion those many years before, seeks revenge. It is, however, precisely the nature of her malevolent penetrative gaze that proves to undermine her seeming strategic and 'moral' impregnability. In a narrative line that resonates with eroticism, and the motif of the gaze, the viewer has witnessed a strange encounter between Brian and an unknown woman. They stare at each other across the geo-ideological space between her apartment window and Brian's penthouse room at 28 Barbary Lane. Using binoculars to effect this transaction, they undress for each other at a prearranged time each evening, exposing themselves to mutual arousal – simultaneously subject and predicate. This erotic ritual of reciprocal voyeurism is presented also for the gaze of the viewer, implicated in the problematic context of desire and its alienated displacement. It is also significant that one of the two initiates is a woman who, corroded by rejection, sublimates her own desire in and through the manipulation of another's longing. Equally, he represents the ideological dilemma of the man who has been alienated from desire and its fulfilment through serial sexual adventurism – itself a displacement of emotional and ideological loss. Ultimately, Anna is able to thus counter Betty Ramsay's threat of exposure with a counter-threat to expose her identity as the 'secret woman' to Brian.

Armistead Maupin, in exploring and re-constructing a San Francisco of allegorical meanings and narratives fulfils one aspect of the role of the author of any fable – that of moral critique and subsequent enlightenment. Maupin is clearly not engaging in conventional moral analysis and he also avoids the narrow constraints of the proselytiser. In these two series he seeks to create an alternative fictional world that is characterised by diversity, choice and the individual journeys that are navigated through that world. Whilst seeking to celebrate the potential for liberal experimentation and expression that the San Francisco of that period provoked, he is equally alert to – and reflective upon – the implications for its citizens of issues of personal integrity, freedom and responsibility. The characters and class within 'Tales of the City' who are most exposed to his bitingly funny satire and critique are those, whether gay or straight, who chose deception, denial and manipulative games while simultaneously enjoying the fruits of the city's Atlantean garden.

Maupin's drama might also be viewed, from a certain perspective, as exhibiting aspects of Foucault's concept of the heterotopia: an imagined alternative site of transposed sexual identities and power relations. In this respect, my discussion of Maupin's construction of San Francisco carrying with(in) it Atlantean signifiers opens up the viewing of the series as a whole as a nostalgic displacement of longed-for sexual liberty and freedom: a culturally mediated heterotopia. As I also alluded to earlier in this chapter, there is a corresponding context in which the notion of this construct as a pleasured space – a 'Garden of Eden-as-unhindered erogenous pleasure' – might yield interesting readings from a Kristevan viewing position. In that respect, the signifiers employed within the dramatisation of Maupin's text might be read as communicating in and through an essentially semiotic process:

> The semiotic is fluid and plural, a kind of pleasurable creative excess over precise meaning, and it takes sadistic delight in destroying or negating such signs. It is opposed to all fixed, transcendental significations; and since the ideologies of modem male-dominated class-society rely on such fixed signs for their power (God, father, state, order, property and so on), such literature becomes a kind of equivalent in the realm of language to revolution in the sphere of politics. The reader of such texts is equally disrupted or 'decentred' by this linguistic force, thrown into contradiction, unable to take up any one, simple 'subject-position' in relation to these polymorphous works.[1]

I am not wishing to propose some simplistic or clumsy intention in terms of Maupin's stated intended aims as the author of the original texts(s). There is no evidence for such a reading and it would run contrary to the principal theoretical and methodological strategies of this book. Furthermore, it would be inappropriate in the context of this wider study to attempt to engage in any extended, detailed discussion of Kristeva.

Nevertheless, the *schema* of 'Tales of the City' functioning as a counter-cultural destabilising of dominant, homophobic readings of gay and lesbian sexuality does carry a clear measure of currency and evidence, I hope I have demonstrated within this chapter. Furthermore, the resonance of that viewing position becomes of even greater and comparative value when applied to the performative aesthetic of 'Queer as Folk' which is the subject of the next chapter.

I want to conclude this analysis and discussion of the first series with a quotation from Maupin himself:

> When *Tales* was first published in book form its audience was largely gay and male. Then, reader by reader, it built a following that grew to resemble the demographics of the novel itself, leaping barriers of age, race, gender and sexual orientation…. That's why I cringe a little when some bookstores restrict this book and its sequels to the Gay and Lesbian section. Don't get me wrong, I'm proud that I've been openly gay for over twenty years – and aware of the impact of my homosexuality has had on my work – but my writing has always been intended for everyone…. To aim for anything less would be to betray the spirit of joyful inclusion that makes life what it is on Barbary Lane.

Note

1. Terry Eagleton (1995), *Literary Theory*, Blackwell, p.118.

4　A Manchester Heterotopia?

'Queer as Folk'

In this controversial drama series from Red Productions and screened on Channel 4, fundamental assumptions about the construction and representation of homo/bisexuality in contemporary television are exposed and challenged. In doing so, it is my belief that the series, with its two-episode sequel, explores ongoing ideological tensions within the broader Gay/Lesbian/Queer Community. In endeavouring to explore these issues, I shall be drawing upon certain aspects of Foucault and Queer Theory. In particular, I want to begin by addressing the ways in which the series offers a fictional construct of Manchester's Gay Village: Canal Street, and to consider the extent to which that construction might be read as an example of Foucault's concept of the heterotopia. Towards the conclusion of this chapter, I will consider the performative aesthetic of 'Queer as Folk' in comparison and contrast to that of 'Tales of the City' in order to explore issues regarding the fictional representation and portrayal of Gay, Lesbian and Queer sexuality.

In her fine and provocative paper, 'Queer Geography,' Affrica Taylor makes the following observation:

> Taken from the Greek, 'hetero' means 'other' or 'different,' and 'topia' means place. Thus heterotopia literally translates as 'places of difference.' But there is another layer of meaning, one that involves the effect of misplacement or displacement.... I want to retain this double meaning as I think that it is important to keep in mind that difference or otherness is always about displacement. Foucault himself described heterotopias as "something like counter-sites, a kind of effectively enacted utopia, in which the real sites, all the other real sites that can be found within the culture, are simultaneously represented, contested and inverted"[1]

Manchester's Canal Street, like San Francisco's Castro District and Sydney's Oxford Street are geo-ideological spaces of gay, lesbian and queer formations. Within these spatial locations, there lies the possibility of the disruptive play and exhibition of sexual identities and activities which have historically been marginalised in terms of silence and/or absence: "The love that dare not speak its name." Therefore, Canal Street, which is a central and defining location and site within 'Queer as Folk,' functions as a heterotopia: a longed-for performative utopia, which interestingly also serves as a kind of 'imagined city.'

Intriguingly, there is effectively a kind of double take in the representation of this area in the television series. The imagined city is re-imagined through the mediating filter of the programme-makers. Furthermore the use of this fictional construction of the imagined space as a focal site, potentially challenges the ideological position and gaze of the given viewer. In narrative positional terms therefore, the geo-ideological space of the dominant heterosexual interest is moved to a location of relative marginality. Through this process, it is that heterosexual formation that carries with it a quality of strangeness or alienation. This phenomenon is explored and communicated with some considerable humour when Vince enters a straight pub to meet up with work colleagues for an early evening drink. As he approaches the pub, he delivers an ironic travelogue account of his approach and entry to Stuart via mobile phone:

> Vince: Straight pub. It's true, everything we've ever been told. Everything except flock wallpaper. Can you believe it? They've got toilets in which no one's ever had sex!

Vince knows that the principal reason for the after work drink is for some of the older female shop assistants from the supermarket – where he holds a junior managerial position – to try and match-make a meeting between him and Rosalie, a new young assistant. Even as Vince tries to navigate this situation, complicated by his own closeted sexuality in his work environment, he and Rosalie are able to negotiate a friendly conversation in the context of his obsession with 'Dr Who' and a shared passion for 'Coronation Street.' Both television series have a gay/camp iconic cult status. As he talks to Stuart in the aftermath of this slightly surreal encounter, Vince bemusedly admits to his friend "In some parallel universe, I just met my wife." This ironic sense of the constructed-ness and relativity of both identity and sexuality very much characterises the post-modern nature of the series and its narrative strategies. Nevertheless, within the macro-frame of that construction of characters and location, there is a counterpoint of a questioning search for a notion of moral coherence, fixedness and commitment within gay and lesbian relationships. This narrative line is most evidently and consistently expressed by the character of Cameron, Vince's lover, exercised in direct dialectical conflict to what he views as Stuart's damagingly irresponsible and manipulative hedonism. I shall explore the nature and implications of this dialectical struggle in a subsequent section of this chapter.

Queer as Sequinned Space

In the opening credits to the series, and to each subsequent episode, there is a coloured montage of shifting crimson and scarlet serving as a backdrop for a similarly shifting network of glittering golden lights, a kind of sequinned spermatozoa. In symbiotic tandem with this visual aesthetic is a pounding, rhythmic musical signature theme which is percussive and punctuated by a celebratory whoop of anticipated pleasure. An out-of-camera-vision voice introduces the opening spoken narrative text. The camera cuts to a full frame, portrait shot of Vince who addresses the audience through a direct-to-camera narrative. He is shot against a primary colour background and proceeds to tell the viewer that it is Thursday night in 'Babylon' – a club with classic gay credentials in Canal Street. Vince's narrative continues in exuberant counter-play with the musical signature theme as the camera work invites the viewer's gaze upon an geo-ideological journey along the canal edge. Images abound and explode upon the retina of intimate male coupling and a surging sense of movement, unrestricted energy and confrontational display. This is a visual grammar and aesthetic of a love that, far from daring to speak its name, positively screams its mobile telephone number, like some outrageous queen, at the viewer. This rampant collage of desire and sexuality is signified in terms of consumption and arguably a form of decadent exhibitionism. For whose interpretative gaze is this display intended? The controversy following on the screening of the first episode, focusing principally on Stuart's predatory seduction of the under-age Nathan, was extensive. *The Guardian* (24.6.99) carried a short feature on an inside page entitled 'Gay drama censured for explicit sex scenes':

> Channel 4's gay drama 'Queer as Folk' was censured yesterday for its use of explicit scenes, including one of a schoolboy having sex with an adult man. The Broadcasting Standards Commission ruled that the under-age sex scene and another involving three men having sex together exceeded acceptable boundaries. Channel 4 argued that the illegality of the relationship between the adult man and the boy was as valid a subject for television drama as any other illegal act such as murder or theft. The troilism was crucial to illustrate the promiscuity of the main character, the broadcaster said.

I discuss the implications of these issues in more detail in the final section of this chapter and also my concluding chapter. As a temporary postscript to this debate, it is worthwhile noting the National Viewer's and Listener's Association (founded by Mary Whitehouse – the paradigm of meridian reactionary values) letter to the Independent Television Commission (24.2.99) which alleged that "this programme is calculated to influence public opinion at a time when the age of homosexual consent is being debated in Parliament." The ideological framing and signing of the programme's visual aesthetic – if calculated provocatively to disrupt both right field homophobic positions and centrist 'tolerance' of homosexuality – had clearly fulfilled its aim.

Later in the first episode, there is a marvelously evocative signing of the city space which seeks to reclaim the spaces of the city from a gay perspective. On this occasion, the location is not the self-defined, identity-based space of Canal Street, but the rooftop of a Manchester city hospital. Stuart and Vince have arrived with Nathan, Stuart's sexual trophy, in tow, to visit and view a truly queered space within a maternity ward. Stuart, having agreed to provide a sperm donation for a child for a lesbian couple, has now arrived to see the newly born baby boy. Around the maternity bed icon of mother and child is an assembled group of butch and femme lesbian friends and supporters. As one of them remarks with acerbic camp irony to Stuart, when Nathan belatedly appears at the ward door, "So, you both had a child on the same night."

The camera cuts to a slow, sweeping panoramic view of a mid-distant Manchester skyline, the pulsating array of distant night-lights evoking associations of the visuals of the opening credits. Stuart is seeking a space in which he can struggle to come to terms with the implications of the birth of his surrogate son. As he and Vince stand together on the roof top edge, they perform a wonderfully funny and ironic re-enactment of an enduring camp icon from recent popular film – the cruciform coupling of Kate Winslet and Leonardo Di Caprio on the bow of 'The Titanic.' Even as Vince complains that "I'm always Kate Winslet," there is – for one evocative moment – an image of transposing and transforming queer sensibility across the city landscape below. Like a gay paradigm of the Christ of the Andes, the image is set against the midnight cartography of Manchester, simultaneously separate from, whilst signed across, the dialectic of the lives of its inhabitants. This is no simplistic or idealised penetrative icon but, carrying within it the ongoing tensions between Stuart and Vince, signifies issues of identity, desire and commitment within their relationship. Within 'Queer as Folk,' the agenda is not one of liberal assimilation of difference or even the 'positive' representation of sexual identities and behaviours defined by the dominant paradigm as 'minority' or 'other.' Nowhere is this expressed more completely and uncompromisingly than in the penultimate narrative sequence in which Stuart and Vince prepare to leave Canal Street, Manchester and – ultimately – Britain. In a visual narrative of pulsating and daringly surreal virtuosity, Stuart and Vince prepare Nathan for their imminent departure. In doing so, their narrative status assumes the proportions of Prospero and that of the deus et machina as they intervene – through wiping the frame of the viewing camera – to transform Canal Street from day through to night. I want to quote from this sequence extensively in order that I might deconstruct its treatment of character, location and ideological purpose:

Nathan: You're coming back, though.

(Stuart looks at him. Growing in strength. He walks away from the jeep, slowly, taking the centre of the street)

Stuart: Come back to this? The ghetto. Alleyways stinking of piss, beggars in every door, straights and students coming to look at the freak show. And every idiot saving all week, saving their stupid wages from their stupid jobs to come here and shoot their load with some stranger –

(In walking, he wipes frame – Cut to – and keeps talking, the same scene, continuous, Stuart, centre of the road, Vince in the jeep.... Around them Canal Street at midnight, transformed. Stripped of people, but every pub and bar shining with colour. And light bouncing off the canal itself, so that the entire height of the walls shimmers with reflection, movement, never still. Stuart at his most powerful)

Stuart: – and just you look after it. This stupid little street, it's the middle of the world. On a street like this, every single night, anyone can meet anyone. And every single night, someone meets someone. (It's as if the speech is continuous, Vince stepping down from the jeep, with the same strength as Stuart)

Vince: It's all yours now. All of them, all the poofs and all the dykes and all the people in between.

(And this time Vince wipes frame – Cut to – and as Vince clears the shot, he's filled the street with the one thing missing, the people…. Music pounding out of the pubs, but just a constant beat, accelerating our own music)

Vince: And this lot. They'll shag you, they'll rob you, some of them might even love you. And they'll all forget you, in the end. Just stick with your friends, and you'll be fine.

(As he finishes, he's alongside Stuart)

Stuart: You fuck it up. Then I'll come back.

Entering into this territory in which, as a subsequent script direction says, "Anything can happen now," the impact of this climactic moment as a precursor to the denouement of the series' narrative and thematic strands is lucidly clear. The stylistic marking of this territory serves to foreground the heightened, generic construction of the series as a whole. Equally, it is also an apex of simultaneous strength and weakness within the overall narrative construction. By this I mean that in its post-modern evocation of the transcendence of material conditions, it may both explore the fluidity and freedom of its ideological spatial constructs, while diminishing the influence and relevance of those material conditions inherent within the production of its themes and characters. In elevating Stuart, and ultimately Vince, into a kind of mythic status, there is a serious risk of operating a wish-fulfilment ideological strategy, in which desire subsumes the problematic demands of the city and its individual lives represented by the series. Of course, there is also an unmistakable sense of self-dramatising camp bravura in Vince's "… some of them might even love you. And they'll all forget you in the end." These torch song sentiments might be read as uncomfortably sentimental, in the context of a series that has striven to sustain an uncompromisingly honest account of sexual desire and identity within an urban/city context. I will return to these considerations in the context of the concluding section of this chapter.

I now want to turn to a detailed analysis of the principal characters and some of the key narratives in which their construction might reveal both authorial and broader ideological concerns within the series.

Stuart Alan Jones

Vince: He doesn't do boyfriends… he doesn't give a toss about anyone.

(Explaining Stuart to Nathan)

For much of the first series, and indeed well into the sequel, the character of Stuart is constructed in such a way that his predominant mode is communicated as a predatory, sexual adventurer who is only ever validated in the act and climactic consumption of sex. In this respect the character is almost a kind of late twentieth century gay, metropolitan Byronic hero: a fascinating ideological compound of Romantic masculine transgression with a post-modern denial of self, except in the flux of desire and its consumption. He is very much the pivotal character against which all other characters are positioned and measured. He is, in this way, a barometer of ideological sexual and ethical indicators, both in terms of the gay/queer/lesbian community that populates the series, and also as a provocative disrupter of the centre/right heterosexual field. The uncompromising sense of his own raison d'être is, I believe, initially revealed in the powerful speech that the character is given in the sequel to the first series. This is in the context of Stuart's own closeted sexual identity with regard to his own family. His sister, Marie, is aware of his gay sexuality and has previously urged him to come out to their parents. However, Stuart is placed in a position in which, ultimately he must confront his family with his sexuality in a savage response to an attempt to blackmail him by one of his nephews, Marie's son Tom. Whilst child-sitting for the two young boys, Thomas has logged onto an internet gay male sex pornography site on which he sits and watches two men engaged in mutual fellatio. As soon as Stuart realises what has happened, he rushes to turn the computer screen off. However, his seemingly innocent nephew plans to use this opportunity to exploit his uncle for money, threatening otherwise to expose him. Stuart responds with characteristic directness by holding a struggling Thomas headfirst over a flushing toilet. This is the background to the scene in Series Two where Stuart is helping Marie to move into her new home. Thomas begins to pressurise Stuart into contrition and a presumable financial payment by making allusions to his uncle's 'male friends.' However, when Stuart's father asks his son to help in assembling some shelves, he uses the opportunity to launch a devastating 'coming out' that is simultaneously a confrontation of the boy's latent homophobia:

> Stuart: We don't do hammers, and nails, and saws. We do joints and screws, but that's different.
>
> Margaret: Who does?
>
> Stuart: Queers. (Beat) Because I'm queer, I'm gay. I'm homosexual. I'm a poof. I'm a bum-boy batty-boy backside-artist bugger, I'm bent, I am that arse bandit, I lift those shirts, I'm a fudge-packing shit-stabbing uphill gardener, I dance at the other end of the ballroom, I dine in the downstairs restaurant, I'm Moses and the parting of the Red Cheeks, I fuck and I'm fucked, I suck and I'm sucked, I rim them and wank them and every single man's had the shag of his life, and I am not – (beat) – a pervert. If there's one twisted bastard in this family, it's that little blackmailer, so congratulations, Thomas. I've just officially outed you.

This hugely powerful speech is in effect a litany of all of the predictable, commonplace euphemisms for homosexuality from a homophobic viewpoint. In consciously and defiantly defining himself in those pejorative terms, he is almost shaman-like exorcising their power to oppress, injure and denigrate their subject. At the very core of this strategy lies the angry radicalism that informs the reclamation of the derogatory term, queer, as an expression of uncompromising, politicised reaction to the dominant, reactionary value set:

> The Queer movement was a call to resist continuing harassment by government, the media and queerbashers, to denounce the feeble establishment response to AIDS, and to assert the revolutionary potential of kinky sexuality. It condemned the complacency of many lesbians and gay men, especially those who have found convenient niches for themselves and who believe that keeping quiet may lead to social acceptance.[2]

I do not want to engage in a simplistic or reductionist deconstruction of the fictional character of Stuart. However, I assert that he embodies, in a very fundamental and strategic sense, a discourse of unsettling and uncompromising queering of both homophobic and bourgeois gay/lesbian viewing spaces. When he accuses his long-term friend Vince of being a "straight man who likes to fuck men," this is a corrosive and scorching challenge to the hegemony of sexual orientation and its expression. Queer can only exist in terms of the framework of repressive binary positions, which must postulate 'straight' as normal, normative, coercive and heterosexual:

> The project for queer historians… is to judge the meaning of sex in any given historical location and to trace the development of notions of identity and sexual selves from within discourses of acts and pleasures…. The homo-hetero binary still continues to clamp down upon sexual excess and insists upon clear sexual distinctions between perverse and normal sexual behaviour and between male and female sexualities.[3]

Whilst it is difficult and unwise to ascribe consistent motivations to a character whose construction so often serves as a provocative, disruptive strategy, there is, nevertheless, a premeditated display of sexual excess and its absolute requiting within the character of Stuart that appears to 'necessitate' constraint. This issue subsequently represents a major ethical dilemma within both the constructions of the character and the programme. As Stuart insinuates in his biting accusation of his friend, this dilemma is not simply explicable in terms of binary gay/straight positions – even liberal/progressive ones – but that the signifiers of straight and gay will both contain inherent clauses about the ideological positioning of any condition defined as 'straight.' Following on from a Foucauldian view of the constructed nature of all sexual behaviours and the absence, ultimately, of any fixed centre, Stuart may be read as both an expression of unconstrained sexuality without centre, and a potential ethical and ideological anxiety regarding that expression. What is significant however, from a cultural materialist reading of the character, is that the economic placement and status of the character parallel these markings of pleasure, excess and its gratification. Therefore I would argue that Stuart is only able to function in the post-modern dialogue of the deconstruction of centred positions using that strategy as an ideological superstructure predicated upon an economic and material base. Therefore, the power relations of Foucauldian sexual politics are replicated and facilitated by the economic relations and purchasing power of the protagonist. This analysis is evidenced at various points in the meta-narrative and also as a transcendent material presence throughout the series. This ideological and interpretative space is signed as 'invisible.' There is an assumption that Stuart's wealth – as evidenced in his warehouse-conversion attic penthouse and four-wheel drive vehicle – is a given material condition. Furthermore, there are subliminal associations of this economic excess as fetishised commodities. This inevitably has implications for the men with whom Stuart has sexual relations. A brutally clear example of the consequences of the character purchasing men for sex is in an early episode of the first series, where Stuart surfs the Internet to buy sexual gratification in the form of a man known in trade terms as 'Good Fuck.'

Significantly, in addition to being defined in the reductionist terms of his saleable commodity as a recipient for sexual gratification, the computer screen reveals a disembodied, reified 'classic' male body. When the man arrives at Stuart's flat, there is some confusion when the infatuated – but under age – Nathan arrives at the same time. When Nathan asks who the other man is, Stuart, of course, can only define him as 'Mr Goodfuck' – a demeaning diminutive that gives Stuart pleasure in utterance in his role as dominant purchaser. It is also significant that the man – middle-aged and defined in dialect and manner as northern working-class – objects to being introduced in this way and reproves Stuart with, "Colin. My name's Colin." With Stuart dismissively expecting Nathan to disappear into the night, it is Colin who once more reproves Stuart's selfishness in terms of the boy's age and his consequent vulnerability on the night streets of Manchester. Stuart, albeit rather reluctantly, takes Nathan down to the streets below and gets him into a taxi. This sequence ends with a temporarily reflective Stuart returning upstairs to his apartment to find Colin lying naked, waiting for him. When Stuart says that he's changed his mind, Colin is aggrieved. Stuart responds with a characteristic "I never promised anyone anything." This might almost prove to be Stuart's self-acknowledged *leitmotif* throughout the series. Nevertheless, he also proves to be true to form when, seeing Colin getting dressed again, he re-thinks his initial decision and leaps upon him in a frame that concludes the episode. There are many other numerous examples throughout both series, which re-position Stuart constantly in terms of a kind of amoral detachment from the men with whom he has casual sexual encounters. As Cameron, Vince's short-lived committed partner says accusingly to Stuart in the context of what is a power struggle between the two men for Vince's affections, "It's sex. Everything's sex with you. There's no such thing as Vince. He doesn't exist on his own. You don't let him." I want to explore these tensions and conflict between Stuart and Cameron as both a means of extending my analysis of Stuart's character and also as a means of entry into an investigation of Vince's character. Furthermore, the entry of Cameron into the series is in the context of the death of Phil, a gay man and a drinking and social companion of Vince and Stuart. The circumstances of his death and its aftermath introduce other important ethical and ideological concerns into the series.

Phil is, like Vince, a likeable and essentially pragmatic character. He appears with Stuart and Vince in the opening sequence of episode one and shares Vince's simultaneous envy and criticism of Stuart's sexual exploits and the implications for their social lives. There is an aura of uncomplicated directness surrounding Phil, which stands in direct contrast to the more impenetrable agendas motivating Stuart. It is in the context of yet another usual night out drinking, dancing and seeking sex that Phil meets his death. Interwoven with three other narrative lines – Stuart picking up two attractive young men and enjoying a sexual threesome – and Vince, in a scene redolent with inherent pathos and comedy, 'copping off' with a guy only to be ultimately frustrated. The third inter-cut narrative sequence is a bleakly funny account of the hugely camp Alexander with his partner Dane, going in search of a sexual threesome with a desperately seedy character, to an equally seedy back street doss-house with the unlikely name of The Dolphin Hotel. They have been escorted back to these dismal lodgings by O'Hagan, a leather-clad character who proves to be a mortician's assistant with a darkly comic preoccupation with death, pain and his pet snake. The use of these three narrative lines to provide a counterpoint to the circumstances of Phil's death is most effective, especially in the interplay of casual sexual activity with a sense of danger mediated by a richly dark humour. Through this editorial and directorial device, the sudden, unexpected death of Phil takes on an even more shocking significance. Vince, having discovered that his pick-up is suffering from an exotic infestation of his bowel, telephones Stuart on his mobile, a call which he takes but doesn't respond to as he lies with his two lovers watching a video of themselves enjoying erotic, sensual sex. Simultaneously, the narrative inter-cuts to Alexander and Dane growing increasingly scared as their pick-up recounts in gory detail the means of pinning shut corpse's eyes which involuntarily open. Meanwhile, the narrative, which seems most innocuous and ordinary, proves to be one in which the search for sex with a stranger ends in a tragic death. The camera shows Phil hailing a cab in the night streets of Manchester, only to realise that another guy, Harvey, has also flagged it down. Deciding to share the taxi together, Phil invites Harvey back to his house in Fallowfield where they are clearly going to spend the night together. The atmosphere of quiet but pleasurable expectation is confirmed when Harvey asks Phil if it's all right to use drugs – heroin – as a prelude to them having sex. Phil, who doesn't use drugs, nevertheless agrees in a spirit of understated tolerance. However, when Phil is invited – and agrees – to snort a line of the heroin, he collapses into a paroxysm, dying within minutes on his kitchen floor of a heart attack. Harvey panics and, without telephoning for an ambulance or help, takes a handful of cash from Phil's wallet and disappears.

At the funeral, Vince is obliged to keep a promise he had made to Phil to read a poem – actually to read the lyrics from the classic camp trash anthem: 'D-I-S-C-O':

> Vince: Cos it was last Easter. Phil had found this bruise on his leg, he said, that's it, I'm dying, I'm off, wrote all this down. His last request. Turns out he bumped his leg on a stepladder. But he chose this, he wanted something… appropriate. (Reads, unsure at first) D.I.S.C.O, I say, D.I.S.C.O. She is D, desirable….
>
> (The congregation starts to laugh, getting the joke (especially the 'she'), some crying at the same time. And Vince warms up, like it's Shakespeare)

Vince: She is I, irresistible, she is S, super-sexy, She is C, CRAZY CRAZY, She is Oh, Oh, Oh, I say D.I.S.C.O.

(Everyone's loving it, in just the way Phil intended. But Vince sees Mrs Delaney looking at him. She's not laughing, she's bewildered, lost. Like the congregation knew her son better than she did)

The mix of embarrassment and pathos is both poignant and funny. However, Stuart trying to pick up an attractive young man during the service underscores even this dimension to the commemoration of Phil's life. After the service, at the wake back at Phil's parent's house, there is a serious and poignant scene between Mrs Delaney (Phil's mother) and Vince. Struggling to understand the terrible circumstances of her son's death, where he had been lying for four hours before being found, she says to Vince

Mrs Delaney: (Upset) – but you didn't see anyone? That night. You didn't see who he was with?

Vince: There were loads of us, we had some friends up for the weekend. Sort of lost track of him.

Mrs Delaney: Did you…? (Stops) None of my business.

Vince: What?

Mrs Delaney: That night. Did you… 'cop off'?

(Beat. She smiles, which allows Vince to smile)

Mrs Delaney: Philip always said that, Cop off.

Vince: I didn't, no.

Mrs Delaney: So…? What's the word, what would Philip have called that? Unlucky. So that makes Philip lucky. Because he certainly took someone back home.

Vince: It was just some bloke, God knows it was. He ran away, so – he was prob'ly scared, he must've been-

Mrs Delaney: But tell me – because I can't stop – (Struggles to compose herself, upset) D'you think a woman would have run?

Vince: … sorry?

Mrs Delaney: If he'd taken a woman home.

Vince: How d'you mean?

Mrs Delaney: (Distress building, in tears) If my son had been straight. That's the word, straight, if Philip were straight. I don't know, Vince, you tell me, what...? He'd have found some woman? At the age of thirty-five? Some woman he'd never met? He'd take her home? He'd take heroin with that woman? Would he?

Vince: (Very quiet) It was a mistake, it's got nothing to do with being gay –

Mrs Delaney: Hasn't it? At thirty-five? Philip? He'd find himself at thirty-five taking heroin with a casual fuck if he was straight?

Vince: ...he could do.

(Silence. Mrs Delaney, calmer, drained)

Mrs Delaney: Well, I suppose. What would I know...? (Sudden terror, overwhelmed by the memory) Four hours he lay there, and I had to see him – (Suddenly walks out) Thank you, people to see –

Within Mrs Delaney's quietly anguished question lie a Pandora's Box of unspoken, latent preconceptions, prejudices and readings of stability and commitment within gay relationships. It is precisely that sense of centredness, commitment and security that, it transpires, Cameron is both looking for and believes he can offer to Vince. This, inevitably, is eventually to bring him into direct personal and ideological conflict with Stuart. It is in the context of this scene at the wake that Vince meets up with Cameron who introduces himself as Phil's accountant. As this embryonic relationship begins to very slowly develop, Stuart and Vince decide to visit Phil's house to remove any evidence from his gay life-style that might cause his parents further suffering. Stuart's concern for the sensibilities and feelings of others leads Vince to observe to him sardonically, "People should die more often if it has this effect upon you." At this moment, Stuart shows a surprisingly open admission of reflective concern and awareness of others, only for it to be undermined in his final sentiments:

Vince: She knows he was gay, she's always known.

Stuart: Yeah, but imagine you're dead and your mother goes through your things. Goes through your porn stash – d'you want your mother seeing that? Well, not your mother, a normal mother. (Beat, looks around the room) The poor bastard. (Quieter) I was thinking, I'll get a spare set of keys, for the flat. So you can have them. (Smiles) Come and save me, Vince.

Vince: (Smiles) Yeah. You can have a set of mine.

Stuart: (Brisker) Oh, like anything's going to happen to you. Right. Porn. And I told you, he was a crap shag, came in two seconds flat.

Vince is initially very reluctant to respond to Cameron's advances towards him and it is, ironically, Stuart who eventually acts as the catalyst for his friend to agree to a dinner date with Cameron at an exclusive restaurant. This setting, with its quiet, understated elegance, is in direct and sharp relief to the brash colour and music of the Manchester Canal Street scene. Cameron is Australian and is defined both as a geographical outsider but also by his age, professional status but – principally perhaps – his disengagement from and disillusionment with the gay scene. Indeed in a later scene, he says to Vince, "The problem is it all starts to look the same. Same men, standing in the same clubs." Jealous of Cameron's growing emotional and ultimately sexual bond with Vince, Stuart seeks to undermine and destroy the relationship. First of all, he attempts to make a pass at Cameron himself and is quietly but expertly rebuffed. Undaunted and with mounting and venomous tenacity he begins a war of attrition in which he seeks to turn Vince against Cameron – a conflict he eventually wins. However, this is not before a critically important scenario in the final episode of the first series – the occasion of Vince's thirtieth birthday party that is hosted at Stuart's apartment. There is a wonderfully funny, almost Brechtian moment, when Cameron arrives with Vince at the apartment, with Vince having to feign surprise at what has been organised as a 'surprise party.' One of Vince's principal dialogue signatures is the exclamation of "Oh my God!" and this is exploited to superb effect as he practises his entry into the flat with varying practised tones of disbelief to colour that exclamation. In its very pleasurable evocation of Vince's friendly, even naive, good-humoured temperament, it is also very funny as an example of the rehearsed nature of performative social roles.

The visual code of the party location is celebratory and communicated in terms of the mix of gender and sexuality in pleasured interaction. Alex performs a Spice Girls number in drag and Nathan and his boyfriend Dazz unwittingly drink from Bernard's urine sample as a punishment imposed by Hazel for their impudence. However, the party also serves as a site for the next stage in the struggle between Stuart and Cameron for Vince. Stuart usurps what is intended as a surprise gift for Vince from Cameron by telling Vince that he is going to receive a Mini car from his lover. This then places Vince into another situation where he must rehearse his "Oh my God!" Simultaneously Stuart has sought to upstage Cameron's generous gift by purchasing the original K9 remote controlled robotic dog from the classic 'Dr Who' series. It is significant that these two gifts represent both the differing intentions of their givers but also their view of Vince in relation to themselves. He remains the perpetual subject in relation to both of them. However, there is at least the possibility in his relationship with Cameron that Vince may be able to grow and mature, as Cameron has previously, and angrily, said to Stuart about his dominant influence:

Cameron: …You live your life by sex. Your terms, your conditions, sex. That's all Vince is waiting for, cos that's all you give. And don't tell me you didn't know. (Less angry) Look, I can just go, I don't think he'd even notice. But he's worth the chance. He deserves the chance, doesn't he?

Stuart: So what am I supposed to do?

Cameron: Leave him alone.

Stuart: He's my friend, he's –

Cameron: (Angry) Just leave him alone. If you're any sort of friend. Cos there's no such thing as Vince, he doesn't exist on his own, you don't let him. Just Stuart and Vince. All the time. (Beat, more honest) And I like him. So maybe I'm stupid. But I really like him.

However, the final and seemingly self-destructive blow that Stuart enacts is to invite Rosalie – Vince's drinking partner from work – to the party without Vince's knowledge or consent. In terms of the drama's narrative, the entry of Rosalie into the enclosed and, for her, alternative world of the party, serves also as a device for confirmation of the dominant homosexual reading of the space that has been constructed as normative throughout the series. Vince is clearly seriously shaken by her arrival and there is a moment of precarious cross reading of the situation as he – still in public denial of his sexuality – attempts to steer himself and Rosalie away from the party. However, Stuart is not to be robbed of his perverse victory and, introducing Cameron to Rosalie as Vince's boyfriend – 'Cameron says Vince shags like a rabbit' – he deliberately seeks to punish Vince and Cameron through causing maximum disruption and embarrassment. His strategy seems to have worked as a distraught, embarrassed and angry Rosalie says to Vince as she leaves, "You're just a liar, Vince. You're a liar and – (Gives the word such venom) and you're a poof. You're a dirty little poof." I shall continue my exploration of the dynamics of the interaction and relationships between Vince, Cameron and Stuart in the following section focusing upon the character of Vince Tyler.

Vince Tyler

Stuart: Watch me.

Vince: Yeah. You'd like that. Spent years watching you.

(Queer as Folk 2, Part Two)

The challenging and problematic relationship between Vince and Stuart is at the very core of this series. The two characters have known each other for sixteen years and, on one level, there is a curious kind of metaphorical sado-masochism to its dynamics. This power relationship positions Vince as the recipient subject whilst Stuart is an unrelenting dominatrix, critiquing his erstwhile friend's character, looks and sexual activities and, indeed, any other area of Vince's life. Inherent to these dynamics is the fact that Stuart, who boasts of having had over two thousand sexual conquests, has never had sex with Vince. Nevertheless, in Episode Two Stuart narrates an early sexual experience with Vince when they were teenage boys, sixteen years ago. The story is told to others in the 'Via Fossa' – one of Canal Street's principal club bars – and in its public setting, is designed to demean Vince and exalt Stuart

> Stuart: We're in his bedroom, we must've been fourteen, and Vince has got the *Radio Times* –
>
> Vince: Oh don't tell this story, don't!
>
> Stuart: And we come to this photo and we're both going phwoaaarh, guess who it was? Barry Sheene! On his motorbike!
>
> (Phil is howling with laughter)
>
> Vince: In his leathers, God, I'm shamed –
>
> Stuart: Not even black leather, it was red and cream, and we're going, cor, look at him, then we're sort of groping ourselves, then Vince gets it out, not bad either –
>
> Vince: Oh fuck off –
>
> Stuart: I said give's a go, so I'm giving him a wank, nice and slow, we're looking down at Barry Sheene –
>
> Phil: Oh my God, you've had each other!
>
> Stuart: No, I'm just about to unzip when his mother comes back, he's jumping up, shoving it back in! And that was it.
>
> Vince: See, that's not sex, it's not sex if you don't come!

There is the occasional but potent indication from Vince that he longs for a sexual relationship with Stuart. This becomes a very powerful, subliminal theme throughout the entire series. As I have already established, from Cameron's point of view, Stuart uses this longing and unrequited desire as a means of retaining control within the relationship. There are also consistent references across the episodes of Stuart saving Vince until he is an old man and can't carry out his sexual adventures any longer. When Vince and Stuart are clearing out Phil's house, the implications of Phil's tragic death both trouble Vince, whilst also acting as yet another opportunity for the subtext of power, identity and desire within their relationship to disclose itself. As Vince stacks up a pile of pornographic videos, he says with some bitterness, "Gay man's legacy, that's what we leave behind. Pile of trash." Stuart's response is firstly to test Vince's feelings by saying that he's found pornographic photographs of children in Phil's belongings. He follows up this tasteless attempt at gallows humour by then saying that Phil had kept dozens of photographs of Vince. Clearly exploiting his friend's emotional vulnerability, a moment of rare compliment disrupts their discourse:

Stuart: ... There's about three dozen, hidden away with this stuff. Just photos of you in the pub, and having a laugh. But dozens of them.

Vince: He hasn't....

Stuart: Course he bloody hasn't! You twat.

(Vince very pissed off: he defends himself, for once)

Vince: Piss off. As a matter of fact, I'm dead good-looking, I was told.

Stuart: Well you are.

Vince: (Thrown by a compliment from Stuart)... oh.

Stuart: Let's go.

After the traumatic ending to Vince's thirtieth birthday party following on the Rosalie scenario, it appears that the relationship between him and Stuart might finally have been placed beyond strain. However, in Episode Eight, Stuart takes the initiative in trying to achieve a reconciliation between himself and Vince. Typically, the contact is made via their mobile phones, a recurring motif and means of instant – if impersonal – communication throughout the series. Furthermore, the mobile phone itself carries with it material connotations of economic upward mobility. Frustrated and perhaps threatened by a continuous mobile phone conversation between Vince and Stuart that interrupts his first dinner date with Vince, Cameron closes the sequence by throwing Vince's phone into the canal. Cameron's purchase of a new telephone for his younger lover is yet another example of his economic status in their relationship – a status that Vince increasingly views as reflecting an increasing and intrusive emotional control.

Thus, when Stuart and Vince meet for a conciliatory lunch at 'Via Fossa,' the conversation immediately turns to Vince's relationship with Cameron – the fundamental element of Stuart's strategy, one imagines:

Stuart: How's Cameron?

Vince: He's great, yeah. Wants me to go on holiday, Melbourne, sounds good.

Stuart: The poor sod. Give him six months, he'll be able to name all the Doctor Whos. In order. (Pause. Then fast) William Hartnell, Patrick Troughton, Jon Pertwee, Tom Baker, Peter Davison, Colin Baker, Sylvester McCoy.

Vince: What about Paul McGann?

Stuart and Vince: (Together, an old joke) Paul McGann doesn't count.

The conversation continues with Vince asserting that his relationship with Cameron was "a bit of a love job" until, unable to sustain Stuart's unspoken but confrontational silence, he suddenly erupts with:

Vince: It pisses me off though. The first one to say 'love,' he's in charge. Puts him in charge. I dunno, it's all a bit... grown up. (He expects Stuart to laugh at that. But Stuart just watches him) You're supposed to ask. If I love him.

Stuart : You can't. You can't even respect him. He loves Vince Tyler, so that makes him stupid. The moment he said it, it all just died.

(Vince tries to resist his own latent realisation of his anxieties about his relationship with Cameron as Stuart comes in for the kill:)

Stuart: You've done nothing, Vince. You go to work, you go for a drink. You sit and watch cheap science fiction. Small and tiny world. What's so impressive about that, what's there to love?

Vince: ...yeah.

Stuart: It was good enough for me.

Stuart's combination of devastating critique as a prelude to the unexpected and uncharacteristic – if oblique – admission of his own feelings towards Vince, perfectly captures the emotional confusion and latent vulnerability at the heart of their relationship. This scene with Stuart proves to be the catalyst shortly afterwards in this final episode of the first series, for Vince to break with Cameron. The final issue that precipitates Vince walking away from the relationship is mundane and domestic – a problem with a squeaking door on Cameron's gift – the car – with him saying to Vince via mobile phone, "It's like waiting for a kid to tidy his bedroom. I paid for the bloody thing, I'll take charge of it." This demeaning of Vince and the positioning of him as a material and emotional dependent proves too much for him. He offers Cameron a final chance of redemption, although it's one that Vince knows his lover cannot fulfil: the reciting of the catechism of all of the actors who've played 'Dr Who.' When, exasperated, Cameron says to him, "What the hell does it matter?" the significance of that dismissal of a personal – if trivial – component of Vince's past and present proves conclusive. Vince pretends that the mobile phone line is breaking up as a poignant and ironic means of bringing the relationship to an end, "Sorry, what? It's breaking up. We're breaking up, sorry…." Locking the keys of the Mini inside the car, Vince walks away literally and metaphorically from a kind of emotional commitment masquerading as yet another form of dependency.

However, perhaps the most crucial encounter between the two men, in terms of the complex dynamics of their relationship, comes in the penultimate episode of the second series in a scenario involving Alexander and the death of his father. Earlier, in Episode Six, there has been an exterior scene in a shopping precinct where Alexander, in the company of Nathan, Cameron and Vince, calls out to a respectable middle-aged couple who walk past with their shopping. As he continues to shout hello at them, their response changes imperceptibly from a simple ignoring of him to a point, at which he becomes, effectively, invisible.

Following on from this scene, Alexander's father is taken into hospital, critically ill and close to death. Conscious, perhaps, of his own strained relationship with his father, Stuart, with Vince's support, urges Alexander to go and visit his father in hospital before he dies. Alexander, deeply wounded after years of rejection and denial, is vigorously opposed to seeing his father. Nevertheless, Alex eventually relents, "All right. I'll go and spit on the bastard, then you'll see," and Stuart drives the three of them to the hospital. The ensuing scene in Part One of the sequel is a compelling and marvelously acted scene, resonant with anger arising out of the calculating manipulation and denial exercised by Alexander's mother upon her son:

> (And when they meet, it's so neutral. No fireworks. Alexander's calm, no performance – not hiding his camp, it's like something's just dead. Mrs Perry exactly the same, a secretary fixing an appointment with a stranger. Vince and Stuart stay a few feet back)

> Alexander: How is he?

> Mrs Perry: Sleeping.

> Alexander: So, what, d'you want me to wait?

> Mrs Perry: Thought we could have a word, there's a tea bar. One or two things to sort out. (of Vince and Stuart) In private.

> (She heads off, Alexander follows. Stuart doesn't even hesitate, he walks with them, and Vince follows)

A scene then follows in which we discover that the sole purpose for inviting Alexander to the hospital is for him to sign away any claims on his father's substantial inheritance. Alexander proceeds to sign it, despite Vince urging him that he should "Read it first, you want to get a lawyer, that's not going to stand up in court." For Alexander, this final, formal and heartless ritual of rejection from his own family, predicated entirely in terms of their homophobic prejudice, leaves him quietly devastated. It also becomes the first stage in a scenario that unwinds with savage intensity, culminating in a moment of violent, cathartic retribution enacted by Stuart. Stuart confronts Mrs Perry in the hospital corridor and she returns his accusative gaze with barely concealed contempt. This non-verbal confirmation of her position in relation to her son and the two men is sufficient for Stuart to move into a dumb show of savage intensity and threat:

(Violence in the air. Very slowly, he brings his arm up, straight, pointing at her head. All his strength, everything he is, concentrated in that arm. Two fingers out. His hand is a gun. She's transfixed. Scared of him. The gun pointing. Stuart's stare, taking aim. Her terror. Then he just relaxes, opens his hand and brings it down. And he smiles)

Stuart : Maybe next time.

(He turns, walks off. Vince runs after him, catches up)

Vince: There's no point in making it worse –

Stuart : Coward.

(Stuart pushes himself forward, not quite shoving Vince aside, but making it clear that he won't walk alongside him. Like Vince has let him down. And Vince knows it. Vince slows down his walk, as though defeated, watching Stuart stride ahead. The growing distance between them)

This scene, with all of its lingering subtext of discrimination and violent retribution signals what will become perhaps the central defining narrative of the series. It concludes Episode One of 'Queer as Folk 2' and provides an ideological and thematic basis for the final evolution of both Stuart's and Vince's characters. Following on from the scene in the hospital, Alexander begins to make a number of pill overdose suicide attempts. This desperate expression of the emotional and psychological pain of estrangement that Alexander is experiencing is the final catalyst for Stuart. He proceeds to devise a means of revenge on the mother – the blowing up of her car. This terrifying argosy of retribution places an almost impossible strain upon the relationship between Vince and Stuart

(Vince looking at Stuart, scared, horrified. Stuart wired, emotional, more dangerous than we've ever seen him)

Vince: You don't even like him.

(Silence. Desperate)

Don't. (Silence)

Let's go home. Come with me.

Stuart: Does she deserve it?

Vince: You'll make it worse.

Stuart: Does she deserve it?

    (Silence. Then:)

Vince: You can't.

Stuart : Watch me.

    (Vince makes his decision. Colder, cutting himself off)

Vince: Yeah. You'd like that. Spent years watching you.

    (And Vince turns and goes)

Stuart: Coward.

    (Vince keeps walking, breaks into a run. Stay with Stuart. A wild grin, almost glad that Vince has gone; now he can do anything. He shouts after him:)

Stuart: Coward!

This profound tension between these two characters epitomises, in the most heightened and even theatrical way, the ideological tension between a politicised queer sensibility and a quasi-assimilationist gay position. In a scene of extraordinary oppositional resonance, signed in the visual aesthetic of a massive fireball scorching through the quiet night air of suburban Altrincham, Stuart blows up Mrs Perry's car, parked on the road outside her house. He has made no attempt to disguise or hide his presence and, indeed, rings her door bell moments before the car explodes:

    Mrs Perry: I'd appreciate it if you didn't come to my house. I don't think we've got anything to say to each other.

    Stuart : Just one thing. (A whisper, gleeful) Bang!

    (And her car explodes)

Stuart then proceeds to walk slowly away to his jeep where his baby son, Alfred, is strapped in the baby seat. This strange inter-mixing of the suburban and the domestic with an act of terror designed to shake bourgeois suburbia to its foundations is potent indeed. Is there a significance to be read in the placing of the son in the geo-ideological location of this moment of violent disruption of the screen of normative, bourgeois social life? From Stuart's viewpoint, one might construct that the child's presence locates Stuart's anticipated positioning of his son within the broader ideological framework of oppression and its dissent.

When, in a subsequent scene, Stuart arrives at Nathan's sixteenth birthday party on Canal Street, Vince is already there, seeking both to distance himself from Stuart's actions and simultaneously sensing an opportunity to provide his friend with a potential alibi. In the following short sequence following on Stuart's arrival at the party, the dialogue again captures perfectly the kernel of opposing views about the marking of queer/gay resistance to the dominant homophobic paradigm:

Stuart: She deserved it.

Vince: I know, but. Just tell her to fuck off, you're always telling them to fuck off –

Stuart: It's not enough any more.

Vince: It is! You can't go and…(Pause. Calmer) There's people relying on me. Mum, and that house, I end up paying the mortgage every other month, that lot don't earn tuppence. I can't start…. (Pause) You're on your own

Stuart: (Colder) Suits me. You're just straight, Vince. You're a straight man who fucks men, that's all.

(Pause. Then, keeping calm)

Vince: I'll phone you.

Stuart's assertion that, "It's not enough any more" is a powerfully succinct expression of a viewpoint that is no longer – if indeed it ever was – interested in strategies of assimilation with the dominant, oppressive ideological construct. Significantly again, Stuart's revolutionary instincts and actions are contextualised from within a position of economic status and power. Equally significant therefore is Vince's heartfelt pragmatism about his own economic status as material support and provider for his mother Hazel and the others who share her house.

After the disastrous birthday party, Vince is both ashamed of his own actions and also anxious that Rosalie will 'out' him at work where he has remained closeted. The implications of this precarious strategy have been highlighted in the first series when the female staff, including Rosalie, have observed two young gay men walking affectionately down a supermarket aisle together. Up to this point, Vince has been following their movements around the store, clearly sexually interested in one or both of them – although they are unaware of his gaze. As the couple passes by Vince and the others, she mimics their sexuality in a gesture encoded within the heterosexual vocabulary of derisory contempt for the 'queer' – the 'limp-wristed' hand gesture. In a moment of excruciating compromise, betrayal and embarrassment, Vince is acknowledging their crude denunciation of the couple by returning a smile of acknowledgment and complicity to the women. As he does so, the two young men turn around and are clearly bemused at Vince's actions in relation to them. Thus, when he sees Rosalie laughing and giggling with her fellow female workers at what is clearly his expense, he fears that he has now become the recipient of their derision:

Rosalie: It was your tie.

(She's standing in the doorway, quiet. Her dignity is worse than her temper)

Rosalie: There was a man on Changing Rooms last night, he was wearing the same tie. We were laughing at your tie.

(Vince just smiles, nods, awkward. Beat)

Rosalie: I've not said anything. In case you're wondering. If you're ashamed, then... that's up to you.

Vince: I'm not ashamed.

Rosalie: You're not exactly proud, Vince. (Beat. She hands him a folder) That's from Carter, he wants it back Monday.

Vince: Yeah, thanks.

(She could go, but she hesitates. A sad smile, because she did fancy him)

Rosalie: It's not that bad. The tie.

Vince, realising Rosalie's affection for him – expressed in her unwillingness to 'out' him at work – and clearly challenged by her stand over his pride and honesty, finally comes out later in the same episode (significantly, it is to Marcie):

Vince: Marcie, can you take that to wages?

Marcie: What did your last slave die of?

Vince: A good beating. It's for Simon Carter, d'you know him? Black hair. Sort of Fox

Mulder look, he's got the best arse in the shop. Put in a word for me. I've always fancied him.

(Marcie gobsmacked)

Vince: Run along.

(And she does. Vince gives Rosalie a smile, saunters back the way he came. King of his domain)

I will conclude my discussion and analysis in a synthesis of the characters of Stuart, Vince and Nathan in the context of the following section exploring the construction of the character of the third, and youngest member of the triumvirate defining the central space of the series.

Nathan Maloney

Nathan: Cos that boy over there. Blue shirt, white T-shirt, dark hair, with the blonde girl, him.... I'm in school with him, right. His name's Christian Hobbs and d'you know what he does? He finds a boy, and if that boy's a bit quiet, if he's a bit different, Christian Hobbs kicks his head in. He kicks them and he calls them queer. That boy there. He beats us up cos we're queer.

(Episode 8)

Much of the original controversy surrounding this series focused on the character of Nathan, principally in respect to the character's age – fifteen – and his involvement in sexually explicit scenes in Episode One. I believe that of the three central characters it is perhaps Nathan who is least successfully developed and who seems to be more evidently a schematic vehicle for other thematic and narrative concerns. Certainly one does witness some development in terms of the character's emotional and sexual journey, and this is most clearly located in terms of him emerging as a younger prototype of his 'mentor' Stuart. Stuart 'cops off' with Nathan in the opening moments of the first series, with Nathan, absolutely infatuated with his older lover, likening that initial sexual encounter to looking up into the 'face of God.' Significantly, Vince reads Stuart's motives quite clearly and endeavours to halt his friend's preparations for what will clearly represent sex with an under-aged minor. Nevertheless, Stuart insists that Nathan must be asked for his choice, and that choice culminates in him spending the night at Stuart's apartment. Stuart insists upon driving Nathan to his school the following day, again, despite Vince's protests. Stuart's jeep has been vandalised overnight by some young boys who have spray-painted 'Queers' on the driver's side. It is a moment of wonderful confrontational verve when Stuart drives his jeep headlong down the driveway to the school, scattering dawdling school children everywhere. As they arrive at the main entrance into the school buildings, Nathan's close friend Donna is introduced, along with a jeering crowd of rowdy boys. The clash between Nathan's sexuality and his personal life are exploded into the public arena of school. Furthermore, Stuart's endemic confrontational style ensures that the ideological delineation of spatial/sexual identity are unmistakably marked:

> (Lots of school kids are watching, lads laughing, taking the piss, as Nathan has to get out in front of them. He's mortified, but shame doesn't matter, he's got to talk to Stuart)

Stuart: Thanks, then. Off you go, first lesson, Home Economics.

Nathan: (Quiet, desperate) Can I see you again?

Vince: Let's just go.

Nathan: Can I see you again?

Stuart: You can see me now....

Nathan: I could meet you tonight –

Stuart: God knows where I'll be tonight, I could be anywhere, I could be in Ipswich –

Boy in Crowd: Come on boys, give 's a kiss.

Stuart: (At the boy, savage) I'll give you a fuck, you tight little virgin, you won't be laughing then.

Vince: We're going! Now! Stuart, just shut your face and drive –

Whilst it's clear that Stuart has no intention of seeing Nathan again, his sexual conquest – consumed and driven by desire – proceeds to search him out and this becomes a strong and central narrative line throughout the first series especially. Navigating that attempted relationship becomes the narrative spine for the development and plotting of Nathan as a character. An important character within the exposition of Nathan's development and the themes of home and school is Donna, a young Afro-Caribbean girl. Her character serves as a very useful means of both enabling Nathan to confide and reflect upon his journey of sexual awakening and as an important counterpoint of marginalised identity and experience. This is communicated with great economy and some latent humour in a scene between the two characters in Episode Five. At this point, Nathan has left home after his mother has confronted him about his sexuality. Even as she has genuinely sought to understand and accept her son, Nathan has not yet the maturity to acknowledge or respond to her efforts. Donna chides Nathan for not appreciating the seriousness of the situation that he is in:

Donna: It's not brilliant! Listen, school hears about this, you'll have Education-Welfare down your back. Happened to Billy Valentine. They put him in care, he disappeared, he went to Cardiff. And he had real problems.

Nathan: I've got real problems!

Donna: Oh like what? Like your mother's been going through your things, big deal.

Nathan: She knew everything, she'd been spying.

Donna: So? She's your mother, it's her job!

Nathan: She thinks if I move back home, I'll go back to normal. Like I'm sick, and I'll get better.

Donna: She never said that –

Nathan: Donna, you don't know her. You don't know anything, cos you're straight, right, you're part of the system, right? You're part of the fascist heterosexual orthodoxy.

(Nathan jogs ahead, Donna's just wry, amused)

Donna: I'm black and I'm a girl, try that for a week.

Disappointingly, and worryingly, Donna remains effectively the only black character in the series, apart from the fleeting view of a black teacher who, perhaps out of moral cowardice and compromise, allows the homophobic taunting of Nathan both before and during lesson time. I will return to that scene later in this section as it represents the climactic moment of Nathan's self-initiated coming out at school. I am not arguing, of course, for some dreadfully misguided and patronising liberal notion of 'ethnic quotas' of characters within contemporary television drama. It does seem to me of huge significance, however, that the geo-ideological spatial construction of the city and its urban identities in 'Queer as Folk' remains so resolutely white and predominantly bourgeois. I shall return to this matter in my concluding chapter.

The continuation of Nathan's journey of self-discovery and self-expression within school is largely constructed in terms of his seemingly binary opposite – the construction of Christian Hobbs as a white, aggressively heterosexual and homophobic bully. The conflict between these two characters is heightened and textured by a scene in the first series where Nathan and Christian become engaged in a sexual encounter. Nathan has followed Christian down to the school changing rooms where his adversary is mopping the floor as some form of punishment. Nathan offers to help him in the context of seeking to make a sexual pass at him. Then, in a scene signed with the erotic subtext of latent arousal and menace, Christian begins to recount an incident of alleged sexual frustration:

Christian: We're behind the house, no one's looking. I've got this fucking boner and she's grabbing it. I'm like, yes, I'm going oaaarh. She's scooping down, she's got me balls an' all. Then she's like pulling. Gripping dead tight. Then she stops, she's got to go home, she fucking stops. (Grabs his own crotch with a hard on) Christ, I'm packing it. (He draws on his cigarette. All the time, not looking at Nathan. Then he sits back, head back, grabs his crotch again, still hard, groans. Then he lets go, stays head back, eyes closed. Like it's a signal)

Within minutes, Nathan is masturbating a sexually aroused Christian and brings him to a sexual climax. Again, apart from the inevitable controversy that such an explicit scene evoked, the scene more significantly returns to the Foucauldian notion of the construction of sexual identity and, by implication, sexual activity. The encounter between Nathan and Christian does not therefore need to lead to earnest or bewildered considerations of whether or not the homophobic bully is or isn't gay/queer. Rather, this scene shows that sexual activity is constructed in terms of its social and cultural context and is authenticated solely in terms of its performative enactment. So, from within this viewpoint, the notion of the ideological defining and positioning of sexual activity is subject to strategies and discourses of power relations. This is an argument that I have already made earlier in this chapter in analysis of the material placement of Stuart Alan Jones.

Returning to the scene between Nathan and Christian, what is of most significance is not, I believe, the issue of constraining that encounter in hetero-homo binary terms. Neither is its explicit nature of paramount importance, other than being the visual exhibition of a crucial moment in the negotiation and formation of power relations. It might be argued, in terms of the dominant cultural and material positioning and privileging of the power relations between the oppressor and the oppressed, that they are crucially, if only temporarily, fractured and usurped. This fracturing in the context and function of pleasured desire and its fulfilment creates an alternative and revolutionary interpretative space, that allows for the reconfiguration of ideological positions otherwise predicated as given, inevitable or 'natural.' Within the relationship between Nathan and Christian therefore, this temporary undermining of the prevailing dominant relations between the two boys becomes both potentially disruptively liberating, whilst simultaneously, as in all revolutionary struggles, precipitating sometimes violent conflict. It is not surprising therefore that the next principal viewing of Christian is with his gang proceeding to beat up a smaller and younger boy nicknamed Midge. Given Nathan's traumatic disruption of Christian's dominant hetero-aggressive, oppressor role, it is entirely appropriate that it is Christian's sudden realisation that Nathan has witnessed the oppression that stimulates him into more violent action:

(Nathan and Donna watch as the mates tug at the bag, taunting him, like they're trying to push Midge into a fight. And they're calling out: poofter, shit-stabber. So far, it's not too rough, only potentially violent. But then Christian catches Nathan's eye, holds the look for a second. Then Christian launches forward at Midge)

> Christian: Fucking queer. (He kicks Midge on the back of the knees, so Midge falls on the floor. Nathan and Donna keep walking)

It is later on in the series, as Nathan must learn to endure and overcome the strategies of oppression at school, that he witnesses Christian and his girlfriend, Cathy, at the 'New Union' in Canal Street. For Nathan this becomes a significant moment in his self-empowerment, a critical moment in a process that carries not only personal but political resonance. Nathan, Donna and the others are enjoying a night out at the pub when Nathan sees Christian and his girlfriend. Worse for Nathan, Christian looks across and smiles at Nathan as if they are friends. Initially his anger disempowers him and he makes to leave the pub saying to Donna, "What's the point of staying here?" For Nathan at this crucial point, his sexual identity, located within a spatial position defined as gay/affirmative, is intruded upon by the penetrative presence of his oppressor. If Nathan leaves, he is signaling a concession to that oppression which will predicate further intrusions. Equally, and significantly in terms of the politics of both this scene and the series as a whole, if he stays and returns the patriarchal, positioning smile of Christian, he effectively colludes in the meta-narrative of oppression. It is hugely significant that Nathan chooses to resist and confront by making eye contact with Stuart:

> (Eye contact. On Stuart, then Nathan… connected across the distance. Keep the moment of suspension going, as though Nathan suddenly sees everything clearly. Nathan turns to look at Christian (who's now so attentive to Cathy). Nathan looks at the stage. He looks across at Vince and Cameron, now back with Hazel, Bernard and Alexander. And then he looks back at Stuart. It's like Nathan grows in height. Inspired)

> Donna: You coming, then?

> Nathan: What, like I've been driven out? What's this place for, Donna, what's it for?

Thus Nathan makes his decision to go up onto the stage, seemingly to perform as a karaoke participant. However, it is not someone else's script or song that Nathan is to sing. Rather, it is the moment of performative self-enactment and assertion, a proud and courageous self-scripted moment. Nathan, in choosing to 'out' Christian's virulent homophobia within a geo-ideological space of resistance, carries the struggle and the battle back into the territory of the oppressor and his attempted colonisation of the gay/queer/lesbian location. Significantly, Nathan does not 'out' Christian's pre-evidenced sexual activity. This in itself reflects an important consequence of his self-empowering positioning in that it secures and signals ideologically produced excess. Out of that excess, Nathan is enabled to consolidate his renewed position of power in the struggle, in terms of the offering of patronage, predicated on a position of earned privilege. I want to offer a slightly extended version of the quote with which I opened this section dealing with Nathan

Nathan: Cos that boy over there. Blue shirt, white T-shirt, dark hair, with the blonde girl, him.... His name's Christian Hobbs. And Christian Hobbs, d'you know what he does? He finds a boy, and if that boy's a bit quiet, if he's a bit different, Christian Hobbs kicks his head in. He kicks them and he calls them queer. That boy there. He beats us up cos we're queer.

(And only now, we've reached 90% silence (never 100%), the Union staring at Christian. Hold the silence, eyes drilling into Christian. Then Bernard stands, stronger than we've ever seen him)

Bernard: Oy, Sunny Jim! That's your cue to fuck off out. (During all of this, Cathy Mott's been humiliated. She grabs her coat, about to go. Christian automatically goes to follow, she turns, hisses "Piss off!" Cathy walks out, Christian turns back to look at Nathan. Furious. But now Nathan's smiling. He looks so much older)

Nathan: Plenty more I could have said, Christian. And that's a favour.

Of course, this is one encounter and one victory in the struggle that Nathan must engage in to establish and assert himself and his sexuality. I now want to complete this important element of the construction and function of Nathan as a co-central character within the series by briefly discussing the further developments within that ideological struggle of identity and desire.

The inevitable counter-attack occurs and moves towards a climax in the second series when Christian, in the security of his own spatial territory at school where he is furthermore supported by his gang, seeks to wrest back the initiative and punish Nathan. In the first scene outside of a classroom, Christian and the gang taunt Nathan loudly and without restraint, even in the hearing and presence of the teacher about to take the class. Nathan endeavours to secure a precarious position of resistance in what is a hugely threatening situation for him:

John: (Grabs crotch) Oh yeah, d'you want it? D'you want some of this? Come on, AIDS boy, suck me off.

Christian: He's got a stiffy, look at him.

Nathan: (At Christian) You'd know all about that.

(A Teacher, middle-aged man, comes up to the classroom to unlock the door and lead them in)

Christian: He fancies me! Sir, Nathan Maloney fancies me! Tell him!

John: He's a poof, sir, he's a queer.

The scene continues to rise in provocative abuse, with the teacher failing to intervene until Nathan explodes with a violent "Piss off!" to his attackers as they attempt to steal his bag:

(And now the Teacher turns round, severe)

Teacher: All right, Nathan that's enough of the language.

Nathan: Me?! What about them?

Teacher: I said that's enough,

Faced by this counter-victory for Christian, Nathan continues to realise that he must find a means and strategy to exercise a comparable self-empowerment to that which he discovered and used in the scene at the 'New Union.' In a scene shortly after this one, he finally manages to find a way of countering their oppressive behaviour towards him, through the pro-active, public queering of the dominant ideological space. Nathan finds himself with the same teacher at registration a few days later and again has to suffer the audible homophobic abuse from the others: "How was the party? Did you get it shoved up your arse all night?" Nathan has now reached a point of no return where he recognises a counter-offensive tactic open to him in the context of the calling of the register. In time honoured fashion, the teacher calls out the pupil's names and they reply with a cursory "here." When the teacher calls out "Maloney," Nathan responds with, "Queer":

(Beat. Silence. The Teacher looks up at Nathan, his authority challenged. Cold:)

Teacher: I beg your pardon.

Nathan: I said queer.

Teacher: I'm aware of that –

Nathan: Oh that's a miracle! Cos they say it, and you don't hear a thing!

Teacher: I don't think I like your tone of voice –

(Nathan not shouting, absolutely in control)

Nathan: I don't like yours. And if you want to make something out of this, sir, that's fine with me. Go on, send me to the headmaster, I'd love it, cos there's plenty I can tell him. And get my mother in, she'd love it, she'd love to meet you, sir, d'you want to do that? Go on. Take it further.

The teacher backs down in the face of Nathan's courageous confrontation of his silent complicity with the bullies. By reclaiming the pejorative, defining language of his oppressors and translating it into a term of proud assertion, Nathan has secured at the very least a breathing space. More importantly, he has learnt a crucial strategic lesson in the political warfare of sexual identity and its expression.

Happy Families?

> Stuart: D'you know why they chose me? Cos I'm rich, and cos I'm handsome as fuck! And that's all! She said so, that fucking Lisa. I'm just a gene pool to them, I'm just spunk!
>
> (Episode Two)

> Cameron: (To Stuart) What is it, a family? All those people gathered round, your own little make-believe family. If you think that's a family then you're fucked.
>
> (Episode Six)

In this, the final section of the chapter, I want to examine the ways in which notions of family and family relationships are constructed in the series. In doing so, I shall be addressing the following sub-sections, based on thematic character clusters in the main:

• Stuart, Lisa, Romey and Alfred.
• Vince, Hazel and Bernard.
• Nathan, Janice and Roy Maloney.

In earlier parts of this chapter, I discussed other examples of problematic family relationships in terms of Stuart's relationship with his parents, sister and nephews and Alexander's traumatic experience of his parental relationships. Clearly those discussions and analysis offer a useful background and context for the material in this final section.

At the beginning of the series, discussed above, the viewer discovers that Stuart is the surrogate father for a baby boy, his chosen name being Alfred. This is in the context of an established lesbian couple, Lisa and Romey, wanting a baby. It is Romey who carries the baby, impregnated through a sperm donation from Stuart. Romey and Lisa are white and bourgeois with Lisa having employment as a successful solicitor. The delineation of these characters carefully avoids dominant ideological stereotypes of butch and femme with the accent being rather on their effective cultural assimilation with the dominant hetero-culture. Ideologically therefore, they are 'Stonewall' rather than 'Outrage' or 'QueerNation.' As Russell Davies says in his script directions for their first appearance in the maternity ward, "Lisa is a classic lipstick lesbian." The choice of name for the newly-born baby is a consequence of a camply humorous discussion at the bedside when Stuart, pointedly wanting an 'ironic' name for the baby, suggests Alfred and turns to Vince for his thoughts. Vince, with an encyclopaedic knowledge of popular film and television culture, he is able to do a masterly reference check on the name:

> Vince: Alf Roberts, Alfie, Michael Caine, Alf that American sitcom with the puppet – bit dodgy, but that's forgotten by the time he's in school, unless they run it on cable, I bet it's on Bravo. Oh! Alfred's the name of Batman's butler, marvelous. Good name.

Thus, with his name established to have the appropriate camp, ironic credentials the baby is called Alfred. Like sensible liberal progressives, the two women have made good use of Lisa's legal expertise to draw up contracts ensuring that Stuart will support the baby financially. Furthermore, there is the contractual expectation that he will also spend leisure and parental care time with his child. The fact that issues of care and parenting have to be legislated for Stuart becomes the reliable predictor of both his self-centred lifestyle and, indeed, for continuing conflicts and tensions between the lesbian couple and Stuart. Immediately after the scene in the maternity ward, and just prior to the 'Titanic' motif discussed earlier in the chapter, Vince and Stuart find themselves alone on the hospital rooftop. In what becomes a character dialogue-signature for Stuart, he has to undermine and counter-score any expression of parental feelings:

> Vince: It's weird isn't it? (Silence) I mean he's real, just seeing him, it's like... I don't know what it's like, I mean it's brilliant, but it's weird.

> Stuart : Most expensive wank I've ever had.

Stuart finds the demands of having to share in childcare duties extremely problematic and this undoubtedly brings tensions into the relationship between himself, Lisa and Romey. However, the real and ultimately serious tensions between the two women comes from when a third party enters their home – a black post-graduate student called Lance Amponah. Initially Romey offers him accommodation in their shared home, but this leads to increasing insecurities and tensions within their relationship. The principal consequence that arises from these tensions is Lisa becoming jealous of Romey's relationship with Lance, a relationship that is to lead to Romey agreeing to marrying him in order that he can stay in Britain. There are two consecutive scenes in Episode Seven which are crucial to the exposition of both the inherent vulnerabilities within the lesbian relationship, and the drastic lengths that Lisa is prepared to go to in order to try and salvage that relationship. Having been regularly, and with some considerable justification, chastised by the two women for his emotional irresponsibility, Stuart takes some pleasure in reversing that dynamic in the following scene. He and Lisa are walking through the park, pushing Alfred in his buggy:

Lisa: Don't pretend you're not bothered. The moment she marries him, your child will have a new father.

Stuart: I'm much more interested in why it bothers you.

(Pause. Lisa hates being vulnerable in front of him. But needs must)

Lisa: He's moved in permanently. Just in case the Home Office checks up. He's got things in our bedroom – her bedroom. Just in case.

Stuart: (Delighted) He's sleeping with her! Oh my God, they're having sex!

Lisa: Stuart. I have every good reason to believe she's a lesbian.

Stuart: Have they? Have they shagged?

Lisa: (Ignores him) She's put his name on the deeds to the house. Just in case. It's her house, she can do what she wants. (Beat, more edgy) I've been living there for six years. Paying half the mortgage. With nothing in writing.

Stuart: (Enjoying her discomfort) And you the solicitor.

Lisa: If Romey and I split up, I'd get nothing.

Stuart: Aah, and I thought this was a love story, it's just a mortgage.

Stuart's ruthless glee at Lisa's predicament is used as a subtextual means of critiquing the material values underpinning her relationship with Romey but also, inevitably, the extent to which such considerations become inextricably intertwined with emotional needs and insecurities. In terms of these considerations and, indeed, my earlier comments concerning the couple's social and cultural assimilation with bourgeois norms, the dynamics of distrust and sexual envy/insecurity are indistinguishable from an equivalent heterosexual couple. This carries important connotations in terms of the construction and signing of the principal lesbian relationship within the series. The predominant straight liberal reading of both homogeneity and tolerated difference in terms of gay/lesbian relationships is exposed as a misreading, and possibly an avoidance of, the prevailing bourgeois, material values that appear to dictate the domain of Lisa's relationship with Romey. Therefore, in terms of notions and strategies of tolerance or assimilation, it seems rather as if there is a depressing familiarity of self-interest, even in intimate and social relationships which might more usually be expected to carry alternative constructions. In respect of the dynamics between Lisa and Romey, their relationship is signified in terms of dominant hetero-bourgeois paradigms, rather than offering any form of radical, alternative social formation.

Lisa proceeds, in the following scene, to ask for Stuart's help in her plan to subvert Romey's attempts to marry Lance:

Lisa: First six months we went out, she wrote to me all the time. She thinks letters are romantic, it's the sort of thing she does. Still writes to me now, like it's some sort of record. The thoughts of Romey Sullivan.

Stuart: (Grins) Lesbian letters. Can I read them?

Lisa : I doubt it, it's joined-up handwriting. But they'll make the Home Office see things in a different light. (Gets out an official letter) Here's the address, it's a Mrs Lake, she's in charge of Lance's visa application –

Stuart: Hold on, why've I got to send them?

Lisa: These could only have come from inside the house.

Stuart: You send them!

Lisa: You're in and out of that house all the time. And, of course, you're a malicious bastard.

Stuart: We could send them anonymously.

Lisa: They've still come from inside the house, someone's got to take the blame. And Romey's going to be furious, she'll never forgive you. But she's got a very good solicitor to remind her that she can't deny the father access.

Stuart: So it all becomes my fault – ?

Lisa: (More direct) I look after that kid every day, every night he's screaming the place down, you owe me.

Stuart eventually sees his relationship with Nathan as a means of getting the letters sent to the Home Office from outside of the house. Nathan negotiates a position with Stuart in which, following on Stuart's attempt to seduce him as a means of securing Nathan's compliance, Nathan explains that he will do it without the incentive of sexual favours, if only Stuart will ask him directly. This arrangement is secured and events unfold according to Lisa's expectations. After a violent scuffle in which Lance punches the arresting officer, Romey is distraught and assumes that Stuart is the perpetrator, only to be doubly shocked to discover that it is Nathan who has sent the letters. This whole network of deception and betrayal creates a depressing scenario of lives and relationships compromised through insecurity, self-interest and guilt. Furthermore, while Lisa has secured her aim of maintaining her placement in the relationship, its future is surely problematic, predicated as it is on deception, guilt and a corrosive insecurity.

The construction of family in relation to the social grouping of Vince, his mother – Hazel – and Bernard, her lodger, represents an interesting example of a signing of 'family' which is, perhaps, the most socially cohesive and supportive. Interestingly, it is this social format that is able to welcome and assimilate others from outside its defined constituents. Consequently, when Nathan experiences difficulties in his own nuclear family unit, it is Hazel and Bernard who agree to allow him to lodge with them for a time. However, it must be said that Vince doesn't wholly support their altrusim as he is only too aware of the economic strain placed upon them as it is. This family unquivocally represent the economic placement and ensuing hardships of Manchester's white-working class. Hazel and Bernard are both unemployed and they are obliged to carry out poorly paid 'home work' in which, amongst other things, they are paid a pittance to make down-market Christmas Crackers. Paid on a piece-work basis, it's a form of exploitative cheap labour, recognisable in Dickens' novels of a century earlier. Vince is obliged, therefore, to support them financially, keeping him bound to a conventional construct of a managerial career at the supermarket where he works. There exists a strong contrast between the material conditions that define the lives of these characters in comparison to the signs of wealth and excess attendant upon Stuart.

There is a very funny scene in Episode Two where Hazel is introduced for the first time. The setting is the 'New Union' pub and Stuart, Vince, Phil and Nathan are enjoying a night out:

(On the stage – a line of men and women, old, young, fat, thin, miming the actions to Rolf Harris's 'The Ladies of the Court of King Caractacus' – an old crowd pleaser. From the crowd, Hazel clambers up, elbows her way into the middle, joins in)

Phil: Just in time, would you look at that old slapper?

Stuart: She needs locking up.

Vince: Some people have no shame.

Nathan: (Trying to join in) She's like a twat isn't she?

Stuart: That's Vince's mother.

Nathan: (Thinks it's still a joke) Yeah, like, imagine if she was, a proper twat like that.

(Cut to – Hazel. She sees the boys, waves)

Hazel: Vinnie!

Vince: Mum.

    (Nathan's horrified. Stuart pretends to be cold, offended)

Stuart: Just be careful next time.

Vince: I don't mind honestly, she's off her head.

Phil: We don't see your mother down here, Stu. Funny, that…. How are they, Mr and Mrs Jones? Still waiting for the Golden Boy to get married?

Nathan: (Suddenly) Cos like my mother, she'd kill me if she knew I was here, like we're watching Emmerdale and Zoe Tate was having that lesbian wedding, and my mother stood up and turned it off.

Phil: That's not homophobia, that's good taste.

The positioning of Hazel in the social and cultural world of her gay son and the ease with which she is accepted and assimilated is one of the most uncomplicatedly affirming narrative strategies within the series. Her pragmatic generosity towards others and sheer sense of life and energy is compelling and believable. This character plays an important strategic role in negotiating Nathan's painful and problematic coming out in terms of his family life. A warm and mutually affirming relationship develops between Hazel and Janice – Nathan's patiently loving mother, who seeks to support her son's sexuality, even in the context of the emotional confusions and difficulties that this process inevitably entails. In the following scene, Janice confronts her son about her concerns, even as she lets him drive her around to the 'Cash and Carry':

Janice: …have you got a boyfriend?

    (Silence, as that·sinks in. Nathan stares ahead, driving, dying inside. Janice barely leaves a pause, keeps going, all of this unplanned)

Janice: I'm not really asking, you don't have to say, but…. And I don't mind, I really don't mind, but I'm not daft, love. You're going out at night, you're not round at Donna's – and I'm not having a go, I'm just saying – I'm sorry, love, go on, pull into the side – (He keeps driving. More honest) You're fifteen years old, that's what I'm worried about, you're fifteen. I don't know where you're going. I don't know what you're doing –

Nathan: (Anguished) I'm not doing anything, I'm not –

Janice: All right. I don't mind, I'm just saying, it's not being gay, I don't mind about that –

Nathan: I'm not, all right?

Janice: Okay, look, that's enough, pull in here.

(He's about to pull in, but Janice can't stop herself)

Janice: So who's Stuart?

In the context of Nathan's continuing and complete infatuation with Stuart and the latter's continuing display of brutal indifference towards him, Vince feels angry when Nathan arrives at Hazel's house in search of accommodation, following on the scene above. Vince knows all too well that Stuart is responsible for the situation developing this way, and recognises the additional financial burden that it will place upon Hazel and, effectively, himself:

Stuart: Pack him off home.

Vince: You do it, he's your problem.

Stuart: Fuck off, Vince. (Heads for the door) I'm going for a piss. (He goes)

Hazel: We should phone his mother, she'll be frantic. What if he's lying now, what if he is in danger?

Bernard: It's cock. That's all it is, cock.

Vince: Thanks for that, Bernie.

Bernard: Fifteen, and your mother finds out, it's not (indicates inverted commas) 'gay,' it's not 'homosexual,' it's cock. Your mother knows you like cock. (Beat) And fair dos. It is revolting.

Bernard's bleakly and crudely 'Freudian' analysis of what is at the core of the problem shows an example of a working-class homosexual man who is clearly in a mix of self-loathing and frank acknowledgment of the centrality and potency of the phallus. Bernard is an odd kind of surrogate partner to Hazel and yet there is genuine, robust humour and warmth between the two:

Hazel: You know you're getting old when the drama queens start looking younger.

Nathan: (Plaintive) Can't I stay here then, just for tonight?

Vince: He's stupid enough, he could run off.

(Hazel looks at Bernard)

Bernard: Christ, does that mean I'm sleeping with you?

Hazel: You know you want it.

The acceptance and good humour that characterises this alternative family structure is certainly preferable for Nathan in terms of his relationship with his father who remains virulently homophobic. Significantly, it is Stuart who – as in the situation with Alexander previously discussed – insists upon driving Nathan back to his home to try and forge a relationship with Roy Malone, his father. As Stuart says to Nathan

> Stuart: Nathan, your mother and father know. You don't know how lucky you are. Go and argue, go and shout, go and – go and watch telly with them. I don't care. Just get in there.

However, as Stuart prepares to give Nathan a kiss goodbye, Roy Malone arrives in his car and with murderous intent begins to smash into the back of Stuart's jeep. By nature and status an unassuming deputy bank manager, he is now consumed with rage:

> Roy: Nathan, get inside the house. (At Stuart, voice building) He's fifteen years old. He's fifteen. That boy is fifteen!
>
> Stuart: (Loves the danger) So? That jeep's only six months, and you've still gone and buggered it!
>
> Roy: You little bastard –

Realising the level of danger and potential emotional and physical violence that he's helped to incite, Stuart reverses manically in his jeep to rescue Nathan and drive him away.

Although Nathan attempts an eventual return to his home and a proposed reconciliation with his father, motivated by his sense of self-affirmation following on his 'outing' of Hobbs at the pub, his return home lasts only as long as it takes for his father's disgust with his sexuality to be expressed:

> Roy: You've made your mind up, and it's obvious there's no stopping you. It's Helen I'm worried about, she's ten years old, she's a child. I don't want her head filled with notions.

Nathan: Like what?

> (Close up Roy, right in Nathan's face: rage and fear in his eyes)

– A Manchester Heterotopia? 'Queer as Folk' –

Roy: As far as Helen's concerned, the anus is for shit. Got that?

(And Roy walks out. On Nathan, struck dumb. Pull out on him, just standing in the kitchen, suddenly young again. The house around him seems small and dark)

The complex problems and issues surrounding the relationship between affirming and expressing a gay/queer sexual identity within a wider social environment which, despite changes in legislation concerning, for example, the gay age of consent, are powerfully communicated in these encounters between Nathan and his father. I shall return to some of these issues in my concluding chapter.

'Queer as Folk' will undoubtedly and unsurprisingly prove to be a landmark television drama, not only in terms of its depiction of fundamental aspects of both gay/lesbian/queer sexuality, and in its uncompromising attempt to explore and discuss ideological tensions within the diverse expressions of those sexual orientations. In this very important respect, it is of special interest to consider the contrast between 'Queer as Folk' and 'Tales of the City,' both broadcast on British television within a relatively short space of each other.

It seems clear to me that 'Queer as Folk' represents a much more unswervingly confrontational perspective and attack upon assimilationist positions both within and outside of the gay community. Its extravagant and uninhibited visual grammar of gay sexual behaviour is in vivid contrast to 'Tales of the City' and 'More Tales of the City' in which the visual depiction of gay men naked together is restricted. Furthermore, whereas the viewer/audience sees Michael and Jon in bed together after their first sexual encounter, there is never any visual display of their active sexual relationship. Equally, in those scenes in 'Tales'/'More Tales' where the predatory nature of casual sexual relationships in the San Franciscan Bath Houses is being explored, the gay male characters are presented with towels strategically draped around their lower bodies and genitalia. Furthermore when, for example, Jon is picked up by Beauchamp at a Bath House, their imminent sexual intimacy is alluded to rather than exhibited. Equally significant I believe, is the searing satirical treatment – with its attendant social critique – that Maupin applies to the status-ridden, prejudicial attitudes and activities of the Gay 'A-List' constituents. Throughout both series, Maupin's, and the production team's treatment of issues of gay sexuality is informed and defined in terms of a plea for tolerance, acceptance and assimilation, counterbalanced by Maupin's wryly acerbic, but compassionate, humour.

By contrast, the dominant performative aesthetic of 'Queer as Folk' is, as I have evidenced and discussed in this chapter, much more fully uncompromising in its exercise of a visual display of sexual pleasure and consumption. The construction of its principal fictive characters is accordingly more complex, allowing for a wider range of the play of binary oppositions. Within that geo-ideological terrain of contradiction and indeterminancy, multiple closures are exposed for view and interpretation. I shall return to these issues in the final chapter.

I want to conclude with an extract from an article by Michael Collins published in *The Observer* on 30 January 2000:

So what was the real impact of the series? If television programmes really can change lives, and change views, the all-dancing, all-rimming first episode of this series was a contender before its opening credits had hit the screen, such was the fanfare that heralded its arrival. Also, emerging as it did at the tail end of the century, it was perfectly pitched. Here was a gauge of how a homosexual lifestyle had become accepted in the eyes of the straight world, and Britain in particular. A hundred years before it was the criminal act that put Oscar Wilde in Reading gaol; now it was in the nation's living rooms, complete with soundtrack, and, subsequently, video, DVD and book.

Notes

The following articles/papers are all published in the excellent anthology edited by Medhurst and Munt (1997) *Lesbian and Gay Studies – A Critical Introduction*, Cassell. Page references refer to that volume.

1. Affrica Taylor, A Queer Geography, p. 8.
2. Alan Sinfield, Identity and Subculture, p. 209.
3. Judith Halbertsram, Sex Debates, p. 332.

5   'Homicide – Life on the Street'

In this final case-study chapter, I want to turn my attention to the long-running popular American television police drama series, 'Homicide – Life on the Street.' Set in the east coast city of Baltimore, this television drama explores issues of policing within an American urban environment of a mix of ethnicity, class and race. Based on David Simon's best selling book *Homicide – a Year on the Killing Streets*, the series enjoyed a form of cult status and following within America. In Britain it was screened on Channel 4 in a post-midnight slot, usually broadcast as a single hour-long episode at about one-thirty in the morning. The scheduling of the series in Britain at this time clearly carries with it connotations of perceptions of the show and its audience, which I will discuss in my concluding chapter.

In his exhaustive and informative account of the making of the series, *Homicide: Life on the Screen*, Todd Hoffman seeks in his opening chapter to place the series in the wider historical context of post-war American society and the genre of the police series within American popular culture:

> The 1960s and early 1970s was a tumultuous period when such inversions seemed to be the rule rather than the exception. Civil rights, Vietnam, new moral standards, drug use all exerted unprecedented pressures on a justice system few people had had realised was on the verge of breakdown.... African Americans had to protest in the streets to achieve nothing more than the dignity and respect promised by the Bill of Rights.... Rifts within American society – between races, classes, generations – were becoming more visible and vocal. They had always been there but now they were making the nightly news. Police, shown whaling away on anti-war activists who were asserting their own concept of patriotism and blacks who had the effrontery to demand equality, were seen defending a political status quo that was fading fast.[1]

Within this social and political environment of reaction to long-standing, structural inequalities and injustices within American society, the notion of what constituted justice, law and order and its legitimate enforcement, became of growing critical interest, within the dual arenas of political debate and popular culture. The complex and problematic nature of the causes of crime, especially in the American inner city amongst poor black and white communities, began to be moved towards the centre of the debate. This process had inevitable consequences, in terms of popular television drama, of raising issues of the construction and representation of class, ethnicity and race within those programmes. Furthermore, if the previous decade's assumptions about the function and role of the police within society and television drama were now being challenged, how would those traditional stereotypes of unimpeachable, paternalistic and reactionary policemen be reversed and transformed?

In the case of 'Homicide' one important element in terms of the piece's stylistic and generic texture of authenticity lies in the circumstances in which Simon's original book was written. A reporter on the newspaper *The Baltimore Sun*, Simon established a fine reputation for himself as a crime reporter. Having spent four years in this work, he then requested a one-year sabbatical to shadow the Baltimore homicide unit. Despite some serious and enduring reservations by some serving policemen in that unit, Simon was finally given the permission he sought. The result is a compellingly written piece of investigative journalism that also serves as a unique, primary source social document of policing within the environment of a contemporary American city. Its principal characters also take on a distinctly fictional signification, both through Simon's crime-thriller style – reminiscent of Ed McBain – and, more pragmatically, in the transposing of real officer's names into fictional identities. The following short extract conveys a characteristic and idiosyncratic sense of the piece's texture and tempo:

> One in the morning, heart of the ghetto, half a dozen uniforms watching their breath freeze over another dead man – what better time and place for some vintage Landsman, delivered in perfect deadpan until even the shift commander is laughing hard in the blue strobe of the emergency lights. Not that a Western District midnight shift is the world's toughest audience: you don't ride a radio car for any length of time in Sector 1 or 2 without cultivating a diseased sense of humour. "Anyone know this guy?" asks Landsman. "Anyone get to talk to him?" "Fuck no," says a uniform. "He was ten-seven when we got here." Ten seven. The police communication code for "out of service" artlessly applied to a human life. Beautiful. Pellegrini smiles, content in the knowledge that nothing in this world can come between a cop and his attitude.[2]

The beat and tempo of Simon's account – cool, urban and played almost like a jazz riff, communicates a strong sense of effectively stylised disillusionment and disconnection from the murder and its investigation. The narrative is mediated through and from a viewpoint of dispassionate masculinity. The piece also evidences the internal vocabulary of the homicide unit, predicated on the basis of sub-cultural institutionalised codes. For example, from the inherent and given status of the narrative voice, uniformed policemen are linguistically and ideologically diminished to the singular 'uniform.' Equally and far more disconcertingly, the dead victim is signed and de-valued within a procedural scale of numeral codification: 'Ten Seven.' The very numeric code designed to signify a vehicle out of service becomes, effectively, the nomenclature for a dead human being. In the process, the human being becomes dehumanised, a manageable and wearily predictable commodity.

Baltimore is viewed within America as an unglamorous and frankly, unfashionable city. It is also a relatively small city of 800,000 inhabitants. Nevertheless, it has a much bleaker and chilling reputation as one of the country's major locations for murders. As Hoffman (p. 43) observes, in 1988 when Simon completed his sabbatical, there were 234 murders. From 1990 onwards, there were over 300 murders committed each year, with 1993 claiming the bleakest notoriety as the year in which homicides reached their highest figure of 353.

In my discussion and analysis of this series, I evaluate certain specific episodes in the chronological order in which they were broadcast. Each of these episodes featured in Season Six, broadcast in America during 1997–98 and broadcast on Channel 4 in Britain in the following years 1998–99. I have chosen to evaluate each episode separately because of the issue-based narrative drive of the series as a whole. Inevitably however, there are some important sub-plot and recurring thematic concerns that run across and through individual episodes. Therefore, where necessary and appropriate, I extend my discussion across the broadcast time boundaries of individual episodes. Each episode, as discussed, will be given its title, episode number, teleplay author(s), story line author(s), director and original American broadcast date.

602. Blood Ties (2)

TELEPLAY: David Simon
STORY: Tom Fontana and James Yashimura
DIRECTOR: Nick Gomez
BROADCAST DATE: 24 October 1997

This episode is the middle episode of a three part special, which focuses upon issues surrounding race, ethnicity, power and justice within contemporary Baltimore. I want to base my own short discussion of this episode upon those themes whilst placing them within the meta-narrative of the episode and Series Six.

The background to the plot line of this episode is that two killings have taken place – one, the murder of Melia Brierre, the maid of a successful, local black businessman and benefactor, Felix Wilson. The second killing is arguably also a murder but is perpetrated by the young white Homicide detective, Kellerman, against a notorious black gangster and drug dealer, Luther Mahoney. Kellerman has alleged that he shot Mahoney at point blank range in order to save the lives of another officer, Lewis, and himself. There remains the strong and likely possibility that Kellerman effectively murdered Mahoney, who had his hands held in surrender when the detective fired. This incident happened in the previous series. While the motives for Kellerman's actions remain suitably ambiguous, one clear possible interpretation is that the detective has taken upon himself the moral role of judge, jury and executioner in killing a local criminal known to be responsible for many drug and vice related crimes. The second principal sub-plot in this episode relates to the seemingly casual, remorseless murder by a New York-based criminal of a criminal associate at a baseball game in Baltimore.

The investigation of the murder of Brierre becomes the catalyst for a vivid exposure of latent racial tensions and prejudices within the Homicide squad. It also serves as the means by which anxieties about racial and ethnic sub-cultural power bases threaten the impartial execution of justice. Within the Homicide squad, the four African American characters are Frank Pembleton, Al Giardello, Meldrick Lewis and a new recruit from the Sex Crimes Squad, Stivers. Lt Al "Gee" Giardello is the Homicide commanding officer and is played with a potent sense of quiet authority and moral dignity by Yaphet Kotto. As his name suggests, Giardello is of African American and American Italian parentage, an embodiment of the multi-cultural and multi-ethnic construction of Baltimore as an urban space. Detective Francis Xavier Pembleton is, perhaps, one of the most enduring and important characters across the entire six series history of this television drama. Played with a searing sense of internalised conflict set against a social code of dispassionate detachment by Andre Braugher, Pembleton is in some ways the signing of moral anxiety within the ideological problematics of policing within the series. Significantly, Pembleton is constructed as having grown up in a Catholic environment and this sense of interior ethical conflict is expertly explored throughout the second series, especially in the episodes 'Something Sacred' and 'Mercy.'

Pembleton is an experienced and, in terms of conviction-rates, a successful officer within the squad. His construction – along with that of Giardello in particular – is significant in terms of the intelligent and articulate black protagonist, driven by a passionate sense of justice and yet painfully aware of the complex geo-ideological environment in which he and the others must function.

It is therefore a moment of unexpected moral and professional crisis when Detective Peter Gharty (a white middle-aged detective of American Irish background) confronts Pembleton. Gharty challenges Pembleton by accusing him of compromising his professional judgment by allegedly protecting Felix Wilson (a successful black businessman and benefactor) and his family from interrogation. What makes Gharty's outburst and strategy even more pertinent is the character has only recently arrived in the squad at the start of Season Six. Gharty is therefore a relative outsider and this position within the narrative is significant in terms of the hierarchical code of loyalty and deference within the squad. It is not surprising, therefore, that Gharty's accomplice in angrily challenging Pembleton's motives in the Wilson/Brierre case is another newcomer, Detective Laura Ballard. The fictional (and actual) Homicide squad is predominantly male and the character of Ballard becomes an important means of female and feminist discourse within Series Six. The following extract from this episode communicates the latent anger, insecurity and racial prejudice that underlies some of those empowered to discharge justice with unconditional impartiality. Just prior to the following dialogue sequence, Giardello has entered, seething with a barely-restrained anger that someone from within the squad has leaked information to the local newspaper, *The Baltimore Sun* which has proceeded to besiege the Wilson household. Pembleton clearly suspects either Ballard or Gharty of providing the leak:

Gharty: No hard questions, then, for rich swanks, eh, Pembleton?

Bayliss: Hey, Gharty, whose house you in? Frank here has cleared more cases than the two of you ever will in a lifetime.

Gharty: This is his house? I'm a guest?

Pembleton: The Wilsons have done nothing wrong. Then again, why should that matter to you two?

Gharty: They're black, they're rich, so all bets are off. Anyone else would be in the Box, sweating.

The 'house' is a euphemistic expression for a space that is essentially marked in metaphorical and ideological terms – the Homicide squad itself and also Pembleton's position within that site of mapped jurisdiction and law enforcement. However, the 'house' also signifies a site defined in terms of its literal and ideological ownership by a specific interest group, defined in terms of race, ethnicity or even business activities, legal or illegal. Gharty, older than Pembleton and from another 'house', namely, the the American Irish community (which has had its earlier historical political dominance in Baltimore) cannot abide the thought that his presence either in the squad or the investigation is as a 'permitted guest.' As Series Six unfolds, the viewer discovers that Gharty is an intriguing mix of an almost sentimental reactionary value-frame with a life-earned sense of human decency and tolerance. The reference to the 'Box' is a direct allusion to the principal interrogation room, which is unremittingly claustrophobic, with one of its walls serving as a two-way mirror for silent and hidden surveillance of suspects. Pembleton, consumed by an inner rage and even disbelief at Gharty's and Ballard's accusations, returns their latent racial prejudice by presenting them with two dominant white racist stereotypical perceptions of African Americans:

Pembleton: …Because we all know that black men can't control themselves when it comes to loose shoes and tight clothes…. So you can prove once again that you can take the nigger out of the ghetto, but not the ghetto out of the nigger, is that it?

These dual icons are of the sexually promiscuous black man, potent beyond 'civilised restraint,' and, consequent to this, the savage binary construction of the black person, 'nigger', as innately 'criminal.' Accordingly, within this pathological 'rationale,' the criminalised, sexually promiscuous 'niggers' are the inevitable 'cause' of the ghetto conditions in which so many of them invariably live in contemporary urban America. Pembleton's counter-offensive argument powerfully foregrounds the historical ideological construction of the African American as a fiction. This Americanised 'Caliban' serves solely to rationalise the historical economic imperialism of slavery, and its developed expression within the social and economic formations of twentieth century capitalist America. Gharty proves to be most reluctant to relinquish his allegations as the following extract reveals:

Gharty: What, the Wilsons are going to suffer? They got half the City Hall and you and Girandello in their pockets.

Pembleton: Excuse me? I'm in someone's pocket?

Gharty: Hey, this is Baltimore. They're black, they're successful. That's the deal, end of story. This is your city Pembleton, your house, your department, your rules.

Pembleton: Oh, so it wasn't that way when the Italians ran it, or when the Irish owned it? How many favours have been called in, in the name of the 'Knights of Columbus and St Michael Society?'

Gharty: Oh, so that makes this all right?

Pembleton concludes this scene of high drama and violent emotions by suggesting to Gharty that he goes and bemoans his ethnic group's 'loss' of the city with other American Irish, offering, with withering sarcasm, to buy a round of drinks for them to commiserate each other. Significantly, he also agrees to bring Felix Wilson in for questioning about the murder and for the businessman to take blood tests to clear himself of suspicion.

In a scene charged with the emotional and ideological sub-text of the preceding scene, Pembleton interviews Felix Wilson in the 'Box' with Giardello watching from the secrecy of the surveillance mirror. Giardello is a personal friend of the Wilson family and his character also represents a signifier of a hard-earned status as a successful black businessman. Pembleton, considerably younger than these two other black men, equally needs to believe that any accusations made against Wilson – a generous benefactor of community projects for inner-city African Americans – are wholly without foundation. It is, therefore, with an almost tangible sense of shock that Wilson admits, in the face of having to provide a blood sample, that he had had sex with the maid prior to the party on the night when she was murdered. Giardello, recovering from his own sense of shock, nevertheless argues from a liberal moral position, that while Wilson's actions may represent a moral lapse in terms of his private relationship to his wife, that does not in itself constitute a crime. In the episode following on from this, the last in the three-part special, it transpires that Wilson's son, Hal, committed the murder. Hal has had a love affair with Melia and murdered her on discovering her sexual relationship with his father. However, and most crucially, their testimony is rendered inadmissible in any proposed court trial as they have only agreed to be interviewed by Frank on the basis that they are not previously advised of their rights. This complex web of compromised loyalties, predicated and confused on the basis of a sense of ethnic loyalty, makes for compelling drama. Furthermore, as in much of this fine series, the ethical and ideological implications of personal narratives and choices within the meta-narrative of wider political and historical discourse are left deliberately unresolved and problematic.

604. Birthday

TELEPLAY: Julie Martin
DIRECTOR: Alison Maclean
BROADCAST DATE: 7 November 1997

In this episode, a young white American woman, Grace Rivera, is found raped and beaten and close to death. These circumstances lead, through a bitterly dark irony, to a conflict of territorial self-interest between the Homicide and Sexual Crimes units. Another new recruit to Homicide, the young and brash Detective Paul Falsone, is keen to prove himself and assert his worth – and professional 'masculine authority' – by claiming the case for his own unit. Furthermore, he rashly promises to Giardello that he will secure a successful resolution to the case, a bravado for which the seasoned Giardello severely reprimands him. One of the two key narrative concerns and journeys within this piece is Falsone's revelation of a more sensitive awareness to others than is usually visible in his social intercourse of assertive machismo. That this sensitivity is developed and exposed in relation to his questioning and growing friendship with Grace – who dies at the end of the episode – focuses attention upon the central ideological discourse. This represents the issues involved in the construction of a young, attractive female character, and the implications of her attack and eventual death. This discourse challenges the ideological assumptions inherent in the dominant patriarchal viewing of the single woman whose personal life is defined in terms of alcohol and casual sexual encounters. In terms of this reflexive self-critique of the construction of female identity and the legitimisation or otherwise of that female behaviour, the character of Julianna Cox, the Chief Medical Examiner, becomes significant. In what has become a stylistic signature piece of the series, the discovery of Rivera's body is presented through a staccato series of jump-cut editing in which the images of her social evening prior to the attack are communicated in a stylised blue-green light. These are juxtaposed with starkly edited frame shots of her broken and bruised body, the finding and presenting of the almost still-frame images juddering, as if in traumatic aftershock of the act of violence. At this point, while dealing with an important aspect of the programme's performative aesthetic, I would like to discuss in a little detail the opening credits for each episode. To the programme's regular viewers, the discordant juxtaposing of sampled images of maps of Baltimore, x-ray skeleton victims and the Homicide badge icon, present perhaps a reassuring and recognisable journey of aesthetic style and ideological form and content. The following attempt to communicate the rapid-fire jump-cutting of the mediated transmission of images can only itself be an approximate map:

> View from interior of police-car/window/rain
> Blue light. Police badge. Police car.
> Black and white negative map of Baltimore with the streets carrying a subliminal reading of arteries.

Blue light. Green eye pupil – text: SUSPECTS
Gold whirl of fingerprint – text: INVESTIGATE
Scarlet/golden backdrop of lettering – text: 911 REPORT
Subliminal signing of a Homicide report.
Rapid collage of gun images – text: EXHIBIT B
Rapid cut and insert of head and shoulders of female victim (blue lit) – text: EXHIBIT A and CRIME SCENE.
Scarlet background with hand holding police badge. Text superimposed over this image: suspect apprehended, DETECTIVE, MOTIVE
Rapid cut/glimpse of Police badge once more
Rapid cut to (actor/character staring directly, impassively to camera/viewer) list of principal characters with actors' names given in scratched white lettering – at end of this sequence. Cut to –
Golden fingerprint superimposed over text: evidence, SUSPECTS. Cut to
Green background (also rapid-cut superimposition of victim's face). Collage of written report fragments – dislocated fragment words e.g. text: PRINTS, WEAPON, INVESTIGATE. Cut to –
Abstract purple collage – x-ray negatives of victim's body, fractured, dislocated. Cut to Coroner's instruments and text: MULTIPLE CONTUSION, CORONER, autopsy, poison. Cut to
A sudden rush/splash/wave of blue light – an unstable visual signing of the text HOMICIDE, a white gloved hand brushing finger-printing powder across the surface of the viewing surface, voice in background, impersonal, distant, 'Homicide.'

I wanted to present a detailed textual account of the opening credits as I feel they powerfully express the interweaving of the show's aesthetic concerns and signature within its ideological terrain. This geo-ideological terrain is one of disjointed, dislocated images and texts depicting the oppressive, dangerous and alienated location of a struggle to define and execute strategies of law enforcement and social order within the reified ideological climate of late capitalist urban sites.

As Falsone, like some post-modern Lone Ranger, seeks to find Rivera's attacker, a visual narrative journey ensues of stylised, slow motion images of the homicide squad checking the various bars where she might have been drinking on that fatal night. In another potent aesthetic signature from the series, this visual narrative is accompanied by a sound track of a haunting folk-rock refrain in which the line 'Love is easily forgotten' provides an evocative counter-point to the implacable routine of the police search for information. The sequence closes with a breathtaking panoramic view of the Baltimore city skyline at night.

In effective and challenging contrast to the main narrative plot is a revealing glimpse into Pembleton's private life as his wife is suddenly rushed into hospital to give birth to their child. However, when Frank arrives at the hospital to see his wife, he discovers that she has gone into the Emergency Room because of dangerous complications for both herself and the unborn baby. As he sits in the waiting room with his long-time police partner, Detective Tim Bayliss, who has driven him to the hospital,

Pembleton observes to his friend, "I've never been here before…. I'm a husband and a father and I should have been with my family tonight." This clash of loyalties between his commitment to his work and his family are brought into sharp relief in the context of possibly losing his wife and their baby. These conflicts help to define the person within the (albeit metaphorical) uniform of public service. His wife and their new son pull through but the incident marks a new and, one imagines, lasting attempt to try and prioritise his wife and family, against the demands of a job that brings him into unrelenting contact with brutal reminders of mortality.

An interesting relationship develops between Falsone and the slowly recovering but traumatised Grace. He is quietly and carefully seeking to help her identify a possible suspect and she tells him of the sad routine of her social life in which she, to use her own phrase, "keeps on kissing frogs" in order to try and find a "prince." However, this is no trite sentimentality on her part as she is only too aware of the depressingly chauvinist similarity that marks the men she meets with in bars:

> Rivera: Some jerk makes a pass, all you want to do is get away, but you're in the living room, you're a little 'buzzed,' so you have sex anyway. Sometimes it's easier than saying no. So you wake up the next morning, take a shower and kind of convince yourself that it doesn't matter.

> Falsone: This is different.

> Rivera: Not for me. You go looking for revenge. You've got to admit that something happened to you. It wasn't your choice. I can't live with that image of myself.

This internalising of blame or responsibility for the violent crime committed against her brings one into dangerous and psychologically predictable territory. That is, the victim of violent crime and/or sexual assault imagines that they've somehow brought the event onto themselves. This is given added impetus when the victim is a woman in the light of the perverse patriarchal view that a woman who chooses to socialise independently without being defined/legitimised by the male presence of the husband/boyfriend/partner is somehow wilfully vulnerable – and dangerous. This oppressive and reactionary viewpoint is so deeply culturally encoded and familiarised as 'true' that Julianna finds herself agonising over a drink in a bar, articulating her concerns to John Munch, a Homicide officer who also has joint-ownership shares in the bar:

> Cox: Nothing's ever black and white is it? Not that being drunk excuses in any way what that bastard did to her, but in some little, finger-pointing corner of my mind, I can't help thinking that she let herself be vulnerable. It could have happened to me if I'd been in that condition.

In his efforts to secure a conviction, Falsone acts upon intelligence from another officer and a suspect, Gantz, is arrested and interrogated. With a record of violent sexual assault against women and having been in the bar where Rivera was on the night of her attack, he seems a strong suspect. When Gantz says, with languidly ugly satisfaction, that he'd savagely beaten an earlier victim because, "I wanted to leave her something to remember me by," Falsone suddenly attacks him violently, punching him in the face. Whilst none of the other attendant officers attempt to intervene or restrain Falsone, Giardello is furious that his actions would invalidate a successful conviction. Further investigations reveal that Rivera's attacker was in fact the barman who'd befriended her and bought her drinks. He carries a bite mark on his arm where she had struggled to defend herself before falling into unconsciousness. When Cox is able to provide a perfect match between the teeth marks and Rivera's own mouth, a triumphant Falsone goes off to the hospital to tell her the good news about the conviction. It is with some shock that he, and the viewer, discover that Grace has died from a delayed blood clot on her brain.

The final sequence of this episode links together the themes from the main narrative with the sub-plot concerning Pembleton and his wife. There is a very moving visual sequence in which the camera pans slowly along the line of newly born babies in the maternity unit – signifiers of a provisional innocence and of an equally provisional hope for future human lives and endeavour. This is powerfully and cruelly juxtaposed with the image of Juliane shaving the head of the dead Grace in order to carry out a post-mortem. To a melancholic soundtrack of a song whose recurring line states: "This is how we should be/ This is the world that's at my door," the picture slowly dissolves to show the murderer in his prison cell, followed by an equally leisurely dissolve to Gantz eyeing up another potential female victim in the bar where Grace had spent her last evening. Finally, the camera takes the viewing gaze to 'The Board' – the white melamine board where each officer has their name printed along a horizontal line at the top. Underneath their names are placed the names of the victims whose deaths they must try, in Pembleton's words, 'to avenge.' The victim's names are written initially in red removable felt-tip pen. Only when they become 'solved cases,' is the red lettering replaced with black. This image of the board with its formal ritual of the signing and marking of human lives is a powerful *leitmotif* within the series. The final image of the visual narrative sequence is the precise and careful translation of RIVERA from red into black ink, the tragic irony being that in being signed from 'victim' into a 'resolution,' she has died. While Falsone has achieved his rash promise to secure a conviction for her attacker, the episode concludes that he has lost someone for whom he'd begun to care.

606. Saigon Rose

TELEPLAY: Anya Epstein and David Simon
STORY: Eric Overmeyer
DIRECTOR: Nick Gomez
BROADCAST DATE: 21 November 1997

In this powerful and bleakly violent episode, some of the issues of both the perception and representation of race and ethnicity explored in 'Blood Ties' are returned to with savagely uncompromising candour. A Vietnamese family who run a Baltimore restaurant called 'Saigon Rose' are brutally gunned down in their own restaurant as they sit down for a hard-earned meal at the end of their working day. The name 'Saigon Rose' carries a special subliminal meaning for an American television audience, it being the pseudonym of a North Vietnamese radio propagandist broadcaster during the Vietnam War. The first viewing of the dead bodies, disfigured by the violence of close-range bullet impact and drenched in blood, is provided through the following visual narrative sequence. The camera pans slowly over each dead body from the camera point-of-view of a gaze – that of an investigating officer – looking down upon them, dispassionately. As each body is framed by the camera, the flash of the police camera cataloguing their brutal deaths is accompanied by a loud staccato thud of the flash gun. Each successive framing of the body is punctuated in this way. When Cox is asked by one of the police officers on the scene if she is OK, she replies with grim stoicism, "My chosen profession." Two of the family, a young son and daughter, survived the murders because they were working in the kitchen at the back of the restaurant. In addition to the death of their family, an off-duty policeman who has worked as a security guard at the restaurant has also been murdered. At the initial scene-of-crime investigation, a black female uniformed police officer arrives to give assistance. Named Antoinette Perry, she lives in the district and offers Pembleton and Bayliss some local knowledge to help catch the murderer. When the two survivors give a positive identification of Perry as one of the two murderers, the plot begins to descend into a dark labyrinthine web of pathological psychology and the wider implications of the 'Affirmative Action' campaign. This is a campaign, informed by liberal notions of plurality and equal opportunity, by which peoples from non-white racial and ethnic groups are actively recruited into the police force. As the widow of the dead off-duty officer remarks to Pembleton and Bayliss, "She [Perry] was 'Affirmative Action,' thought she was entitled to everything on a silver platter. Larry said she was a lousy cop. There was no other way she could get upon the Force."

The routine checking of Perry's file in the light of the survivor's identification and the widow's bitter observation confirm that Perry's record as a police officer is indeed poor and scattered with disciplinary reprimands. As the grim realisation of Perry's guilt and complicity becomes depressingly and unmistakably clear, it provokes Giardello to say to the investigating officers, "One off-duty cop kills another and the family they work for? I don't know, but the thought of this churns my stomach." When the listening Meldrick adds that the colour/racial identity of the murderer is going to prove controversial, Giardello continues by asserting, "I am more concerned with the morality of the department than I am of the Media." The nature of the mass killing of an innocent family and off-duty officer has a huge and traumatic impact upon a Homicide squad seemingly anaesthetised by their work against such an emotional reaction. In a visual narrative sequence of haunting sadness and bleak beauty, it is as if this emotional trauma is given an aesthetic form. The camera point-of-view lingers unbearably slowly as it tracks along each murdered individual family member. This time the location is not the restaurant-turned-bloodbath but Cox's autopsy room. Each victim is framed in a bleakly surreal head-and-shoulders portrait, each looking strangely at peace in the steel blue light of his or her sterilised objectivity. It is as if the camera lingers in pain and disbelief at the appalling consequences of Perry's pathological, violent actions. The camera then makes a slow fade to a view of Perry walking up the steps of the police station's main entrance, seemingly just another officer. She has been called in to be interrogated by Pembleton and Meldrick, but under the guise of them consulting her for local intelligence about the murders. Meanwhile her cousin has been arrested on the suspicion that he was her accomplice. As he admits to being an accessory but not the murderer, the killings are revisited once more, but this time through the visual device of a mid-distance camera point-of-view of the restaurant from the street outside. As his out-of-vision narrative describes the context of the murders, the viewer sees a lightning flash from each gun shot light up the late night midnight blue of the restaurant's interior, with a Brechtian sense of alienated distance. The flash and sound of the gun shots is eerily reminiscent of the earlier scene when the bodies were framed by the police camera flash. Perry eventually admits under cross-examination that she was the murderer. It then transpires that she has murdered her father too. Here is an attractive and articulate young black woman in the possession of a pathological sense of being marginalised and rejected by the world. Perry's character, played with chilling longeur and icy rationality by Camille McCurty Ali, is also a complex construction and signification of racial/ethnic representation. In this construction, comfortable white liberal assumptions about the tolerated nature and presence of the racial/ethnic 'other' are profoundly challenged. In this way, the potentially patronising and simplistic ideological viewing position at its base is exposed. Nevertheless, one might also read the complex dialectics of her construction as an unconscious exhibition of white liberal/centrist anxieties about both the essentialist 'nature' of the racial/ethnic 'other' and its undermining of the efficacy of affirmative assimilationist strategies.

For the other characters in this episode, the principal emotional impact rests upon Pembleton and Cox. Cox has earlier admitted to a form of emotional 'giddiness' in the face of these appalling murders, articulating the dreadful process of recognising physiological similarities between the family members as she carries out her autopsies. This 'giddiness,' a kind of bleakly manic humour, is clearly a psychological displacement for her sense of profound shock about these tragically innocent victims. She endeavours to share this obliquely with Kellerman over a drink at Munch's bar:

> Cox: I was contemplating a career change. Maybe I'd like to take a year off – write a book or something?
>
> Kellerman: A book? About what?
>
> Cox: What I do for a living and why. (Beat) I can't figure that one out.
>
> Kellerman: You don't know?

Cox: I'm not so sure. I thought I did but....

Kellerman: It'll be a best seller. The public love gore. They can't get enough.

Cox: Yeah? Well, I got gore galore.

In addition to this dialogue extract subtly communicating Cox's deepening sense of pain and shock at the work that she does, it also functions in a self-reflexive way to comment upon David Simon's writing of his own book, *Homicide – a Year on the Killing Streets*. In terms of the proportion and graphic representation of violence in this television series, Kellerman's cynical observation that "The public love gore" is disturbingly reinforced by Hoffman's account of a crisis that the series faced in its third season. Hoffman describes how NBC had only committed to thirteen episodes and it was unclear whether the series would close mid-season. Following a series of three episodes in which, for the first time, Homicide officers themselves were victims of violence:

> Fontana was initially uncomfortable with introducing such explicit violence, in the event that they were renewed and would have to continue from that point. "Those who favored this course were convinced that it would create an emotional wellspring in which all the characters would be able to participate and from which we'd learn new things about them" he recalls.... Although he liked the episodes at the time, in retrospect Braugher has mixed feelings about the direction they presaged, "We were sinking neigh unto death when they were shot, and suddenly we got a spike in the ratings. Now we're shooting people every week."[3]

Kellerman's observations about the public's appetite for 'gore' is confirmed by Braugher's acknowledgement that the introduction of more explicitly violent scenes – in the context of the series suffering in the ratings and facing closure – resulted in significantly improved ratings and the survival of the series. Braugher's character, Frank Pembleton concludes the 'Saigon Rose' episode by having a drink with Meldrick and the barmaid, a vivacious older woman called Billy Lou. Like Cox, Pembleton has been seriously affected by this case and seeks a similarly oblique means of displacing his pain and confusion:

Pembleton: When you were a kid, did you believe in guardian angels?

Lewis: I don't think I gave them much thought, Frank.

Pembleton: Really? Well, if you were a Catholic, you would.... I used to try and catch them out of the corner of my eye, real quick.... Billy Lou, did you ever believe in guardian angels when you were a kid?

Billy Lou: Still do.

Pembleton: Yeah? You a Catholic?

Billy Lou: Performance artist.

These concluding sentiments represent the only sense of light relief within what may prove to be one of the series' most harrowing and challenging episodes.

607. The Subway

TELEPLAY: James Yoshimura
DIRECTOR: Gary Fleder
BROADCAST DATE: 5 December 1997

In this episode, Pembleton's inner conflict and agonising over the nature and implications of his work and identity as a seasoned Homicide officer is taken into even more challenging territory. It is also an episode in which, in dramatic terms, there is relatively little explicit action or plot development following the traumatic incident at the episode's opening, in which a young white male, John Lange, is pushed under a subway train in the early morning rush hour. While the character survives this initial trauma, it becomes immediately clear that he is mortally injured and has only a short time left to live. In what is a piece of inspired narrative structuring, those remaining minutes of the character's life are effectively lived out in 'real time' for the rest of the episode.

In the opening sequence, the viewer receives one of the relatively rare, longer exterior shots of Baltimore the city. Beginning with a mid to long distance shot of the harbour and a distant skyline, a passenger ferry traverses the eye-line and skyline from right to left. The camera then pans fairly leisurely to a different mid distance shot of early morning commuters. The camera then closes in upon the character of John Lange, just another commuter making his daily journey into work. He kisses a young woman (whom we later discover is his girlfriend) goodbye and she embarks upon her early morning run around the harbour area – something that becomes a narrative device for this episode's sub-plot. The following visual narrative sequence shows Lange moving briskly, almost slow running, as he moves to get his train to work. As he weaves in and out amongst the other travellers, the camera catches and follows him through the visual filter of the railings of the subway, creating an effect of splintered, disrupted visual reception of his movement. This sequence is accompanied by the musical soundtrack of a folk group busking in the subway. In precise timing with the increasing intensity of his descent to the subway train platform, the visual narrative moves into a rapid jump cut montage of slow motion images of dense bodies crowding for the imminent train and Lange trying to push his way through. It culminates in a nightmarish moment of bodies stumbling and Lange falling, a mosaic of speeding train, voices screaming and Lange plummeting to the ground.

Although how Lange has fallen under the train is initially uncertain and deliberately ambiguous, it transpires that he has been the random victim of a character called Larry Biedron. Bayliss interrogates Biedron at the scene of the crime and discovers that he is mentally ill and has served time in a psychiatric hospital in Chicago for a similar offence. Meanwhile, as this sub-narrative unfolds and reveals itself, the principal narrative focuses upon the dramatic relationship between Pembleton and Lange who is trapped from the waist down between the train and the platform edge. In two excellent performances of subtle nuance and complex emotional range, Andre Braugher and Vincent D'Onofrio plot and navigate a relationship signed by a sense of quiet despair, blistering anger and a growing sense of impending mortality and imminent death. At one powerful moment an angry and bewildered Lange looks up at Pembleton and says, "So what am I? Some lesson in bad luck?" As Falsone and Meldrick are instructed to try and find Lange's girlfriend before he dies – a task which proves to be desperately and tragically futile – the trapped man becomes increasingly angry and bewildered beyond restraint at the events that have suddenly brought him close to death. The only person that he can project these turbulent emotions onto is Pembleton. With an eerily effective resonance of the Antoinette Perry case, he jibes Pembleton using racist terms: "You're just some moke." Lange angrily denounces Pembleton in terms of his impotence in the face of these circumstances. Crucially, he venomously alleges that Pembleton is only there as a 'token' black police officer who has only succeeded on the basis of positive discrimination. Seeing immediately the anger and hurt that this has caused to his sole confidante in a world he is soon to leave, Lange apologises. By the end of the episode, the two men are sharing a strange intimacy framed in terms of mortality, empathy and a sense of shared shock, disbelief and impotence to change or affect these events. In the final moments before the train is eventually moved, causing his immediate death, Pembleton is holding Lange's hand in support. In his final moments of life and consciousness, the previously bellicose Lange implodes into a final recount of a transcendent image from nature, which a deeply shocked Pembleton seeks to share with Bayliss back in the police car:

Bayliss: You all right? (Beat. Long pause)

Pembleton: Did you ever notice that when the rain is coming, the leaves on a sugar maple [tree] will turn over?

Bayliss: No.

Pembleton: Learn something new every day. (Beat) The guy. He said to me, "I'm OK."

As a quietly distraught Pembleton and Bayliss drive off from the scene, the camera picks out Lange's girlfriend, still running, arriving at the subway station oblivious either to the tragedy or the identity of its victim. Within this image, there is a profound resonance of the relationship between the city and its inhabitants. Within the alienated discourse of the dynamics of contemporary city life, trains continue to run, commuters board them, the ferry crosses, a young woman runs its streets, while a citizen – murdered in some malevolent discourse of 'Fate' – is methodically taken away, his name effortlessly translated from red into black.

608. All is Bright

TELEPLAY: Raphael Alvarez
STORY: James Yoshimura and Julie Martin
DIRECTOR: Matt Reeves
BROADCAST DATE: 12 December 1997

Taking its title from the line in the popular Christmas Carol, 'Silent Night,' this episode opens with John Munch and Meldrick Lewis – joint owners in the bar venture – bedecking the interior with Christmas decorations, while Munch is on his knees scrubbing the floor.

The laconic Munch, played with a deceptively easy sense of world-weariness by Richard Belzer, is ruminating with bitter irony on the position he finds himself in:

Munch: What's a nice Jewish boy like me doing on his knees at the altar of Donner and Blitzen? Christmas isn't even a Christmas holiday any more. It's all about retail.

Lewis: You're so cynical Munch. The reason why we're putting the spit and shine on our bar is so that we can get money from the Christmas crowd celebrating the birth of our Saviour, hopefully visiting us here in our humble inn and knocking back a few beers.

Munch: Your saviour, not mine.

Billy Lou: Come on John, it's the spirit of the thing, the gesture that counts.

(Lewis and Billy Lou leave him a few moments later)

Munch: (Remarks to himself) The 'Chosen People?' (Slight beat) Yeah!

Munch's cynical observations about the commercialisation of Christmas and his sharply laconic sense of himself as a Jew, as an outsider, are interesting reference points. Munch's rough-hewn, stonily implacable features, rarely if ever crease with emotion. His sense of his ethnicity is keenly felt and, when articulated, expressed with concise and uncompromising feeling. In a later episode entitled 'Secrets' (which I will refer to in my concluding chapter), Munch takes unexpected exception to Lewis' casual remark that someone might expect better justice in a supposedly neutral country such as Switzerland:

Munch: Don't go trusting the Swiss, it seems like they spent World War Two scheming money from my dead relatives. I don't like their chocolate, I don't like their cheese – don't go talking up the Swiss to me!

Munch becomes a key character in the principal sub-plot in this episode in which his estranged wife arrives with news of her mother's death, seeking solace and support from her former husband. As it becomes clear that, contrary to her daughter's belief, her mother was profoundly disliked by the New York literary circles in which she moved, Munch reveals a tenderness and sensitivity towards his wife which is quietly moving.

However, I want to focus my principal discussion and analysis of this episode upon the central plot line which concerns a young woman, Rita Hayle, who, it transpires, has killed her ex-boyfriend who has given her AIDS. Within this scenario, both the suffering and stigma of the AIDS victim becomes vividly and painfully clear, as well as the prejudice that serves to alienate those who suffer.

The murder victim, Philip Longley, is found on the floor of a suburban laundrette with a broken neck and, strangely, with signs of what proves to be domestic bleach around his mouth. When Julianne Cox reveals through her autopsy that he was also HIV-positive, Ballard and Gharty go around to the deceased's parents to break the news of his death to them. The two detectives arrive at a scene of almost banal bourgeois activity outside of their quiet residential house – they are erecting a Nativity Crib. This icon of cultural and religious respectability contrasts bitterly with the circumstances of their son's death. In a voice strangely lacking in emotion, his father uses the opportunity to voice the anxieties and concerns of residential, urban, middle-class America:

Mr Longley: Just last week my neighbour across the street, Lou Krenshaw, was held up at gunpoint as he got out of his car.... Round the corner, old Mrs Finney, stabbed in the back for ten dollars in change.

Ballard and Gharty discover that although his mother knew of his illness, she had kept this news from Philip's father. The stigma and shame of AIDS carries considerable currency in the neat lawns of WASP America, especially so because of its ill-perceived but pervasive association with homosexuality. What becomes even more concerning however is the disturbing level of prejudice demonstrated by Falsone when Gharty and Ballard bring in a female suspect, Rita Hayle – one of Longley's former girlfriends – who is clearly and visibly suffering from an advanced case of AIDS. Noticing Falsone's reactions when she is brought into the station, Lewis says:

Lewis: Hey, Falsone, you can't catch nothing by breathing the same air.

Falsone: That's what they say today. Just like they thought Thalidomide couldn't cause birth defects, like they thought the earth was flat....

Lewis: It is flat....

Falsone: I got a kid. I'm trying to get him back now. I'm not taking any chances.

While Gharty himself is initially nervous in the company of Rita, he demonstrates a more decent and pragmatic acceptance of her, gradually growing into troubled concern for her illness and its impact upon her life. As the two detectives are interviewing Rita, Ballard – another young woman with progressive and feminist attitudes – seeks to express some empathy. However, this is bitterly rebuffed by Rita, who proceeds to demolish a comfortable liberal perspective of a condition now under control:

Rita: What do you know?

Ballard: I read the papers.

Rita: So do I. (as if quoting a headline) "Drugs Cocktail Kills AIDS! AIDS No Longer an Epidemic! AIDS Can't Kill You!" As far as my life is concerned, they're wrong. I took those cocktails, detective, I swallowed forty one pills a day.... Their cocktails work for two thirds of the people who need it. For the rest of us, it doesn't do jack. You know how it feels to pick up *Time* magazine and read they think medicine can beat this disease? Do you know how it feels to see Philip Longley walking down the street, looking healthier than ever, a beautiful girl on his arm?

The viewer has discovered by this point that Longley has had a sexual relationship with Rita, deliberately not telling her that he was HIV-positive. Furthermore, he has embarked upon a large number of serial sexual relationships with other young women with a similarly staggering lack of concern. Whilst Ballard clearly has huge sympathies for Rita and sees the 'natural justice' in her actions, Gharty – while deeply saddened and thoughtful – insists upon getting an admission of guilt from her. When she finally confesses to having murdered Longley, the viewer also understands the significance of the bleach traces on his mouth:

Rita: Poor people, people with no money, no insurance, who don't read *Time* magazine, get told a healthy dose of bleach will clean out the virus. So they go down to their basements and down half a bottle and end up in the Emergency Rooms, sick as dogs.... Philip Longley murdered me. (Slight beat) I murdered Philip Longley.

Ballard's identification and empathy with Rita motivates her to try and plead for her not to be charged with murder, given the circumstances of her case. However, Gharty and Giardello argue that, in the interests of the impartial application and execution of justice, she must face prosecution for what was, in the end, a premeditated murder. In much the same way that in the 'Birthday' episode, Cox found herself reflecting upon Grace Rivera's death; Ballard cannot shake off the sense that she too might suffer as a young woman in the context of a sexual affair with a man. Earlier in this episode Rita has spoken with deeply bitter irony about the public media presentation of AIDS awareness:

> Rita: Let me give you a big, big hint? Always wear rubber. Listen to me, I sound like a Public Service announcement! I think they ought to let me do one of those. They've got a load of sit-com stars with their fresh TV faces: "Wanna be cool? Wear a condom!" I think they ought to put my mug up on there instead. I'm guaranteed to scare the be-Jesus out of any kid watching.

Troubled and saddened by this case, Ballard goes to see Cox to arrange for a blood test to check own health and is clearly very thoughtful about the implications of her own private and sexual life. In this episode the sense of vulnerability and exposure to AIDS, and indeed, exploitation of other forms of vulnerability within personal and sexual relationships, is conveyed with great power. The fact remains that a police officer's badge neither makes one immune from those wider social problems of contemporary urban existence nor, in the case of Falsone, from the widespread prejudices and ignorance towards those who suffer from AIDS and AIDS-related illnesses.

612. Something Sacred

TELEPLAY: Anya Epstein and David Simon
DIRECTOR: Uli Edel
BROADCAST DATE: 30 January 1998

This episode explores issues relating to the presence of the church in the inner city, some of the tensions arising from that interface between religious faith and activism, and the seemingly overwhelming social problems of the contemporary American city. The central plot-line of what was a two-hour special episode is the murder of two Catholic priests, both working in poor inner city areas. The opening sequence follows an established aesthetic within 'Homicide – Life on the Street,' by using rapid jump cuts of images of violent crime in the immediate location. In this episode there is an up-tempo inter-cutting of images of the gagged, bound and mortally beaten priest with images of suffering from Catholic iconography: the suffering Christ inter-cuts with the bloodied body of the dead priest.

Ballard is on the scene of the crime and is waiting to interview another priest who might be able to provide important information. When told that he is at prayer, she observes with dark certainty, "Heaven can wait, Homicide can't." Chalked in Spanish on the blackboard of the study where the priest has been murdered is what Gharty is able to translate as, "Teach us how to truly live, God of love, forgive, forgive." This acts as a brutally ironic Brechtian gestus of the scene of the crime, where such ethical sentiments of spiritual growth and forgiveness seem impossibly at odds with the crime-ravaged inner city. It is discovered that the victim, Father Jeneau, had been an active supporter of the Catholic Friends of Central America – a liberal theological network of support for the exiled, poor, political refugees from Central America. This theme is important, focusing as it does upon contemporary perceptions of both political refugees and poverty: stricken economic migrants. The construction of those characters and the ideological debate surrounding that site are important issues in contemporary British and American cultural and political life. Political pressure is placed upon Giardello from high strategic levels within the Catholic Church. He remarks to his squad, "Let's bring in our sinners before the Pope comes calling." The dead priest's home has effectively become a sanctuary for young Guatemalan refugees and two such young men have disappeared following the murder. Inevitably, they become suspects and are arrested by Munch and Kellerman. Meanwhile, another issue enters the narrative in the form of the questioning of the dead priest's sexuality and, more pertinently, of the possibility that he might have sought homosexual relationships with the young men. It is naturally very disconcerting that the constructs of paedophilia and homosexuality are blurred and paralleled in this way. What is equally disquieting is that in presenting this possibility as a fictive frame, the writers touch the raw nerve of widespread contemporary distrust of both organised religion and of the sexual activities of 'celibate' Catholic priests in particular. It transpires that these allegations have come from a self-styled guru of an inner city-based sect, and that the cult leader has been formerly convicted of paedophile activities. All of this contributes to that contemporary moral malaise where the notion of morality in both its public and private locations is delineated as an uncertain and profoundly unreliable site of negotiation. Within this problematic discourse, religion and religious belief becomes another similarly unstable site. This ideological anxiety and its discourse are filtered through the discussions that the investigating officers engage in regarding this case. Once again, issues of ethnicity and personal value systems threaten to intrude upon and disrupt the impartial execution of law enforcement. Gharty (as I've previously established, of American Irish Catholic extraction) is angered and bewildered that the allegations about the dead priest appear at first to be accepted uncritically. He seeks to defend the posthumous integrity of the priest by saying to Ballard, "This is what happens when someone leads a decent, moral life." Pembleton, also Catholic by upbringing, nevertheless displays his characteristic hard-hitting insistence upon ascertaining the truth at all costs, and responds by explaining to Gharty that the statistics of sex-crime offences by priests against young men and boys cannot be discounted. Later in the episode, Gharty recounts his Catholic upbringing to Ballard and admits that, as a young man, he had given serious consideration to the priesthood. When she cautiously and sensitively enquires what prevented him from so doing, he replies with quiet good humour, "I met my wife."

The allegations prove to be unfounded although the uncertainty as to his killers remains. The two young Guatemalan refugees are interrogated. As they recount their version of events, there is a visual re-visiting of the crime. This is explored and communicated through three short jump cuts of the priest's bound and gagged body, cutting to a bird's-eye view of his bloodied corpse and then returning to claustrophobic close-ups. When threatened with deportation back to Guatemala unless they tell the truth, the young men move into desperate panic. In anguished and halting English, one of them makes a pathetic plea to stay in the face of certain arrest and torture should they return, "I love Baltimore, I love America, I love MTV." Present at their interrogation – at her insistence – is a young black Catholic nun and community worker, Sister Dianne Attwood, another worker at the CFCA centre. Her character is constructed in such a way as to be carrier of liberal/progressive values and attitudes, represented most clearly in her affirmation of the refugee's human rights. When, therefore, Homicide decide to detain the two young men as murder suspects, based on the circumstantial evidence of their being present at the site of the crime, Attwood argues vociferously that this represents prejudicial, oppressive and heavy-handed treatment of the two young men. From this moment midway through the first episode, a dialectical debate of liberal, human-rights centred values with the reactionary pragmatism of the Homicide position is enacted. It is interesting and significant that the embodiment of these liberal/radical values is signed as black, female and articulate. To the extent that the Homicide officers – including Ballard – are critically impatient of her position, seeing it as misplaced and naive idealism, one wonders which particular aspects of her fictive signing are most exposed for this reactionary critique. Is it her femaleness, racial ethnicity or, most disruptively, her daring to articulate her historically marginalised identity through a discourse of radical liberalism? Significantly, it is Ballard alone out of the Homicide officers who reflects upon her initial response and questions some of her own subjective, prejudicial assumptions about both organised religion and religious faith. It is also significant that it is with Pembleton that she shares her concerns:

Ballard: Maybe it's easier for me to imagine someone dying of AIDS than what it means to believe in God?

Pembleton: So you're lucky…. In this line of work, be it a mutilated priest or an over-dosed addict, faith only gets in the way, it twists you up. So if you don't have the Almighty to reckon with, you're fortunate…. Work the way you need to and consider yourself blessed.

Within the post-modern indeterminacy of late capitalist geo-ideological urban sites, the moral certainties and ideological cohesion demanded of questioning, uncertain believers such as Pembleton and Giardello paradoxically constitute a kind of existential curse, rather than a blessing.

Following on a full-scale publicity and demonstration campaign orchestrated by Attwood and others, Giardello is instructed by his superiors to release the two young men under the protective house custody of Attwood. The investigating officers are angry and frustrated and their worst fears and suspicions seem to be confirmed when, following their release, another Catholic priest is found murdered. Homicide arrive at Attwood's home, only to discover that the two Guatemalans are not there.

In the second episode of this two-parter, it is eventually established that a local drug-addicted youth in the neighbourhood has committed both crimes and that the Guatemalans are indeed innocent of the crimes. Nevertheless, the unfolding of these dialectical narratives has raised and exposed multiple contemporary anxieties. These include the efficacy of liberal/humanist strategies and the problematic perception of both organised religion and religious belief. Furthermore there remains the issue of the prejudiced assumptions about the ethnicity of the 'other' – especially when that other is either black, female and articulate, or the dispossessed citizens of countries who have suffered though covert American/CIA imperialist strategies.

In my concluding chapter I shall return to some of the issues that I have raised in this chapter and, in the process, introduce some other material for further consideration. Like its British counterpart 'The Cops,' 'Homicide – Life on the Street' negotiates the problematic and unstable ideological terrain of the policing of contemporary cities and urban sites. In so doing, it raises profound questions about the psychology and internal agendas of those Homicide officers who are forced to navigate a journey through complex and ambiguous constructs of personal and public morality and of private and political integrity.

Notes

1. Tod Hoffman (1998) *Homicide – Life on the Screen*, Ontario, ECW Press, pp. 13–14.
2. David Simon (1991) *Homicide – A Year on the Killing Streets*, New York, Ivy Books, pp. 1–2.
3. Hoffman, p. 13.

Sensing the City – Centres and Margins
A Conclusion

To conclude, I want to review my overall thoughts, reflections and provisional discoveries in terms of the five programmes as a whole, and revisit each case-study separately to raise some final concerns. In using the term 'discoveries,' it is not to suggest secure closure in any formal sense. Indeed, one of the principal realisations is that each of the five case-studies defies interpretative closure. This is both a strength and measure of the quality of those dramas. The difficulty, or unwillingness even, of providing secure resolutions of the conflicts and issues that they explore, reflects the complex nature of such issues. And the ideological performative aesthetics through which those themes are treated will not in themselves facilitate reassuring closure. In some senses therefore, like the final chapter of Dr Samuel Johnson's (1759) novella *Rasselas*, this chapter signifies a "conclusion in which nothing is concluded."

Policing the Centre from the Boundary

In both 'The Cops' and 'Homicide,' one of the prevailing concerns expressed is that of a profound moral ambiguity regarding the nature and possibilities of policing in the twenty-first century. This dilemma is accentuated by a clear understanding in both series of the complex interaction of the private person-in-the-uniform with the public execution of criminal detection and justice.

In 'The Cops,' as I discussed at some length in the opening chapter, the performative aesthetic of the series is simultaneously a visually denotative, metaphorical displacement of contemporary policing, with an editorial sub-text that radically subverts the implications of that quasi-documentary style. As Garnett observed in his interview with me:

> The more I work at this game, the more I realise that I want to leave room for the audience to do the work, and the kind of drama I don't like is where all of the work is done for them and it's on a plate. The speculation for the audience about Giffen's past is all part of the audience's relationship with the show. The show is told, in every scene, from the point of view of the police, but editorially the show is not seen from the police point of view – but that is a very difficult tightrope to walk. One of the rules of the show is that we cannot have a scene where we are not taken into it by the police – which is a very big constraint on the writers – so that we see everything through their eyes.

This dialectical interplay between what we, as viewers, are 'privileged' to see through this aesthetic framing device, and the moral and ideological implications of the editorial critique of those events, is powerful, disturbing and compelling. Supported by an impeccably strong cast, an excellent team of writers and with directors, editors and crew of a uniformly high standard, this series has been one of the highlights and landmarks of recent British television drama. That production team and process seeks to implement Garnett's own commitment to a collaborative and egalitarian production ethos:

> For me, dramatic fiction on the screen is essentially a collaborative, social activity, but also I think it would be a pretence to claim that it is a democracy. It isn't. But most of the time, most of the decisions are consensual. What's important is that as far as possible, an opinion should not hold greater weight because of the status of the person who holds the opinion. Sometimes, very occasionally, I'll say I'm sorry, this is the way it's going to have to be.

In terms of the ways in which the urban is sensed through the series, the over-riding geo-ideological landscape is one of unremitting material bleakness. Skeetsmoor, the fictional housing estate on which much of the dramatic action is located, is a grim mosaic of dilapidated public council housing stock, long-term unemployment and a vigilante mentality that evokes a depressing sense of a late twentieth century (north) Western frontier town. The persons in the police uniforms enact a seemingly impossible scenario, seeking to manage their own personal agendas and crises, as well as the problematic task of retaining some semblance of social and judicial order. When, at the end of the first series, PC Danny Rylance disappears like a modern-day Pentheus beneath the terror of a violent mass assault, he is signified not only as some bloody, sacrificial victim, but also a disturbing symptom of deeply entrenched personal and public histories of exploitation and inequality.

This series well deserved the awards it received and, at the time of writing, a third series is in the planning and pre-production stage. In its absolute commitment to an authentic recreation of the deprived urban conurbation of Blair's New Britain, and its unflinching scrutiny of this complex geo-ideological terrain. 'The Cops' represents a crucial antidote to a neutralising, south east England bourgeois viewing of Britain's depressed, post-industrial wastelands.

In 'Homicide – Life on the Street' there is a similar commitment to a hard-hitting, uncompromisingly authentic account of policing within the contemporary American inner city. With Barry Levinson and Tom Fontana as its Executive Producers – responsible for earlier genre-breaking series such as the acclaimed hospital drama 'St Elsewhere' – and the documentary basis of Simon's original book, it's not surprising that the series carries with it an aesthetic aura of authenticity. In its serious issue-based multi-narratives and careful character development and exposition, it is – like its generic predecessors 'Hill Street Blues' and 'NYPD Blue' – a million light years away from the previous generation of 'Starsky and Hutch' style police car chase dramas:

> Television has given us the myth of the raging pursuit, the high-speed chase, but in truth there is no such thing…. The murder police always get there after the bodies fall, and a homicide detective has to remind himself to take his .38 out of the top right desk drawer. Following from this, 'Homicide' has been more about the consequences of murder than anything else has.[1]

– Centres and Margins: A Conclusion –

In examining the 'consequences of murder' the series inevitably exposes and challenges the geo-ideological landscape in which those murders are enacted, and the complex web of cause and effect, which are both symptomatic of and inscribed within that landscape. David Harvey describes that contemporary landscape in the following terms, while asking about what kind of collective, unified political resistance might be mobilised to transform its inequalities and injustices:

> If the historical and geographical process of class war waged by the Republican party and the capitalist class… has feminised poverty, accelerated racial oppression, and further degraded the ecological conditions of life, then it seems that a far more united politics can flow from a determination to check that process, than will likely flow from an identity politics which largely reflects its fragmented results.

There is a sense in which the kind of 'identity-based politics' that Harvey identifies as a symptom of the alienating fragmentation of high capitalism, informs, to an extent, the issue-based scenarios of this series. Those issue-based narratives, while explored by the producers of 'Homicide' with consummate insight and uncompromising candour, might nevertheless be viewed as reflecting an underlying liberal 'check list' agenda, screening the wider historical processes which create the conditions out of which those 'issues' emerge.

This is not to distract from the powerful and distinctive performative aesthetic through which the issues of contemporary American inner city life are mediated. The quality of the acting, writing, direction and editing are all consistently of a very high order. Through its use of the stylised double and triple jump-cut editing process, and its evocative sampled soundtrack of stylised flash gun sounds and contemporary melancholic acoustic folk rock, the series has a stylishly memorable aesthetic signature.

In two episodes from Series Six, the interaction between the domain of public affairs and the personal concerns of the individual police officers reveal some exemplary instances of the wider ideological landscape of Baltimore. In Episode 609: 'Closet Cases,' Pembleton and Bayliss are called upon to investigate the violent murder of a gay man whose body is left dumped in a skip outside of a restaurant known as 'Zodiac.' Owned by a gay businessman, Chris Rawles, an initial interview between him and the two detectives leads Pembleton to observe that Rawles had made a clear pass at Bayliss. As the episode unfolds, the viewer follows the two detectives into pleasured gay and lesbian spaces, characterised by the insistent aural signature of techno-pop and visually signed in terms of the subterranean shadows illuminated by the pulsing of strobe lights. Bayliss, who has just had an embryonic relationship with Cox brought to an abrupt end by her, confesses to his long term police partner and friend that he is attracted to the gay sub-culture with what he perceives as its more evident celebration of life. Eventually, the victim is identified and the rough-living hustler that he had sought to befriend proves to be his murderer. However, this character, Peter Fields, refuses to confess unless Bayliss responds to his taunts in the Box that the detective is sexually attracted to him. In a sequence of vivid emotional power and anticipation, Bayliss, played with superb inner realisation by the actor Kyle Secor, confronts his tormentor and acknowledges his sexual attraction towards the young murderer, and the conviction is secured. This scenario perfectly maps out a territory of constructed and conditional sexual identity and ambiguity in which the limits of formal public execution of the law float and mix uneasily and subversively with the interior space of desire. At the end of the episode, Bayliss accepts a dinner invitation from Rawles, leaving Pembleton concerned, and the viewer uncertain as to his position on the issue of gay sexuality. There is a similar absence of closure as to whether Bayliss' admission to Fields was an expression of personal desire or a professional strategy to secure a conviction.

This prevailing sense of the city as a location where identity, desire and personal choice are subject to a state of flux and indeterminacy that may be viewed as equivalently disconcerting and liberating, is further explored in Episode 619: 'Secrets.' In this episode, two apparent suicides take the viewer into the rarely glimpsed echelons of white, monied, upper class Baltimore society. It transpires that both victims had been members of an exclusive country club, whose owner is Remington Hill. It also becomes clear that the close relatives of both victims have received compromising photographs, one revealing an affair between a middle-aged woman and her teenage babysitter, the other, an incestuous relationship between a prominent Baltimore financier and his half-sister. As the investigation proceeds, what is revealed is that Hill has taken it upon himself to exercise a form of almost sadistically manipulative control over the private lives and morals of the club members. He is himself ultimately murdered by the small-time photographer whom he has employed (through blackmail) to take the incriminating photographs. Thus a dark cycle of judgment and retribution is enacted within the sphere of Baltimore social and cultural life most conventionally associated with moral respectability and power. This exposure of reactionary, manipulative moral intrusion and its brutal consequences conveys a strong sense of the mistrust with which the exemplars of American high capitalist society are viewed in liberal and, increasingly, in other quarters. In the wider debate concerning the nature, causes and location of crime, it is also a chilling and necessary exposure that the framework for this debate is not the sole preserve of the poverty stricken, inner city, working-class African American and white communities.

Liberation, Assimilation or Confrontation?
Queering City Spaces

'Tales of the City' and 'Queer as Folk' represent two immensely interesting and contrasting dramatic explorations and representations of gay, lesbian and queer sexuality within contemporary television drama. Whilst Armistead Maupin has chosen the historical distancing device of placing his characters and narratives in a pre-AIDS San Francisco of the early-mid 1970s, Russell T Davies, the author of 'Queer as Folk,' has equally deliberately located his controversial drama in contemporary Manchester.

As I discussed in Chapter Three, Maupin creates a fictionalised city in a way that defines that imagined metropolitan space as almost allegorical, a site for the evocative meditation of San Francisco at a specific and traumatic juncture in its history as a location for liberal/radical agendas. Both the first series and its sequel, 'More Tales of the City,' possess a kind of charm and sense of ennui, while containing some wickedly funny satire of both gay and straight Californian high society. The series provoke a sense of the city, therefore, which serves as a libertarian fable of the need and virtue of personal and sexual integrity through openness, honesty, tolerance and self-growth. Furthermore, the dangers and perils of denial, deception and the manipulation of others for self-advancement and self-gratification are equally signaled throughout both series. In the characters of Anna Madrigal, Michael Toliver, Mona Ramsey and Mary Ann Singleton, Maupin has succeeded in creating fictional characters who have become enduring – and to many, endearing – icons of contemporary popular American culture.

Of the five dramas under consideration, it is both interesting and significant that 'Tales' is the only one to use the generic form of the 'mini-series' as its means of production and broadcast. This genre, more commonly associated with the mainstream, commercial marketing of popular, sudsy melodramas, no doubt helps to explain the popular success of the series. Equally, if not more importantly, there is a residual liberal optimism within the piece, expressed partly through the growing maturity and tolerance of Mary Ann, and the rapprochement of Michael with Jon, and Mona with her discovered father – 'A man turned girl' – Anna Madrigal.

Symptomatic of this performative aesthetic within the series is the absence of any of the gay men having to confront homophobic discrimination or violence and, of course, the absence of the devastating impact of AIDS. First identified as GRID – Gay-Related Immune Deficiency – the first cases were reported in San Francisco in 1981. By the end of the 1980s AIDS had claimed thousands of lives. The post-liberal years of the late 1970s and 1980s were also marked by the notorious murders of Mayor George Moscone and gay supervisor Harvey Milk. The perpetrator, a former City Hall employee called Dan White, was convicted of manslaughter and served a short sentence on the grounds that an over-consumption of chocolate 'Twinky' bars had overloaded his sugar intake, drastically reducing his capacity for rational self-control. This appalling miscarriage of justice provoked a mass, violent demonstration on the night of the sentencing – known and commemorated as 'White Night.' Finally, when D'orothea and Dee Dee exit the second series with the twins to start a counter-cultural life together, the viewer discovers that they are going to join the Reverend Jim Jones' 'People's Temple,' a San Francisco-based cult. The cult migrated to Guyana in October 1978. Jones then led over 900 of his followers into a mass-suicide – the largest such event of the modern period. Clearly, the San Francisco of 'Tales of the City' might be viewed as an idealised and imagined evocation of the liberal/radical hopes of the pre-AIDS period: a west coast 'Forest of Arden' where the oppressions and insoluble problems of the city might be explored, exposed, and creatively re-enacted.

Interestingly, but perhaps not surprisingly, it was at the 1999 International Lesbian and Gay Film Festival that 'Queer as Folk' had its US premiere. The series sold out at each screening and left audiences cheering. This event was reported in the September 1999 edition of the American gay magazine *Out*, which went on to report:

> [Vince, Stuart and Nathan] are complicated characters but not always nice ones.... As Matthew Parris, the prominent Parliamentary columnist for *The Times*, (who is gay) and an admirer of the show says, "It is paradoxically a sign of the growing self-confidence of gay people in Britain that we are able to take representations that are not positive – the characters are selfish, shallow, unkind and obsessed with sex."... The show regularly drew 4 million viewers, or a 14 percent share (such a percentage would put it just below the top 10 shows in the United States.)[3]

Nevertheless, as I have discussed earlier in this book, the series inevitably provoked a lot of very negative criticism, both from the centre/right but also from individuals and groups within the Gay community itself. *The Guardian* reported on 22 June 1999 that:

> Britain's first gay drama series, 'Queer as Folk', received more complaints than any other programme broadcast on TV, according to a report published today. More than 160 people complained to the Independent Television Commission, mostly about the first episode of the Channel 4 series, which showed a 15-year-old-boy being introduced to gay sex by a promiscuous 29-year-old. In the ITC's history, only Martin Scorsese's hugely controversial feature film 'The Last Temptation of Christ,' also broadcast by Channel 4, prompted more complaints from viewers.... Channel 4... said it remained "extremely proud" of the series. The director of programmes, Tim Gardam, said the series "epitomised our mission to put alternative viewpoints and voices on screen," He continued: "It broke new ground for television drama and provoked a huge response from viewers with the majority very supportive of its style and subject matter."

However, some of those viewers who were not "supportive of its style and subject matter" included high-profile 1980s gay icons such as the singer Boy George, in more recent times, a highly respected DJ mixer. Writing in the *Sunday Express* at the time of the transmission of the first episode, he angrily criticised the series for what he believed to be its irresponsible and gratuitous depiction of gay men and their sexual behaviour. His was far from a single voice and a number of gay men, both scene and non-scene, expressed their concern that homophobic prejudices about gay sexuality would be 'confirmed' and 'proven.' The impact of this predicted response was especially significant at a time when the battle for the repeal of Clause 28 and the equalisation of the legal age of consensual sexual behaviour was at its height. In the June 1999 issue of the British gay magazine, *Attitude*, Russell T Davies hit back at his critics:

> When this all began in November 1997, no one told me there was an agenda. Because there must be an agenda – every gay politician, spokeswoman and militant has shouted at me for not following it. Perhaps it's available in public libraries, or Clone Zone. I don't know, I never looked. Right now, I'd love to see it, this set of rules, as unwritten as the British Constitution and as rigid, dictating what, how and why a gay writer must write. The creation of the series was entirely personal.... And that's where the trouble started. I knew I had to focus. I knew I had to invent specific lives rather than portray the entire so-called community. So where did I look? The clubs.... Some of the men and women who

claim to speak on our behalf would rather this night-life did not exist…. It's more than political correctness, it's far, far worse. It's those old and powerful ghosts, the unholy trinity: Self-loathing, Fear and Shame. (p. 34)

As Jenny Madden observed and went on to discuss in her article. 'Queer as Friends' (*The Guardian*, 1 February 2000), to the surprise of the show's producers and everyone involved, demographic market research revealed that the drama's biggest proportional viewing audience was made up of women. That the series achieved consistent viewing audiences of over four million was solid and respectable, but not spectacular, for a non-mainstream drama scheduled in a late evening slot.

What these issues of criticism, audience demographics and viewing figures illustrates perhaps, is firstly, the relative visibility of what is often uncritically and without proper definition or analysis referred to as 'the gay community.' That no such homogenous grouping actually exists – or exists only in terms of a specific, 1970s-originated, liberal/left politicised ideological position – is revealed in much of the angry debate surrounding 'Queer as Folk.' Furthermore, as discussed extensively in Chapter Four, I believe that the drama has inscribed within its performative aesthetic, a struggle between that liberal/left strategy of disciplined resistance leading towards equality and assimilation, and the confrontational, post-modern queer discourse of "We're queer, we're here and we're not going away." Secondly, there is an unmistakable sense of the growing social and cultural visibility of specific constructs of gay sexuality in metropolitan sites such as Manchester's Canal Street. This visibility is inescapably related, I believe, to the commercial exploitation of selected expressions of those constructs defined in recreational/leisure terms of fashion and music. As I asserted in my discussion of the construction of Stuart's character, this capitalist exploitation of a specific purchasing market delineates 'gay sexuality' as a fetishised commodity, signed by a fashioned display of consumption and excess. There is a considerable volume of research material being generated through the auspices of the ESCR-funded 'Violence, Sexuality and Space' research project. One of the investigative locations for this excellent project is the Department of Sociology at the University of Manchester where Professor Beverley Skeggs and her team, in conjunction with colleagues including Les Moran, Paul Tyrer and Karen Corteen are researching the relationship between safety and gay urban space. It is not possible or appropriate to do justice to the detailed revelations that this long term project is producing, but their discovery and discussion of the territorialisation of gay locations by advanced capitalist development is challenging and revealing.

Arguing that full hegemonic incorporation or assimilation is never possible, with some groups continuing to dynamically position themselves at the edge of controlled centres, Skeggs goes on to assert that:

There is now a need to look to that beyond the incorporated, beyond the availability of already known subject position and identities. The concept of struggle precisely identifies that which cannot be known in advance. It is only in the concrete articulations of living the everyday, in the struggles for future space, that one can begin to understand what it is and what is not beyond incorporation.[i]

The ideological and territorial spectrum ranging from Maupin's warm and wistful evocation of a pre-AIDS libertarian San Francisco – signed by a yearning for openness and tolerance and acceptance – through to Davies' uncompromising display of unapologetic gay sexuality as pleasured consumption, reflects important aspects of the 'Sensing of the City.' Equally, it is interesting that in his post-modern pastiched homage to 'Thelma and Louise,' Davies' Arizona truckstop-based denouement in the final episode, is as much an engagement in idealised wish fulfilment as Michael Toliver's plea for tolerant inclusion in his coming-out letter to his parents. In their respective aims and performative aesthetics, they might both be construed as "articulations of living the everyday... the struggles for future space."

Sensing the City – more than just Holding On?

In this final concluding section, I want to draw together my thoughts on Marchant's 'Holding On' and, in doing so, bring this book to a point of necessary, but provisional, closure.

At the heart of Marchant's fine drama is an underlying sense of moral ambiguity and ideological uncertainty that is also expressed to some degree in the other four case-studies in this study. Interestingly in 'Holding On,' issues of law and order and justice are vividly presented through the narrative focusing upon the murder of Chris. Also, the issues of justice and its construction and implementation are important signifiers of aspects of Shaun's character and narrative. Nevertheless, the presence of the police as the supposed formal and legitimised means of law enforcement and justice are visible only in their absence; the viewer witnesses only the symptoms of the presence of institutionalised racism within both the police and judiciary. This is not in any sense a criticism of the drama, but rather an instance of the ways in which what is figuratively absent from the complex text of the performative aesthetic may be a significant presence in its absence. What is also significant about Marchant's drama is how through its multi-vocal narrative structures and strategies it moves both between the marginal and centre points/positions, while seeking to ascribe equivalent value to those positions. If surviving the city (in this case London) is a central motif to this series, then Marchant seems to argue that it is not only those on the seemingly fragile margins who must 'hold on.' Through the character of Gary Rickey, in his startling combination of outrageous and conspicuous consumption, inner pain and savage satire, Marchant has provided us with one of the memorable dramatic character creations of recent British drama. At the conclusion of his ambiguous, bleakly romantic elegy for the city that ends 'Holding On,' he observes with a wonderfully ironic sense of loyalty to what the city can offer:

> The country's not everything it's cracked up to be – you can never get a taxi when you need one.

The ideological terrain traversed by these five dramas communicates a 'Sensing of the City' which is in turns, poignant, searingly, critically searching and looking to define, in some respects, a very fragile, tentative and qualified optimism. This optimism is never facile but always hugely constrained by the recognition of the complex causes and symptoms of historically mediated, immanently experienced inequality, discrimination and injustice.

Finally, as I hope I've made clear throughout this book, I have not sought to engage in a simplistically reductive, vulgar socialisation of the processes and means by which these outstanding television dramas inscribe and exhibit their ideological histories and concerns. I am conscious, of course, that I have chosen to navigate my analysis through a detailed and, at times, complex investigation of narrative and character formation. I have endeavored to pursue this strategy solely in order to drive my analytical route through the material. I also recognised, of course, that readers without access to video copies of the original dramas would require some means of locating the both the visual and narrative frame.

In using the term *geo-ideological*, I hope that I have developed a critical concept that might stimulate debate and facilitate research by other colleagues in the arena of television drama and cultural studies. It is also my modest hope that this explorative study and analysis may make some useful contribution to this wider and ongoing debate concerning the relationship of popular cultural forms to ideological anxieties and agendas.

I am going to close with a quotation from Alan Clarke that perfectly expresses both my original and ongoing ideological aims and perspective:

> It is important not to isolate the moment of fictional representation from the rest of the lived world. The political forces of society cannot be disentangled from this nexus, the dramas are enacted within the structured ideological field of society… as such, they constitute one of the sites on which ideological struggle can take place and in which the cultural formation can be shaped. [5]

Notes

1. David Simon (1991) *Homicide – A Year on the Killing Streets*, New York, Ivy books, pp.160–1.
2. David Harvey (1993) 'Class Relations, Social Justice and the Politics of Difference', published in Keith & Pile (eds) *Place and Politics of Identity*, Routledge, p.64.
3, S. D'Erasmo (1999) 'You Can't Do That on Television,' *Out* (September, 1999) pp.93–5.
4. Professor Beverley Skeggs *Violence, Sexuality and Space*, p.228.
5. Alan Clarke (1992) 'You're Nicked! Television police series and the fictional representation of law and order,' in Strinati and Wagg (eds) *Come on Down? – Popular Media Culture in Post-War Britain* (eds. Strinati and Wragg), Routledge, p.252.